MADE IN HOLLY-WOOD

MADE IN HOLLY-WOOD

James Bacon

cbi Contemporary Books, Inc.
Chicago

Library of Congress Cataloging in Publication Data

Bacon, James, 1914-
    Made in Hollywood.

    Includes index.
    1. Bacon, James, 1914-   2. Journalists—United
States—Biography.   3. Moving-picture industry—United
States.   I. Title.
PN4874.B22A35   791.43′092′4 [B]   77-75716
ISBN 0-8092-7870-7

Copyright © 1977 by James Bacon
Published by Contemporary Books, Inc.
180 North Michigan Avenue, Chicago, Illinois 60601
Manufactured in the United States of America
Library of Congress Catalog Card Number: 77-75716
International Standard Book Number: 0-8092-7870-7

Published simultaneously in Canada by
Beaverbooks
953 Dillingham Road
Pickering, Ontario L1W 1Z7
Canada

To Jimmy, Tommy, and Margaret Anne, who may grow up someday and discover their old man was a little on the wacky side, especially when they read his books.

Contents

Preface

Writing a book is easy. It's the title that is tough.

This book was written with the working title *I've Never Met a Nymphomaniac I Didn't Like.*

It stemmed from a true incident with the Burtons before they were married. We were all down in Puerto Vallarta, Mexico, where Elizabeth Taylor was trying to get Eddie Fisher's name on a consent Mexican divorce decree. Eddie wouldn't give it.

Not even after Elizabeth offered him $1 million cash.

Richard, Elizabeth, and I—plus a few others—all went to the Oceana bar that night with Elizabeth quite depressed.

At one point in the drinking she commented: "Eddie wants to make me look like a nymphomaniac."

I put my arm around her and said: "Elizabeth, I've never met a nymphomaniac I didn't like."

She laughed. Richard laughed. I laughed, and the rest of the night was merry.

I tried the title out on a hundred people. Everybody liked it, including such diverse people as David Niven and Harold Robbins.

Everybody liked it but my publisher. He said women would not buy a book with "nymphomaniac" in the title. He was right, of course.

I hadn't taken into account the feminist movement. You meet a different type of girl in Hollywood.

Then began our consideration of better than 100 titles—*Son of Hollywood Is a Four Letter Town, Hollywood to Go, Hollywood: Land of the Midnight Sin, Hooray for Hollywood—and Downtown Burbank Too, Hollywood Is an Eight Letter Word, Hollywood Unzipped,* and dozens more.

Finally you get to the point where you don't care if it's called *I Found God While Working for the FBI in Hollywood.*

And then one day, the publisher said: "We got it—*Made in Hollywood.*"

It was short. You could see it on the bookshelves. And the cover would be the nicely rounded derrière of a pretty girl in cut-off blue jeans with "Made in Hollywood" on the back pocket.

That sold me. And I hope it sells you.

JRB

PART I:

THE SUPERSTARS

A sometimes irreverent, sometimes boozy, but mostly revealing look at some of the show-business names we all know—and love.

How Did Frank Sinatra Really Win That Oscar?

Ever since *The Godfather* came out as a best-selling novel and a blockbuster movie, I can't go to Italy—where Frank Sinatra's forebears came from—without being besieged by people with the same question:

Did Frank Sinatra really get his Oscar with the help of the Mafia? Over in Italy, and especially Sicily, the Mafia is big news. Everybody from the chauffeur to the concierge at the hotel assailed me with that question.

I would say by conservative guess that more than 150 people hit me with it. If I could speak Italian, God knows how many would have asked me.

I went right to the source after my third trip to Rome and found out the true story of how Frank won the Oscar for *From Here to Eternity*.

Jonie Taps—that name sounds like a vaudeville hoofing act—was a vice-president at Columbia Pictures for thirty years—and Harry Cohn's confidant and best friend. Jonie is now a vice-president with Southwest Leasing Corporation in Beverly Hills, biggest car rental outfit in town.

"It was late in 1952 or early 1953," recalls Jonie. "Harry Cohn, Beldon Katleman (owner of the El Rancho Vegas at the time), Jule Styne the composer, and I were all in the Hampshire House in New York. Harry kept a suite there.

"This was the time when Frank's voice had given out. He couldn't get arrested in the business.

"The phone rang as we were all talking. I answered it. The operator asked for Harry Cohn. Harry told me to take care of it.

"It was Frank. I told him to come on up to the suite. Harry was furious but I told him Frank was coming up anyway.

"When Frank came in he said he wanted to play Maggio in *From Here to Eternity;* he would do it for nothing.

"That offer got Harry's attention. He said he would think about it and let Frank know.

"After Frank left, Harry said: 'Who in the fuck would want to see that skinny asshole in a major movie?'

"I said: 'Harry, he's the perfect casting. You got Ernie Borgnine playing Fatso. What better than a skinny Italian playing Maggio? He'll have immediate sympathy with the audience. He *is* Maggio.'

"Harry still didn't like the idea and he said: 'Give me one fucking good reason why I should give him this picture?'

"I said, 'You may want Ava Gardner for a picture sometime. She loves Frank and she'll appreciate it.'

"Ava helped out by giving Harry a call and making the same pitch.

"'Harry,' I finally said, 'Give him a test—what the fuck can you lose?'

"Cohn agreed to the test and told Sinatra to do the test scene standing up.

"When the test was shot, Director Fred Zinnemann and Producer Buddy Adler wanted him to do it sitting down. Frank balked, but the two of them assured him they would take care of Cohn. When Harry saw the test, he was furious again because he figured Frank had deliberately disobeyed his orders.

"Adler and Zinnemann took off without once explaining to Cohn that they had ordered Frank to sit down. Frank was left holding the bag.

"I told Harry that Frank hadn't double-crossed him but that Frank wanted to explain what happened himself. Frank then told Harry that Adler and Zinnemann made him sit down in the scene.

"Harry cooled down and signed Frank for $12,500 for the run of the picture. It was barely above scale. Peanuts. Ridiculous.

"Then Max Arnow, the casting director, jumped all over me. He had Eli Wallach for the part. He said: 'What the hell are you doing to me? It's not even your department.'

"What the fuck did I care? Frank got the job and proved me right. He *was* Maggio. Now he's our greatest show business star today."

In *The Godfather,* the Mafia emissary got a turndown from

the studio boss when he relayed the Godfather's request that the Sinatra-like character get the part. The next day, the head of the tycoon's prize racehorse was in bed with him.

"Harry Cohn never owned a racehorse," says Jonie. "The only one in town who did was Louis B. Mayer, and Frank was long gone from MGM by that time."

No wonder Frank and Mario Puzo had harsh words and almost a free-for-all one night in Chasen's.

"Puzo was writing fiction just like Harold Robbins," said Jonie.

When Queen Elizabeth Walked out on Princess Margaret

There's no more fun in the world than watching Hollywood royalty mixing with the real McCoy.

In 1965, Princess Margaret and Lord Snowdon included Hollywood on their official tour of the United States. What happened could have set British-American relations back to George III and the Colonies.

Fortunately, the Princess and her then husband missed most of what happened behind the scenes.

The big affair of the visit was a party at the Bistro, Beverly Hills' most famous watering hole.

Queen Elizabeth of Hollywood—that would be Taylor—and husband Richard Burton drove up to the Bistro in a London taxi, gay, well-fortified and all set to swing with royalty.

I was there because I was traveling with the royal party all the way from San Francisco to Lake Powell in Arizona.

But the Bistro was the most fun part of the trip. Even Princess Margaret said that.

When the Burtons drove up, they were the very first of 100 celebrities to arrive. They were also the first to leave—somber, tight-lipped, and miffed—hours before the arrival of the Princess and her party.

In leaving before the Princess, Richard, a British subject,

committed a serious breach of protocol, but he didn't give a damn. Elizabeth, trying then to become a British subject, went right along with him.

But the Burtons' breach was nothing compared with that of the late Larry Harvey, also a British subject.

Why were the Burtons miffed?

And why did they bypass the luncheon next day at Universal studio, where every important figure in the movie industry paid homage to the royal party?

And why were't they at the WAIF ball that same night— even though they had bought tickets at $100 apiece?

The Burtons obviously were snubbing Princess Margaret.

There was a good reason. Sharman Douglas, daughter of the former ambassador to the Court of St. James, was hostess of the Bistro party.

If the Burtons violated royal protocol, then Sharman was guilty of violating Hollywood protocol. In those days Richard and Elizabeth were the undisputed King and Queen of Hollywood.

Not Warren Beatty, Hope Lange, and her then husband, Director Alan Pakula.

Beatty, Miss Lange, and Producer-Director Pakula sat with the Princess and Lord Snowdon.

The Burtons were seated near the kitchen, something Kurt Niklas, owner and maitre d' of the Bistro would have thought unthinkable had he been in charge of seating in his own restaurant.

The slight made Richard downright pugnacious. One of his table partners was Joanne Woodward.

Knowing Joanne and Paul Newman's close relationship with Director Martin Ritt, Burton started tearing Ritt apart in front of Joanne. The evening ended with Joanne vowing never to speak to the Burtons again. A number of other stars felt the same way about the battling Welshman. Obviously Richard had stopped off at another pub on the way to the Bistro. Also, he hates the English with a passion—as do most Welshmen.

Judy Garland got up to entertain. Her shoe caught on a mike cord and came off. Rupert Allan, her publicist, helped her put it back on.

"She's drunk again," said Richard, whose voice carries across an amphitheater and can certainly be heard in an intimate *boite*.

Judy, as it happened, was not drunk. She entertained beautifully.

When she finished, everyone for tables around stared at Richard, who really couldn't have cared less.

Finally, midway through the evening's entertainment, the Burtons left.

"I thought they would never leave," said Joanne.

Richard, recovering the next day, did send his regrets to the Princess, explaining that his departure was due to an early call for both of them the next day. That was true. Jack L. Warner waits for no Princess when production is under way.

The Burtons were making *Who's Afraid of Virginia Woolf* for J. L.

But it was the first Hollywood party in memory, movie or not, that the Burtons didn't swing until the tables were empty, the dance floor deserted.

And if there was anything the Burtons loved in those days, it was a swinger. Princess Margaret was still swinging at 3:15 A. M. and the royal couple was the last to leave the gay party.

And speaking of gay parties, Larry Harvey pulled a stunt that he had done at several Hollywood parties before. Larry was drinking the labels off the bottles that night, so he took his pants off.

Worse, he took them off in the ladies room, amidst much screaming and hollering.

Fortunately, the Princess hadn't arrived when this happened so there was no serious breach of protocol.

Sharman, with the help of a Secret Service man, got Larry to put his pants back on, else he would be thrown on his ass out the kitchen door.

After that—and in the presence of Princess Margaret and

Lord Snowdon—Larry did nothing worse than dance with the men.

At this, Joan Cohn, widow of the famous Harry Cohn, and Larry's fiancée at the time, got up and left. As she got in her Rolls-Royce, Larry was out on the floor dancing with himself and yelling:

"No one will let me lead."

In Princess Margaret's twenty-one days in the United States, she said openly that the Bistro party was the highlight of the trip.

She was charming at the Universal luncheon as she chatted with Fred Astaire, Rock Hudson, Claudia Cardinale, and Gene Kelly.

But there was another incident there. Jean Seberg was supposed to sit at the royal table, right next to Lord Snowdon.

But someone at Universal goofed and Jean was seated next to the A table, right behind it. It left an empty seat next to Lord Snowdon.

Once again Larry Harvey, fortified on Pouilly-Fuissé, came to the rescue. Seeing the empty seat with Jean Seberg's name on it, Larry sat down next to Lord Snowdon.

"I'm not Jean Seberg," said Larry to Snowdon. "Are you?"

Lord Snowdon took it all good-naturedly, although his laugh did seem a bit hysterical.

The table was filled quickly by Hayley Mills, also a British subject.

Said Sharman Douglas in explaining the mix-up:

"We were told that Miss Seberg wouldn't sit there unless her husband were allowed to."

When Jean heard this, she blew up.

"How dare anyone accuse me of such bad manners?"

Jean thought when she was ushered to another seat, she just wasn't one of the chosen few and said nothing more about it. Until the ruckus.

At the WAIF ball, a drunk meandered up to the Princess and mumbled to her:

"I'd like to buy the little Princess a drink."

Cops ushered him away gently but didn't arrest him. He was one of the biggest names in Los Angeles government. Won't mention his name because he's big enough to have the cops harass you.

The next night Rupert Allan and General Frank McCarthy, producer of *Patton* and *MacArthur,* entertained the Snowdons at a Beverly Hills home.

Only incident there was a definite coolness between the Princess and Shirley MacLaine. Margaret didn't like the way Shirley had danced the night before at the Bistro with Snowdon. The way Shirley snuggled with his Lordship, the place would have been raided if the music stopped.

Next day the royal party left for Tucson, Arizona, and a look at the real America. But that lasted only forty minutes before a whole contingent from Hollywood arrived in a plane. The parties began again.

At Lake Powell in Northern Arizona, the Princess and her party drank $100 worth of whiskey in about two or three hours.

Art Greene, owner of the Lake Powell motel, had a room under the royal suite.

"They were going like hell up there at 2 A. M. I wanted to sleep and was tempted to rap a broom on the ceiling. Then I figured, what the hell? I was a hell-raiser too when I was their age, so let them have their fun."

Who Came First? Bing or Russ?

It's a controversy that will always be with us. Just the other night I got a call from a bar where two friends wanted me to settle a bet.

The one guy said that Bing Crosby got his style from Russ Columbo when both worked in Gus Arnheim's band at the Cocoanut Grove in Los Angeles. He had $100 riding on his bet. The other fellow, of course, said that Columbo got his style from Crosby.

My answer would decide the bet.

Fortunately, I had once gone to the source to settle that argument—although I felt from my own experience that Bing was the favorite.

Around about 1931, when I was a senior in high school in Lock Haven, Pennsylvania, a bunch of us used to hang around a soda fountain and record shop called the Roxy Garden.

We knew every new record as soon as it came in, just like the kids do today with the rock groups.

Big singers of the day were Rudy Vallee, Lanny Ross, Gene Austin, and, of course, Al Jolson.

Then one day a record came in by Gus Arnheim's band. This was still in the early days of radio and it was a mark of distinction in Lock Haven to sit up until 2 or 3 A. M. and listen to the Arnheim band from radio station KFI in Los Angeles.

KFI is still one of the most powerful stations in the nation, and in those days the old Atwater Kent would pull it in from across the country.

So we all knew the Arnheim band. I can remember the record as if it were yesterday. On one side was a song called "Fool Me Some More" and on the other was "It Must Be True."

The latter song, composer Harry Barris was to tell me thirty years later, was written as an obligato to a famous song of the day, "If I Could Spend One Hour With You."

On the record, in minute type, was the notation, "Vocal By B. Crosby."

The first time we played it, every kid in the shop went wild. Crosby was an original. Most singers of the day either imitated Jolson or they sang high tenor, much like Dick Powell was to do in the early Warner musicals.

The same thing was to happen years later with Elvis Presley and Frank Sinatra, both trailblazers.

Soon Bing was out with more solos, also written by Barris, his partner in the Rhythm Boys. These became major hits because they were great songs sung by an exciting new stylist: "I Surrender, Dear" and "Just One More Chance."

By the time we graduated in June 1932, Bing Crosby was on network radio for Cremo Cigars fifteen minutes every night. You listened to him like you listened to *Amos 'n' Andy*.

Just about this time, when Crosby was already getting there, another exciting new singer burst upon the scene with the same style as Bing's. His name was Russ Columbo and when he sang "Prisoner of Love," it was like Sinatra singing "One For My Baby."

And to top things off Russ looked like a crooning Valentino.

Bing was handsome enough but he had ears that looked like the wings of a Boeing 747. For years in the early Crosby movies, Jack Oakie and Richard Arlen, needing an early quitting time to visit a pub, used to pull the glue off Bing's ears. The makeup department had pasted them down so he wouldn't take off like a hawk in flight.

The director inevitably had to call off shooting because it was a two-hour job to make Bing's ears lie down again.

No question that Russ gave Bing competition, plenty of it. But the Crosby personality and versatility soon outdistanced Russ. Bing could sing anything from romantic ballads to hot jazz to "Silent Night." Russ was strictly in the romantic league.

Ironically, Bing and Russ were good friends. They had worked together in Arnheim's orchestra. The competition was mostly among their followers, not between the performers.

Bing's publicity came from his married life with Dixie Lee and his addiction to the sports life. He was an idol of that innocent age of the thirties.

But so was Russ, until his untimely death from a Civil War gun he was showing in his home in 1934. The gun had been a collector's piece for years but no one ever bothered to check if it had a bullet in it. It did.

Russ's publicity in those days came mostly from his romantic life, notably a hot romance with Carole Lombard, then a reigning movie queen who later married Clark Gable.

But over the years, the argument went on. Who came first? Russ or Bing? I heard it debated a hundred times.

Finally one day in the fifties, I looked in the Los Angeles telephone directory—often a good place to find celebrities' phone numbers—and saw the name Gus Arnheim.

Gus, then retired from bandleading, answered the phone and I put the question to him after I identified myself.

"Bing," he said without a moment's hesitation.

"Until Bing came along all male vocalists sounded like something out of an operetta," said Gus.

"I first hired Bing with the Rhythm Boys when they decided to stay in Los Angeles rather than go back east again with Paul Whiteman and his band.

"Occasionally Bing would take off on a solo during the boys' stint with the band. Women went wild whenever he did it.

"I didn't have to be hit over the head to start giving him some solos with the band. Russ was the regular vocalist but he sang in a high tenor style like Dick Powell and the rest.

"Russ also played violin and I could watch him studying Bing's raspy, easy style.

"Soon Russ, while still with my band, starting singing in that new slurring sound that Bing had created. And the women went wild for him.

"You had to tip the maitre d' ten bucks in those Depression days to get a table at the Cocoanut Grove. That's like $100 now but I had two sensations in my band. Bing was the first to leave and then a year or two later, some smart manager got hold of Russ and he became big, too.

"I always figured Bing would go further. Russ was more reserved and Bing was shy, too—until that light hit him. And then he was Mr. Personality.

"But you can take it from me—and I loved them both—Bing originated the style."

Well, that should settle some bar bets.

One of my favorite all-time Bing Crosby stories was told me

by the late Barney Dean, who acted as a gag man for Bing and Bob Hope on the *Road* pictures.

In those days, Bing used to have a home in Pebble Beach, in central California. Barney was up there with him working on some material when Bing said: "Let's drive back to Hollywood."

It was the middle of the night but Barney didn't question him.

About 4 A. M., Bing stopped the car in Paso Robles in a residential area.

"Why are you stopping here, Bing?"

"I want a drink of water," said Bing.

"Drive a few more blocks and we'll find an all-night diner. Where are you going to get water here?"

Bing got out of the car and knocked on the door of a house. Soon a light went on and an astonished housewife in housecoat opened the door and got Bing a glass of water. He thanked her and got back in the car.

"Bing, that was a crazy thing to do. Why did you do it?"

"Because," said Bing, "that lady is going to tell everybody she knows in town that Bing Crosby stopped at her house at 4 A. M. and asked for a glass of water. And not a damn soul will believe her."

Bing laughed and laughed.

Another time, Bing and his drinking buddy, Phil Harris, were grouse-shooting in Scotland. Driving along a Scottish road early one morning to the shoot, Bing spotted a distillery going full blast.

"Look, Phil," said Bing, "there's one damn place that can make booze as fast as you can drink it."

"Yeh," said Phil, "but I got the bastards working nights."

Phil was also the first ever to utter the famous line—since stolen by other comedians—when a slightly inebriated Harris got stopped by the Highway Patrol for driving erratically home to Palm Springs.

The cops took Phil out of the car and told him to walk the white line in the center of the highway.

Phil, in amazement, demurred.
"You mean—without a net?"

Judy

Judy Garland was a little girl who searched a hopeless lifetime for that place where bluebirds fly, then, with one drink
and one pill too many, found it in death.

Her death came in a new home in London's Belgravia
district—an area of bright yellow doors and pretty flowers.

Married to her fifth husband, twelve years younger than she,
Judy had vowed—as she had done a hundred times before—to
make this home and this life a little better than it had been
before.

Judy was one of the most tragic figures in Hollywood history, but you would never know it when you were around her.
To her dying day, she still possessed that delicious sense of
humor that kept her going for forty-seven years.

Liza Minnelli, her superstar daughter, says today that her
most precious memories of her mother were the jokes and the
fun even when the sheriff was banging on the front door.

Even when Judy told me that she had cirrhosis of the
liver—the last time I ever spoke with her—she did it with a
joke.

"What are you doing about it?" I asked.

"I put water in my Liebfraumilch," she laughed. She wasn't
kidding and we both laughed.

Judy, like many people who drink too much, used to have
telephonitis. I have had calls from Judy, usually around three
of four o'clock in the morning, from all over the world. She
would apologize and say she couldn't sleep and just had to
talk to an old friend. I wasn't the only one she called, by any
means.

Never in all those dozens of calls did I ever hear Judy com-
plain or feel sorry for herself. Every call was filled with laugh-

ter. Even a lawsuit for nonpayment of some hotel bill would touch off some humorous repartee.

Yet Judy in her lifetime had little to laugh about.

First there was the stage mother whose idea of discipline for a lackluster performance was to abandon a little girl all alone in a fleabag hotel room where she sat terrified all night on the bed crying her heart out.

Judy's mother always returned in the morning because there was always a split booking in Mauch Chunk or Sioux City that had to be kept.

Then came Hollywood, where Louis B. Mayer, her movie boss, knew he had a gold mine—an adolescent box-office bonanza. But also one with a weight problem.

That's why, Judy told me, Mayer assigned a special cook whose main task was to grind Benzedrine—a diet suppressant that was really speed—into her food.

Judy once confided to me with that bubbly sense of humor:

"I was flying with the bluebirds before Harold Arlen ever wrote 'Over the Rainbow.' I had always thought Mr. Mayer gave me that special cook as sort of a status symbol. Even Garbo didn't have her own cook. My cook was the sweetest, kindest lady I had ever known. I loved her—and she loved me like a daughter. Years later, after I had two mental breakdowns and tried suicide once, she came to me in tears. She said she had been paid to doctor my food. She felt a tremendous sense of guilt for what she had done. She begged me to forgive her. We both cried and hugged and kissed and I told her to forget it. I forgave her."

From the pep pills, which shot her up, the teen-aged Judy naturally turned on the tranquilizers and sleeping pills that slapped her down.

"If there had been a pill that made me go sideways, I probably would have taken those, too."

Five marriages didn't help things, either.

In 1941, Judy married David Rose, the composer and conductor.

"I was fleeing from my mother and MGM," Judy told me.

"David's only fault was that he was too nice to me. I felt he deserved more happiness than I could give him."

She was to say the same thing after her divorce from Vincente Minnelli, the famed director who is Liza's father. Vincente directed Judy in some of her classic movies, *Meet Me in St. Louis* among them.

Then came Sid Luft and thirteen years of the stormiest marriage in Hollywood history. Sober, the two were like teen-age lovers. They loved each other in a crazy way.

Said Judy: "We had a strange kind of affection for each other—like Rocky Graziano and Tony Zale."

But Sid could make Judy work. All her amazing comebacks were engineered by Sid—the Palace, the London Palladium.

All of us were members of the Holmby Hills Rat Pack. One night Humphrey Bogart, patriarch of the Rat Pack, chartered a bus with booze and bartender to make the trip to a Judy concert at the Long Beach Civic Auditorium.

We all got there flying about a half hour ahead of the bus and went backstage to wish Judy well. She had had a few drinks herself and didn't want to go on. In fact, she was terrified of going on.

Luft, strong as a bull, literally pushed her onstage. As soon as she hit that first note, she wrapped the audience around her little finger.

No performer—and this includes Sinatra and Jolson—ever had the love affair with an audience that Judy had.

Critics of Judy's—and there were some—used to say that she cried phonily on cue when she sang "Over the Rainbow," especially when she trembled the line "Why, oh why, can't I?"

"It's true I always cry in the same place," Judy once said when I asked her about it, "but there's nothing phony. They are real tears and real emotion.

"Once I get out on that stage, I am always moved by an audience. I guess it's a throwback to our old days in vaudeville. If we didn't please the audience, we were fired the next performance. And if we got fired, Mama got mad.

"I can only perform one way. Give the audience it's money's worth. Most of all, I want people to like me. 'Rainbow' has always been my sad song. Everybody has songs that make them cry. 'Rainbow' is my sad song."

And when she sang it, she could stampede an audience—any audience—into standing ovations of huzzahs and bravos.

True, a lot of the bravos came from the gays who idolized Judy just like they do Ethel Merman and all the other great belters. That's a problem for psychiatrists to solve.

But most of the fans who cheered Judy were ordinary people to whom she had given a lifetime of happiness. Perhaps she reminded many of them of the innocence of childhood and Dorothy of the immortal *Wizard of Oz.*

She will always be Dorothy, the little girl from Kansas who met up with a cowardly lion, a tin man, and a scarecrow—and danced happily up a yellow brick road to a never-never land that only children know.

Audiences the world over forgave her her peccadilloes when she broke into the first chorus of "Over the Rainbow."

But not always. Not long before her death, a London cabaret audience pelted her with bread rolls and tableware when she arrived onstage an hour late. She never got to finish "Rainbow."

I have never forgiven the British audience for that. That never would have happened in the United States, where even the smallest children who see *The Wizard of Oz* on network television each year love Judy Garland although she's been dead for years.

In her later years, theater managers exploited her. At a New York performance some years ago, Judy came onstage, literally pushed out drunk by a money-grubbing manager.

"She was in absolutely no condition to perform," comedian Jan Murray recalls.

"I was in the audience and so was Vivian Blaine, the star of *Guys and Dolls.* We went backstage immediately and demanded that Judy not perform. The theater manager said: 'The show must go on.'

"What the fuck for?" Jan demanded.

"We'll have to refund the money," said the theater owner.

Jan and Vivian went out and performed instead for Judy. Jan told the audience they could get a refund if they wanted. Not one asked for a refund, showing how devoted they were to Judy.

Amazingly, Mayer, who had Judy under contract, didn't want her to play Dorothy. He wanted Shirley Temple. He called Judy "that big-assed kid."

Mervyn LeRoy, the producer, fought and fought with Mayer and finally won the role for Judy. Her performance ranks with the five all-time great performances in movies—and it's hard to name the other four.

Thank God for Mervyn, who put his job on the line against the most powerful studio boss in Hollywood history.

When the picture became an all-time classic, Mayer of course took all the credit.

Surprisingly, Judy never considered that her greatest performance.

"I honestly never cared for myself in any of the movies I ever made until *A Star is Born*. The night of the premiere I looked at myself on the screen and gave myself the first 'Okay' in my career. I know it sounds a little egotistical but I pleased myself for once."

Judy was a favorite to win the Oscar that year (1955). She was in the hospital awaiting the birth of son Joey Luft. The TV crews were all set up at the hospital but competition was especially tough that year. Grace Kelly won for *The Country Girl*.

But Judy had given the classic Hollywood story an Oscar performance that was hard to beat.

Judy was born Frances Gumm in Grand Rapids, Michigan, literally in a theater trunk. By the time she was two, she was onstage singing with her sisters. Her first song was "Jingle Bells" and the Gumm sisters might have remained that even though Judy took seven curtain calls on her first appearance onstage.

It was one of those acts that was destined for the small-time hick circuits, like the Gus Sun Time. But a lucky booking brought them into the Oriental Theater in Chicago as an opening act for headliner Georgie Jessel. As Jessel recalls it:

"What the hell kind of a name was Gumm? It was okay for Wrigley but not for a garland of beautiful girls like these sisters. I gave them the name—the Garland sisters. I don't know how in the hell Frances became Judy but I sure as hell got rid of Gumm on the marquee."

The act went from Chicago to Los Angeles where the Gumm Sisters—now the Garland Sisters—played both the old Orpheum and the RKO Hillstreet. The sisters as an act made no impression.

Then one night at the Orpheum, Mrs. Gumm brought only Judy to what they called the Monday Night Preview of New Acts.

Mrs. Gumm, the quintessential stage mother who was no dummy in the ways of show business, had Judy come from out of the audience as a new discovery. She was dressed in drab and faded blue denims, a style forty years ahead of its time. But it gave her a waiflike appearance.

People who were in the audience that night in the middle thirties never forgot that child's left-handed stance, waving that skinny left arm as she belted a song called "Rain."

She stopped the show and got seven curtain calls. Then she went out and belted another song and another. One witness recalled:

"No kid should have had this much show business savvy— following a climax with still another climax and another. She was adorable."

She was such a hit that Mrs. Gumm took her out to Universal studios the next day and she was signed for a short with another unknown by the name of Deanna Durbin. Judy belted jazz and Deanna sang classical music.

Louis B. Mayer saw the short and wanted Deanna instead of Judy.

As to how Judy got signed by MGM, there are more claimants to that deed than there are descendants of Mayflower passengers. The most logical choice was Ben Piazza, talent scout and casting director at the studio. Mayer wanted Deanna but didn't act fast enough. He took a trip to Europe first and Joe Pasternak grabbed her instead. The Pasternak-Durbin pictures paid the rent at Universal for years.

Judy, meanwhile, played a hillbilly in a movie called *Pigskin Parade* for Fox. Nothing much happened with her until a big studio party, where she sang "You Made Me Love You" to a photograph of Clark Gable. It was such a sensation that she repeated the same performance on film in *Broadway Melody of 1938*.

Then came all of those Andy Hardy and musical pictures with Mickey Rooney, also born in a trunk.

All told, Judy's thirty-four films over the years grossed more than $100 million. But it required Frank Sinatra, a pal, to give $10,000 to Liza to pay for her mother's funeral costs.

"Everybody made money off of Judy Garland but me," Judy once said in a 4 A.M. phone call from New York. And she laughed when she said it. Funny, my fondest memory of Judy is laughter. Yet her life story could make a better tragedy than *A Star is Born*.

The Secret of Ageless Cary Grant

Most girls would sooner have Cary Grant, age 73, in their Christmas stockings than Robert Redford or any other star you know.

What's his secret? His secret of youthfulness is so simple it's anti-climactic.

"I really don't do a thing except relax and take things easy. I am enthusiastic about my work and the people I work with."

He no longer makes movies but is on the board of directors of Faberge, Inc. He approaches that job with the same enthusiasm he took to acting.

"I am constantly amazed to read that I distill vegetable juices, swim fifty laps daily as if I were training to cross the English Channel, and spend six hours a day in the gym working out."

In truth, Cary only swims. And then only if he feels like it.

"It's the least exertive of exercises and certainly the most pleasant on a hot day. I eat what I like. In fact, I would call myself a hearty eater. Something lucky about my metabolism keeps me from putting on too much weight.

"I fortunately am not a heavy drinker but if I feel like a cocktail or two before dinner, I'll drink. And I love good wine with my meals. I don't smoke but I used to.

"I have a theory that if the world relaxed a little more, there would be no tension in the world. No war. No problems. It took a lot of years for me to reach my present state of relaxation. I had lots of problems over the years but they were Archie Leach's problems, not Cary Grant's." (Archibald Leach, of course, is Cary's real name).

"You might say that Archie Leach sat watching a Cary Grant movie one day and said: 'Why don't I relax like Cary Grant?'

"And I did, forevermore.

"I suddenly realized I had spent the greater part of my life fluctuating between Archie Leach and Cary Grant, unsure of either, suspecting each. Then I began to unify them into one person. With unity came peace and relaxation."

Cary may be a cosmetics tycoon now but he will always be an actor.

When my book *Hollywood Is a Four Letter Town* hit the bookstalls, Cary was the first of the stars I had written about to call me.

"I want you to know," he said, "that I bought your book and like a true actor looked in the index first to see if my name was there. It was and I read all my pages first and I want to thank you. You were so complimentary that I couldn't believe I was that man. Thank you."

One of the crimes in this business is that Cary never won an

Oscar for his acting. The Academy gave him a special one once but that's not the same.

Cary never expected to win any.

"I'd have to blacken my teeth first."

Cary was the absolute master of light comedy on screen—the hardest thing to do. Brando flopped when he tried it in some long-forgotten movie with David Niven.

What Cary did, he did so well that he made it look too easy. That may be the reason why he has never won an Oscar.

"I was in the business so long that I knew what people wanted me to do. That's why I kept doing it. Experience. That's the answer."

Cary is a perfectionist in anything he does. When a Cary Grant movie hits the screen, Cary's performance could only be compared with the great Willie Mays catching a fly ball in center field.

(Threw that in because Cary is a baseball nut. He has a dugout box at Dodger Stadium.)

There was always a lot of hard work before the cameras turned on any Cary Grant movie.

"Acting, actually, is the easiest part of my job."

He's not kidding. On the set, he was the only star I have ever known who personally examined each extra before a scene to make sure they were dressed right.

If the prop department supplied inexpensive prints to dress up a Cary Grant home or apartment set, it so disturbed him that he went home and came back with priceless Picassos or Monets.

Once, working with Doris Day in a movie, she was so impressed with Cary's taste that she asked him to supervise her wardrobe.

When one of his pictures was finished, Cary went back with it to its preview at Radio City Music Hall. All of Cary's movies were previewed at the famed New York theatre.

The theatre, most prestigious showcase in the nation, would buy a Cary Grant movie sight unseen in the old days, but Cary took no chances.

Before the picture was screened in the Radio City projection room, you would find Cary personally seating the theatre management so that they could properly see and hear each word, each nuance, each expression.

"It takes 500 small details to add up to one favorable impression."

Cary's perfectionism explains his many wives. Over the years, I have known all of them. They all say, as if by rote:

"I still love Cary. He's the most charming man I have ever known but. . . ."

Our Girl Got Married on Us

Joan Crawford was my idea of a movie star. She and I were friends for as long as I had been around. Up until her death, I still heard from her all the time, usually by handwritten note.

Before Joan married Alfred Steele, chairman of the board of Pepsi-Cola, she used to go with Milton Rackmil, head of Universal Pictures and Decca Records.

I knew Milton but he always regarded me suspiciously around Joan because of our close friendship.

One day Joan urgently asked me to visit her set out at Universal, where she was making a picture for Milton. I got there as fast as I could. Soon as she saw me, she took me in her trailer dressing room and locked the door.

Turned out she wanted my advice about a story *Confidential* magazine was threatening to publish about her, a story that did not have a word of truth in it.

As I recall, I believe it had something to do with the strict discipline she imposed on her children at home. The story, as threatened, made Joan out to be a Nazi storm trooper with her kids.

Joan didn't spoil her kids like most Hollywood mothers did, but she was a loving and kind mother. A good mother. I knew that for a fact.

She told me who was going to write the story, a well-known Hollywood trade-paper columnist. I told Joan I had enough on him to hang him.

The columnist and the editor of *Confidential* were planning to call on Joan later that day. She was quite worried.

In the midst of all this discussion, a knock came on the dressing-room door. She ignored it and continued talking. The knock turned into pounding. It was Rackmil.

I excused myself quickly and left.

For whatever reason—Joan's charm and candor with the editor of *Confidential*, or a phone call I made to the columnist, dropping the name of some of his boyfriends in the casual conversation—the article on Joan never appeared in *Confidential*.

But Rackmil still wanted to know what Joan and I were doing in a locked dressing room. She pacified him.

Then a few weeks later, I was over at Joan's house drinking vodka with her. Joan is the only person, male or female, I know who can sip straight vodka and tell you what proof it is. It's kind of a perfect pitch for drinkers.

Anyhow, Joan had a date that night with Rackmil, who was calling for her. I started to leave but she asked that I stay while she got dressed upstairs.

Now Joan is the most meticulous housekeeper I have ever known. No maid could get her floors scrubbed clean enough for her. I have seen this glamorous movie star down on her hands and knees scrubbing the floors in her Brentwood home.

That had happened this particular day, so she asked that I take off my shoes as we crossed the hallway and went upstairs to her bedroom.

I left my shoes by the front door and took my glass with me.

I stood there while Joan was putting on her makeup and getting ready for Rackmil, who—wouldn't you know it— showed up early.

The first thing he saw were my shoes by the front door. The next thing he saw was Joan Crawford in negligee at her makeup table and me, coatless, with drink in hand in her bedroom.

I thought he was going to blow his top so I beat another hasty retreat.

Not long after that, Joan eloped to Las Vegas with Steele in his private airplane. I called her the next morning because I knew she had a deathly fear of flying in those days.

"Well," she said, "you know I love this old devil because how else would he get me up in an airplane? We just had drinks and dinner at Romanoff's last night and decided it would be a good idea to elope to Las Vegas."

I had barely hung up the phone when Milton called:

"Well," he said with a certain amount of sadness. "We lost our girl to a soft drink."

Long Live the King!

It was Sunday morning, November 6, 1960, when I got a tip that an ambulance was being dispatched to Clark Gable's ranch in Encino. I lived less than five minutes from there.

As I drove up the long driveway to the Gable ranch, a place I had been many times before, I saw the ambulance attendants loading the King onto a stretcher.

I didn't know whether he was dead or alive until one of the attendants told me he had suffered a heart attack and they were taking him to Hollywood Presbyterian Hospital, a good half hour away.

Somehow I beat the ambulance to the hospital and was waiting when they wheeled him in.

He spotted me. That famous grin and then he said:

"How's the food in this joint?"

It was the last time I ever saw the King alive. He died in the same hospital ten days later from another attack.

To this day, Kay Gable can't figure how I beat the ambulance to the hospital. Thank God, there weren't many cops on the freeways that quiet Sunday morning.

His attack was a particular shock to me because only the Friday before, the King and I had had a long chat on the set of *The Misfits* while we both were waiting for Marilyn Monroe to show up for some process shots. It was the windup day of *The Misfits*.

Gable was the most professional of actors. To him, it would have been unthinkable to have a heart attack in the middle of a picture. There was never a day's production lost because of Gable in any of his ninety movies. And he came to work with a heavy hangover more than once.

That Friday we talked about Marilyn's problem with booze and pills and her various insecurities, but mostly we talked about his becoming a father for the first time—legitimately.

I say legitimately because Gable once had a romance with one of Hollywood's biggest stars during a picture. Not long after the picture, the leading lady "adopted" a baby who is now grown up and resembles her mother more than somewhat. And if you look close, there's a little Gable there, too.

But that is Hollywood legend.

What we talked about that Friday was the impending birth of a baby to his fifth wife, Kay Spreckels Gable, which was due the following March.

"This is a dividend that has come to me late in life," he said as we sat together in the director's chairs. One chair had his name. Mine said John Huston, who was busy trying to get Marilyn to show on the set so he could get the hell out of town and back to his estate in County Galway.

"When I wind up this picture, I'm taking off until the baby is born in March. I want to be there when it happens—and I want to be there a good many months afterward.

"This is my ninetieth picture and it's been a tough one. I'm not doing any more for a long while. I want to enjoy my son,". said Gable.

All through the chat, he referred to the baby only as "he"—and it was hard to conceive anything but a husky boy being born to Gable, a genuine he-man.

After his death I told Kay his widow about the conversation.

"Funny," she said. "You're the only one he ever mentioned to that he wanted a son. He never said it to me."

I said that was probably because Clark, a kind man, didn't want to hurt her feelings if she bore him a daughter.

John Clark Gable, a carbon copy of his old man, was born March 20, 1961. The father got his wish but never lived to see it fulfilled.

To show you how much affection there was for Gable, all of his old friends from MGM showed up within hours of his heart attack at the hospital—even though he had been away from the studio for ten years.

Ken Hollywood, the famous gateman at MGM, showed up with a bunch of off-duty studio guards to make sure the King had peace and quiet.

Howard Strickling, the veteran director of publicity at MGM, took charge of all press relations as media from all over the world converged on the hospital. It was all extra work for all of them but they loved doing it.

"No one but Gable would ever get this turnout," said Strickling. And he was so right. Gable was one of the most genuinely loved stars Hollywood had ever known. He was down-to-earth, a gentleman of the old school who treated the gaffer as kindly and courteously as he did Louis B. Mayer.

He was King of a phony world—but no phony himself.

For some strange reason, Gable never had the trouble with fans that other stars did. I saw him show up at premieres where there were howling, mad fans screaming like banshees. As soon as Gable was spotted, the crowd parted just like the Red Sea in a DeMille epic.

"I don't molest people and they don't molest me."

He truly was the King—and seventeen years later, Hollywood hasn't come up with anyone to take his place.

I guess it was because Gable was all man. Women adored him and men did, too, with a little touch of envy.

Only time I ever saw a fan get overemotional around Gable was when a woman visiting the Paramount lot came around a corner and ran head on into Clark. She fainted. Gable picked her up and took her into his dressing room and gave her some water. She woke up and saw Gable leaning over her. Her reaction was natural. She fainted again.

Gable was a hell of a lot better actor than even his most ardent fans realized. He had come up the hard way in stock and he knew his craft well. But Gable himself always pooh-poohed his acting ability. Once when Jimmy Cagney directed a movie, I asked the King—I always called him that to his face—when he was going to direct.

"Direct? Hell, I haven't even learned how to act yet."

His modesty, which was real, also brought forth another astonishing statement.

One day when he had left MGM and was working over at Paramount, we got to talking about *Gone With the Wind*.

"Hell," he said. "I still don't think I was right for Rhett Butler."

"You got to be kidding, King," I said.

"No, I mean it. I never was right for that part." He was serious, despite the fact we were each on our fifth martini at Lucy's restaurant.

Gone With the Wind swept Oscar—except for Gable. It's hard to believe when you see that movie today, how his performance got overlooked.

Robert Donat for *Goodbye, Mr. Chips* won the best actor Oscar that year.

The picture that Gable won an Oscar for—*It Happened One Night*—was one he believed in—although you will never make Frank Capra believe it.

"Back there in 1934 I had a big beef with Mayer. I was sick and I wanted time off. Mayer didn't believe me—even when I later went to the hospital," said Clark.

"So he gave me the old Siberia treatment. He loaned me out to Columbia. In those days Columbia was on Poverty Row, not the big studio it is today. They thought they were punishing me. I knew different because I knew I was going to work for Frank Capra. Also I knew I was going to do comedy. That picture got me out of a career rut of playing mostly heavies."

Capra has a different version.

"Clark came into my office for a meeting and he didn't even lift his head. He was really pissed off at MGM and Mayer. I kept telling him what the script was all about but he couldn't have cared less. He knew he had been exiled and goddamn it, that was it."

But it's what gets on the screen that counts. Gable gave a memorable performance in that 1934 movie and won the best acting Oscar.

The picture was so successful that it took Columbia and Harry Cohn off Poverty Row and established Capra as one of the legendary directors of the screen.

Gable almost didn't make it into the movies. He was playing Killer Mears in a Los Angeles stage version of *The Last Mile*, the same part his pal Spencer Tracy had made famous in New York.

Minna Wallis, sister of Hal Wallis and one of the top agents of the Golden Era, was Gable's agent. She took Gable over to Mervyn LeRoy, then a top director at Warners. Mervyn also saw the play. Both Minna and Mervyn saw the potential in Gable.

They took him in to meet with Darryl F. Zanuck, then in charge of production at Warners. Darryl recalls that meeting:

"Whenever the publicity department calls me a genius, I always remind them of the time I refused to sign Gable because I thought his ears were too big. Some genius."

Minna then got Gable in a 1930 movie called *The Painted Desert*, starring William Boyd, pre-Hopalong Cassidy.

The picture was shot in Arizona and women visiting the set swooned over Gable. He had, as always, that most marketable of all Hollywood qualities in male stars—balls.

MGM saw *Painted Desert* and immediately signed Gable to a two-year contract. It is not generally known that Clark made twelve pictures in his first year at MGM without creating much of an impact.

Then came *A Free Soul* starring Lionel Barrymore and Norma Shearer. Gable was cast to play the most despicable of heavies. In one scene he slapped Norma, then the reigning star of the MGM lot.

Mayer wanted the scene cut from the picture. He said real Americans would boo Gable. American men didn't slap their women, especially stars like Norma Shearer.

Irving Thalberg, who had more than a passing interest in Norma, argued vehemently to keep the scene in. He won.

Then an amazing thing happened. Women by the thousands, instead of protesting the brutality of the scene, wrote in that they would all love to be slapped around by Clark Gable.

A star was born.

In typical Hollywood fashion, the next few years had Gable slapping women all over the place. That's why he was glad to be exiled to Columbia and *It Happened One Night*.

"I was never typecast after that picture," he said.

A lot of Gable's appeal stems from his Air Force career.

Mayer, publicized for his patriotism, was not patriotic enough to lose his biggest star—not when he didn't have to go.

In 1942, Gable was three years over the draft ceiling. He didn't have all his own teeth and he was drinking too damn much because of the air crash death of Carole Lombard early in the year. Anybody else would have been turned down in that condition—which was okay by Mayer.

Despite all kinds of studio pressure, Gable enlisted as a buck private in the U.S. Army Air Corps (that was before there was a separate Air Force) on August 12, 1942.

He did it with as little fanfare as possible. He was assigned to Officers Candidate School. It was tough for him competing with others half his age of 41 but he survived.

"The one happy thing I remember about the service," he once told me, "was shaving off that mustache and wearing those khakis. For the first time in ten years, I was just one of the mob. I wasn't Clark Gable, movie star."

He went on air strikes over the continent as a gunnery officer and won not only the Air Medal but, more important, the respect and admiration of his fighting buddies.

After the war, Gable returned to MGM and had a series of flops. He was the first to admit it.

He considered *Mogambo* the only good movie he made at postwar MGM and that was a remake of one of his earlier hits, *Red Dust,* with Jean Harlow.

Worse, he wasn't getting rich like a lot of the stars around town were. That was because of MGM's policy of not granting percentage deals to its stars. Gable's salary, while high, was in the ninety-percent tax bracket so he left the studio that had made him a star and for which he had made millions.

I happened to be there the day he left. The place was like a morgue as Gable went around shaking hands with all the little people on the lot. Many of them had tears in their eyes.

"I'm not rich by any means but I'm comfortable. I don't ask much out of life except to be warm and comfortable and be able to eat three meals a day."

And how Gable could eat. Next to Mario Lanza, he had the biggest appetite of any man in the business, but he always kept himself in shape by working around his ranch or hunting and fishing.

He had a down-to-earth quality about him that few stars have. Once I was standing on Sunset Boulevard when Gable drove by in a new Mercedes-Benz, the most expensive convertible you could buy. He saw me and pulled over to the curb to show off the new car, like a kid with a new toy.

"I just walked in off the street and said, 'I'll take that.'

"The goddamn salesman was flabbergasted. I had Alabam drive my old car away while I waited for them to get it ready to drive off."

A few weeks later, he pulled out a 79-cent cigarette lighter from his pocket.

"Remember the day I walked in off the street and bought that Mercedes for $16,000? Well, the dealer called me and said they had a nice present for my wife because I had given them my business.

"Like a horse's ass, I drove all the way in from Encino to pick up this cheap, goddamn lighter." And then the famous grin.

What was the Gable appeal?

He was one of the few in the history of the screen who appealed as much to men as he did to women. Wives adored him and it made their husbands happy that they did.

Gable had come along to exemplify virility at a time when the Depression had sapped a nation.

Both men and women could identify with Gable. To the college coed, he was the moose fullback on the grid team. A man could see those big ears and realize that if Gable could make it, maybe he could, too.

Big-city audiences could identify with Gable's sophistication and the British tailoring of his suits. And always that leer that devastated women wherever they lived.

To small-town America, he was the guy from Cadiz, Ohio, who made good in the big city—but never got the swelled head.

Barbra Streisand Owes Me a Lot

I have a psychic friend who calls me a lot. We first met years ago through our mutual friend, Clifton Webb.

As I recall, Dr. Kenny Kingston the psychic was at the party where Clifton, in his queenly way, asked me to dance with him.

Clifton was quite loaded, of course, but I didn't want to offend him. It would not have been the greatest image for me to be seen dancing with the gay Clifton at a party at Romanoff's filled with all the stars in town. The party was in honor of Vivien Leigh.

So what do you do? I said:

"Clifton, you are probably the greatest dancer the Broadway musical stage has ever known, with the possible exception of

Fred Astaire. How could I possibly dance with such a talent?"

It appeased Clifton, who agreed. Then he turned to Bob Newhart and asked the same question. Newhart's wife saved him.

"Don't dance with him, Clifton," said Ginny Newhart. "He's a lousy dancer."

Next thing I knew Clifton was dancing with Vivien Leigh—and that's why you have never read about this party before.

Not too long after that, Clifton, who was a beautiful man, died. He was gone but never forgotten. Every time Dr. Kingston has a seance, Clifton shows. He once told Kenny that, thanks to me, he gets more publicity dead than alive.

Last year I was down in Houston and got to talking with Gene Tierney, who had co-starred with Clifton in a memorable movie, *Laura*. It was a cocktail party at the home of some billionaire Houston oilman, and casually I mentioned to Gene that I often hear from Clifton.

She did a double take and stared at me with those beautiful panther eyes—and then abruptly walked away and joined another group, meanwhile shooting backward glances at me.

All of which brings me to Barbra Streisand. It was March, 1969, and Kenny the psychic called me as he often does. He opened the conversation thusly:

"I was in the 5800 block of Laurel Canyon last night and ran into Fannie Brice, who was with Clifton and his mother Mabelle. They were all standing in front of Ramon Novarro's old house. Someone had tacked a for-sale sign on it."

Now you must remember, everybody in the foregoing paragraph was dead. Ramon was the latest to go to that Great Screening Room in the Sky.

I played it straight as I always do. As a Hollywood columnist, I mentally noted that it was about two weeks after nominations had been announced for the Oscars. Barbra Streisand, playing Fannie Brice, had been nominated for best actress in *Funny Girl*. The picture had also been nominated for best picture.

"Tell me, Kenny," I said. "Did Fannie say anything about Streisand's chances of winning the Oscar?"

Kenny answered matter-of-factly.

"She was very vague. I don't quite understand it. She said Barbra would not win as best actress but also she would not lose. Strange, isn't it?"

It was indeed strange, so strange that I just kissed it off in the column the next day. Fannie also predicted that *Funny Girl* would not win the best picture Oscar but that another musical would.

That was strange too because *Funny Girl* and *Oliver,* the only other musical, were both made by Columbia. Usually, big studios with two pictures in the running split their vote and knock each other off. *Oliver* was the long shot in the race. *The Lion in Winter,* starring Katharine Hepburn and Peter O'Toole, was the favorite to win.

I put that in the column, also the fact that Fannie, Clifton, and Mabelle went down Laurel Canyon to the San Fernando Valley to meet Rudolph Valentino for dinner at the Valley Tail of the Cock.

Next day all hell broke loose. John Flinn, director of publicity at Columbia Pictures in Hollywood, called good-naturedly to tell me that Ray Stark, producer of *Funny Girl,* was quite upset and warned me that there would be further high-echelon calls.

Flinn, who has a good sense of humor, thought the whole thing rather funny but felt he had to relay the message.

No sooner had I hung up than Bob Ferguson, vice-president of Columbia advertising and publicity in New York, called. He sounded more agitated but, in fairness, he was civil.

Apparently Ray Stark, skiing in Sun Valley, had chewed out his—Ferguson's—ass.

I explained it was all tongue-in-cheek and quite silly to even worry about it.

Within thirty seconds, Stark calls from a phone atop one of the Sawtooth mountains in Idaho. Ray said:

"You have cost me the spiritualist vote in the Academy."

I should have known how seriously producers take an Academy Award nomination. Worse, Ray was Fannie Brice's son-in-law and his wife, Fran, one of the leading social lights of Holmby Hills, didn't like the idea of her mother going to the San Fernando Valley. People who live on the Beverly Hills-Holmby Hills-Bel-Air side of the mountain wouldn't be caught dead in the valley.

Well, came the night of the Academy Awards four weeks later. Barbra Streisand did not win and she did not lose. She tied with Kate Hepburn, the first tie in Oscar history since 1932.

And *Funny Girl* did not win as best movie. The other musical, *Oliver*, did.

But I'm going to reveal something now that may get me forgiven by Fran and Ray Stark. Not long after the psychic's call, Jack Oakie, my pal and neighbor, asked me to drop by the house, which I did.

Sitting in front of Jack was a half-empty bottle of scotch and his Oscar ballot. We finished the bottle and opened another one. Then Jack said:

"I've only seen one picture this year, *Oliver*, and I'm voting for Ron Moody for best actor. You've seen them all, how about filling out my ballot for me?

Scotch has a way of making everything seem logical. I filled out the ballot, although I am not a member of the Academy and ineligible to vote.

I voted for Barbra Streisand for best actress.

Had I not, Katharine Hepburn would have won the Oscar all alone by one vote.

Maybe that's why she tried to run me down with her bicycle over at Nice, France. And I always thought it was because I brought Spencer Tracy home drunk.

Pictures that are made with lots of fighting often are the best. If that's the case, *A Star Is Born* should go down in history with the greatest.

Miss Streisand, who was star and executive producer, fought

with her boyfriend Jon Peters, who was producer. Both fought with Frank Pierson, the director.

In the middle, getting the hell squeezed out of him from both sides, was the immensely talented Kris Kristofferson, a Rhodes scholar turned country singer.

You have read all the accounts of the squabbles on that set. It sounded like World War III.

When I was down in Tempe, Arizona, on location, I fully expected Bob Hope to show up at any minute to entertain the fighting stars.

At one point, with 50,000 rock fans in the Sun Devil stadium of Arizona State, Barbra and Kris got into a fuck-you name-calling contest over live mikes.

Some of the fans thought it was part of the script. Those up close knew it wasn't.

Finally, Kris grabbed me and we went to his trailer dressing room. The day was hot but Kris' Coors beer was chilled. We sat there for a few moments. Kris said: "I wish in the hell I knew who's running this ship."

As the beer and tequila soothed nerves, Kris took up his guitar. He picked out a tune I had never heard before. Words I had never heard before. It had all the hit marks of his other work—"Help Me Make It Through the Night" and "Me and Bobby McGee."

"That's a great song, Kris," I said. "Where did that come from?"

He then went into the chorus of "It Can Never Happen Again."

"You and I are hearing this song for the first time because I'm just composing it. It's the story of my experiences in making this movie."

It took about twenty minutes for him to put words and music together. Then he put down his guitar and went out and did a scene with Barbra without rancor and with such emotional feeling between the two of them, it was heaven to watch.

Kris is already a superstar in the rock and country field.

He's going to be one too in the movies.

He's got balls and talent, too—plus rugged good looks. How can you beat that?

Helpful Hints for Hostesses

In my career as a Hollywood columnist I have been to more parties than Chasen's catering service. Some stand out in my memory as super galas.

One of my all-time favorites was a gala given by Princess Grace and Prince Rainier in 1958 with Frank Sinatra entertaining. It was held in the Sporting Club in Monte Carlo and the guest list read like a Who's Who of French Riviera society. It was so exclusive I wonder how I ever got invited. But Grace and I had been friends ever since *High Noon* and maybe that's the reason.

The Sporting Club in Monte Carlo is a rather compact place, and one rubbed elbows with Noel Coward, Somerset Maugham, King Peter of Yugoslavia, a dozen or so dukes and counts, a sister of a future president of the United States—Pat Kennedy—plus movie stars by the score.

The vodka was especially flown in from Russia; the champagne was a special *cuvée* of Rainier's—plus cases of Dom Perignon, 1955. The caviar was especially selected by Rainier's chef, who made a special trip to Iran.

The only drink not provided by the host and hostess was Jack Daniels, which Sinatra drank in those days. Frank knew sour mash bourbon was hard to come by in Europe and when we left the United States, Frank's baggage included ten cases of Jack Daniels.

His excess-baggage charges cost more than his first-class fare. This was back in the days of the prop planes and if we had hit a headwind over the Atlantic, we might have had to scuttle the booze.

"I'll never forget Maugham and Coward escorting a sixteen-year-old, sweet-faced boy to the gala. It's hard to say which one he belonged to but it struck me as rather obscene.

My dinner companion was Hedda Hopper, who was not royally received by the Rainiers but she was Frank's guest. At one drunken point in the proceedings, Hedda suggested that we dance. That would have been okay except all of a sudden she started to lead me across the floor. I didn't know where in the hell I was going. Hedda headed straight for the Rainiers and then bumped the Prince right in the ass.

"I'll teach those bastards not to speak to me," said Hedda as we danced off. She let me lead now.

I was embarrassed as hell because I was very fond of both Grace and the Prince and didn't relish taking part in Hedda's feud.

Then the show started. An Italian singer preceded Frank and sang his own composition, which was quite catchy.

I was with Joan Caulfield the actress by this time. To hell with Hedda. I always lead when I dance with girls. Joan asked the Italian if he had made a recording of his song. He had and gave her one. She brought the record back to Hollywood and gave it to Ira Cook, then one of the top disc jockeys at radio station KMPC.

Ira loved the song and plugged the hell out of it. Before long both the singer and the song were famous—Domenigo Modugno and "Volare." If it hadn't been for Joan, Domenigo might still be an opening act.

But the one thing that made the party so memorable was Sinatra himself. Frank brought along his pianist Bill Miller, who Frank calls "Sun Tan Charlie." That's because Bill, like most musicians, is night people and hasn't seen the sun in years.

All day long "Sun Tan Charlie" kept urging Frank to rehearse with the band, which was strictly pick-up from Paris, none of whom understood English. Finally, just before show-time Frank went in and rehearsed a total of ten minutes with the musicians.

That night Frank gave one of the finest concerts he has ever

given. I judge every Sinatra performance by that night. Frank
liked it, too. The whole house rose as one to give him a standing ovation. I was sitting next to Coward, that master of English prose, who was on his feet yelling: "It's a gas! It's a
gas!"

Hedda left after the show and soon an equerry came over
and said: "The Prince would like you to join him at his table." Which I did.

As soon as I sat down, the Prince said:

"I would have invited you over much sooner but you were
sitting with that dreadful madame."

I then apologized for what happened on the dance floor.

"Please don't," he said. "I could see that you had no control
over the situation. Awkward, isn't it, when the lady insists on
leading?"

Rainier has a down-to-earth, almost homespun quality
about him that I found quite charming. He looks like a
Prince and is the only absolute monarch left, but it never went
to his head.

A lot of my best parties have been with the Burtons. Was
really sorry to see those two split up.

One Burton party was held in Paris and it was a dilly. The
food and drink were the finest and so were the other guests.
For entertainment, there was the famous nude revue from the
Lido de Paris.

At our table was Aristotle Onassis, with Maria Callas. Ingrid Bergman was there, too.

A good group.

Then a well-known Las Vegas hoodlum spotted me and
came over to the table. I never minded talking to him in Las
Vegas because that town was an open city in those days, no
bloodshed among the boys.

But in Paris, who knew who was going to take a shot at
him?

Just as he was talking with me, a waiter dropped a champagne bottle, which exploded like a shot. I immediately went

under the table. I thought sure some of the boys had scored a hit on my friend.

Burton lifted up the tablecloth and asked what the hell I was doing under the table so early in the evening?

I came out sheepishly, but it was some consolation to find out that my mobster friend was a little shaken, too, by the realistic sound of the exploding champagne bottle.

Another party with the Burtons took place down in Puerto Vallarta, Mexico, after the close of the movie *Night of the Iguana*.

Everybody was drinking tequila and eating hot Mexican food.

John Huston in those days had a beautiful Iranian mistress, about twenty-one, who gave Elizabeth Taylor real competition in the looks department. I was chatting with her when the famous "El Indio" of Mexican films joined us.

"El Indio" works only as an actor now but under his right name, Emilio Fernandes, he was once Mexico's finest director.

Emilio had one problem. He shot his producer and also two newspapermen who wrote something about him he didn't like. That ended his career as a director. What producer is going to hire a director who is such a poor sport?

Well, when "El Indio" sat down next to us, the first thing I noticed was the cocked pistol in a holster strapped to his thigh.

Emilio was drinking tequila like water and it didn't help matters much when Huston came up to me and said: " 'El Indio' goes native on tequila."

I knew he had already shot two newpapermen, so when he turned to me and said: "Jeem, what do you do for a living?" I said:

"I'm in ladies' ready-to-wear."

At that I made a hasty exit and joined the Burtons. Before long I had Elizabeth on my lap and I was imploring her to let me take her away from all this. And Richard was urging her to go.

It was a fun evening. Tequila is a great drink. You never get a hangover, just bruises and cuts when you fall down.

The only wild Hollywood party I ever went to was, believe it or not, down in Athens, Georgia.

I was down there working in a picture called *Poor Pretty Eddie* for a young director named Rick Robinson, who is quite a hell raiser.

We were all staying at one of the local motels and one night Leslie Uggams decided to give a birthday party for her Australian husband, Graham Pratt.

It was very sedate until the birthday cake was cut. Robinson cut a piece and handed it to Shelley Winters, who is quite playful. She threw the cake in Robinson's face. Robinson then threw a piece of cake back at Shelley. In a matter of seconds, everybody in the cast and crew were throwing cake at each other.

It was like a Mack Sennett comedy. All the time a rock band kept on playing music. Some of the young girls took off all their clothes and started dancing nude. Robinson the director took off all his clothes and started dancing naked. This went on for a good half hour. The whole room was naked except me. I couldn't pass the physical.

Funniest thing came when a customer at the nearby bar came in to see what the hell was going on. He was a traveling salesman in town for the night. He saw everybody naked and he immediately shed his clothes and was out on the floor doing the funky chicken with a naked young chick.

Shelley took off her clothes and jumped in the swimming pool but nobody looked.

Leslie, I might add, remained ladylike through the whole thing. She later told me that it cost her $1,500 to repair the cake-throwing damage to the motel.

It really was a spontaneous thing that ended almost as fast as it began.

Peter Lorre and Medical Science

Peter Lorre and I were close friends but I always worried

about him. He had high blood pressure and drank too much, which you are not supposed to do with high blood pressure.

It finally got him—but not before one particularly close call in Spain where he was making the first and only Smell-O-Vision movie for Mike Todd, Jr.

In the middle of the shooting, somewhere in the middle of the Spanish countryside, Peter collapsed.

"I thought he was a goner for sure," said Mike, Jr. "The only doctor around for miles was a village doctor, whom we summoned immediately. I didn't think we had a chance to save Peter."

The doctor came in and went through all the established medical procedures and then decided to put leeches all over Peter's body.

"I was in horror," Mike recalls, "but the doctor said it was the only chance Peter had. Nothing else would work now."

The leeches sucked Peter's blood and, amazingly, his blood pressure dropped. Soon he was sitting up in bed, joking with Mike and others who had come in to witness his marvelous recovery.

Later when I saw Peter back in Hollywood, he commented:

"You put a scene like that in a script, especially with Peter Lorre playing it, and they would throw you out the door. Too bad my friend Bela Lugosi didn't live to hear about it."

A Hollywood Myth Exploded

Let's explode one of the most famous and durable of Hollywood myths—that Gary Cooper was a "Yep" or "Nope" yokel who grunted only monosyllables.

I found out exactly the opposite the very first day I met Coop on the set of *High Noon* at the Columbia ranch in Burbank.

During the lunch hour, Coop and I dropped over to a restaurant called the China Trader. We had a drink or two and then the waiter brought over a water tumbler of tequila.

"It's from Miss Jurado," said the waiter.

Cooper looked at it; then from across the room the great Mexican actress, Katy Jurado, yelled:

"In my country, when we admire someone, we send tequila to their table."

At that, Coop drank the whole tumbler, practically in one swallow.

By the time it hit him, he was up on his chair giving a speech on the good-neighbor policy with our Latin neighbors. No one could shut him up.

Before long an assistant director came over and dragged him out of the place since he was in the first shot after lunch. The assistant gave me one of those nasty looks, as if I had gotten Coop drunk.

He went out the door shouting "Viva El Mexico!"

After that Coop and I became the best of friends. He was the nicest actor who ever lived—and one of the best. The two Oscars he won for *Sergeant York* and *High Noon* were no flukes.

Sometimes you would watch him do a scene with a noted actor and you would wince. He often sounded like a high school junior delivering lines for the annual school play.

Then you would see the same scene on the screen and Cooper would dominate it with a look of reaction and steal it, often from some of the best stage actors in the business.

Coop once explained that to me.

"I know I'm a shit-kicking actor but I've been around this business so damn long that I have learned it all. Guys like me and Duke have mastered the art of movie acting—as compared with acting acting."

And he was so right. John Barrymore once said he would never appear in a movie with Cooper.

"I could eat up the scenery and Coop, with one look or a hand wiping his face, would steal the whole goddamn scene from me. He's the best there is."

The Cooper you saw on the screen was entirely different from the Cooper in person. The real Cooper was witty, urbane, and sophisticated. True, he was one of the real cowboys of the movies but his early education came from the "public" (i. e., private) schools in England. He might wear jeans in his movies, but his offscreen wardrobe was tailored on Bond Street.

Also, he was not the straightforward U. S. Marshal in real life. If anything, Cooper was a roué.

And when he played himself in a delightful Billy Wilder movie called *Love in the Afternoon,* it was a box-office flop.

Coop was quite open about his romances.

His marriage to Rocky Cooper was at times, to put it mildly, quite rocky.

He once told me that during *Saratoga Trunk,* he had a love affair with Ingrid Bergman. Ingrid, such a dedicated actress, had a habit of falling in love with leading men for the duration of the movie. Maybe that is why she has always been so brilliant on screen.

"In my whole life," said Coop, "I never had a woman so much in love with me as Ingrid was. The day after the picture ended, I couldn't get her on the phone."

Once when I had lunch with Cooper in the Beverly Hills Brown Derby, I told him I was leaving the next day for Monaco.

He said: "Say hello to Grace for me but don't mention my name to Prince Rainier. He's hated me ever since we both went after the same model in Paris and I beat him out."

Also in the same Brown Derby, I once accidentally eavesdropped on his farewell to Patricia Neal, one of the most torrid and long-lasting of the Cooper romances.

It was breakfast time—10 A.M. or so—and I walked in the side door of the Derby. The waiter sat me in the booth behind Cooper and Patricia. Cooper's back was to me. Patricia could see me but she didn't know who I was in those days.

Soon, she was in tears. I felt very embarrassed as I could hear Coop tell her that divorce to Rocky was out of the question. His daughter, Maria, had pleaded with him not to leave her mother and he was going to stick it out. It meant the end of his relationship with Patricia.

She sobbed so much, Coop threw a ten-dollar bill on the table and said:

"Let's get out of here."

As he got up, he spotted me.

"Jesus," he said, "did you hear all that?"

"I didn't hear anything, Coop," I said with a look that said his sad farewell was not going to be printed by me. It never was until now. It doesn't matter anymore. Cooper is dead, Rocky is remarried, and Patricia has talked and written openly about her affair with Cooper.

The Beverly Hills Brown Derby was a favorite hangout of Coop's since his office was nearby in the Bank of America building.

His office was on the second floor right above the big bank's vault. Sitting there in the office one day with Coop, I told him he should have cards printed that stated: "Assets over $2 billion."

Cooper thought it was funny at the time.

Once one of Cooper's flings did get into print in *Confidential* magazine. The magazine told how Cooper and the luscious Anita Ekberg had a rendezvous in a Malibu beach house.

The story was written in chronological style: "2:02 P.M., Cooper and Anita, arm in arm, went from the beach into the house. 2:04 P.M., the shades in the bedroom were drawn"—and so on.

The next day I visited Coop on the set of *Friendly Persuasion*. He had a copy of the magazine in his dressing room.

"The sons of bitches put a stopwatch on me," was his only comment.

Coop loved his reputation for taciturnity even if it was manufactured.

"It all started years ago," he once told me, "when I was a guest on Edgar Bergen's radio show. The writers had Charlie McCarthy wisecracking in his usual sophisticated way. I was just the big cowboy who said either 'yep' or 'nope' through the whole skit. It came off pretty funny and caught on with the public."

Coop soon saw the advantage of it.

"Whenever Hedda or Louella would ask me silly questions, I'd just grunt, maybe say 'nope' and that's all. They soon got tired of asking me and I'm still friends with both. You never see my name in a gossip column unless it's something to do with a movie I'm making."

Coop, ever since he did *For Whom the Bell Tolls,* was a great personal friend of Ernest Hemingway. The only time I ever met the famous author it was arranged by Cooper.

Hemingway was living in Ketchum, Idaho, at the time. This was back in the days when the Union Pacific ran a train into Ketchum because the railroad owned Sun Valley then.

Cooper called Hemingway and told him I was coming to Ketchum and he thought the two of us should get to know each other.

"You're both hell raisers," said Coop.

I came to Ketchum on the train and was surprised as all hell to find Hemingway there to meet me. That shows you how much he thought of Cooper.

It was one of the most amazing afternoons and nights I have ever spent, because Hemingway took me immediately to a bar in Ketchum called—if memory serves—the Alpine. We talked and drank all day and all night, it seemed. You could see that Ernest was a regular in the place. He knew every barfly there and they knew him.

One of the few things I remember is Hemingway asking me how long I had been with AP. When I told him about fifteen years at that time, he said:

"That's about ten fucking years too long. You won't learn any more about writing."

Like a horse's ass, I stayed on for another ten.

Also during the night he kept extolling the virtues of Sun Valley. I knew it was around Ketchum someplace but I didn't know exactly how far. Several times during the drinking session he said something about taking me over there. We never made it. He finally poured me on the train going south and I didn't make Sun Valley until twenty years later. Surprisingly,

I found it's only a mile and a half from Ketchum.

I was a Hemingway fan before but that night made me.

Some years later when Cooper found out he had cancer, he told Hemingway about it.

"I'll be in the barn before you," said Ernest.

It didn't quite happen that way. Cooper's cancer took him on May 13, 1961. Hemingway went out with a gun in his hand on July 2, 1961.

When Cooper first told me about that "barn" remark, it made me wonder if Hemingway didn't have cancer too.

I was outside the Cooper home the day he died—a reporter on death watch. All of a sudden, Cooper's dogs—two French poodles and a mongrel—started barking and whining. They were very agitated. I remember my Irish mother once had told me of an ancient folk tale—that the dogs always know when their master's soul has departed. I looked at my watch. It was 12:27 P.M. We waited outside for a good half hour more, a small army of reporters and photographers. Then a spokesman came out and announced Coop's death. The exact time of death—12:27 P.M. I wrote about the amazing coincidence of the dogs. It wasn't long after that that I got a letter from the head of the Duke University School of Parapsychology, who asked me to write a paper on the coincidence.

And thus with dogs barking came the end of one of the greatest of all Hollywood stars. There was only one Cooper. About the only one who is filling his shoes today is Clint Eastwood, who once bore such a remarkable resemblance to Cooper that the secretaries at Universal used to call him "Coop."

Coop was born in Helena, Montana, May 7, 1901, into a part of the United States that was still the Wild West.

His father, Charles Henry Cooper, was a former British barrister who had emigrated to the United States some years before. Later the father became an associate justice of the state supreme court of Montana.

Helena, in Coop's boyhood, was a hell-raising mining town of the Old West, and young Cooper spent much of his time on horseback exploring the rugged country.

The Cooper family was as elite as any could be in Montana. When Coop was nine, he was sent to Dunstable School, Bedfordshire, England, where he spent four years.

"I guess they considered me some kind of freak. Here I was, a kid fresh from a land filled with Indians and gun-toting cowboys, set amidst well-mannered, prim young boys from traditional English families."

But Coop got along fine, although he often recalled: "I was homesick as hell."

Coop stuck it out because his father insisted that he get a proper English education.

The rest of his education came in the public schools of Helena and Grinnell College in Iowa.

No one—not even Duke Wayne—could do a showdown with a gun better than Coop, but he often admitted that the one actual gunfight he had seen as a youth had scared hell out of him.

"I had a job one summer, must have been around 1915 or 1916, driving a jitney bus that took tourists into Yellowstone National Park. Me and another guy who was working with me stopped one day in a little cow town.

"We had barely got there when we heard that two cowhands who had been drinking in the saloon were aching to shoot each other up. Before long they faced each other in the street and walked down hand on holster just like I did in *High Noon* with the guys who were out to get me.

"The guy who was a little soberer than the other got off the first shot. I don't remember whether he killed the other guy or not. I was too damn scared to stick around and find out. I never did like the combination of drinking cowboys and guns."

On screen, Cooper was the most heroic of heroes—and actually he really was—but he once admitted to me:

"If I had lived in the old Wild West and faced up to everything that those guys did, I would have been scared to death."

It was quite an admission from the man who was to say a

week before his death: "I know what is happening is God's will. I am not afraid of the future."

Somehow you know that a guy who faced death like that wouldn't be scared of a cowboy with a gun.

Coop, before he came to Hollywood, was a bona fide cowboy. He spent two solid years on his uncle's ranch doing all the jobs—lonely jobs—that all cowboys do.

"I learned one thing. I wanted a job in town."

And he got one—as a cartoonist on a Helena newpaper. Then he hit for the big time—Los Angeles—and a possible job drawing for an advertising agency.

"I met a couple of guys from Montana and they told me I could get ten bucks a day just falling off a horse. I still dreamed of making it in the advertising business but I kept showing up in those cowboy movies and falling off horses. I thought it was the easiest money I ever earned.

"One day I got a job in a Tom Mix western. At that time, 1923, Mix was the highest-paid western star in the movies. Someone told me he was getting $15,000 a week—and here I was doing all the tough stunts in the picture for $10 a day.

"The most I could make in the advertising business was $10,000 a year. It started me thinking. Although I had acted in some school shows at Grinnell, I had no burning, inward desire to express myself. I just thought the money looked good."

About the same time, there were a couple of other extras around town. They all became friendly. They were Coop, Richard Arlen, Jack Oakie, and Gilbert Roland.

If you worked in a dress-up picture and wore a tuxedo, you got extra pay. There was only one tuxedo in the group. Unfortunately for the six-foot, three-inch Cooper, the tuxedo belonged to the shorter Arlen, but all four shared it.

Coop, who always had financial savvy, hired a cameraman to make a screen test of him for $65. He even hired an agent, unheard of for an extra. But eventually it paid off.

Cooper's biggest asset, however, was his prowess in the sack. He soon became a favorite with all the women. You can't beat virility.

Sam Goldwyn gave Cooper his first big break as the second cowboy in *The Winning of Barbara Worth,* which starred Ronald Colman and Vilma Banky.

Cooper's cock got him his next break—the one that made him a star—in *Wings.*

Clara Bow, the Marilyn Monroe of her day, once put it to me a little more innocently than that, but I got the idea.

"Coop attracted me because he blushed when I teased him."

The two had a torrid romance, much to the dismay of his pal Oakie, who had a secret love for Clara until the day she died. I know because he took me to his home after her funeral and he poured it all out as he tied one on.

Wings made stars out of both Coop and his buddy Arlen. Coop had only a bit part in this great air epic but was so outstanding that exhibitors cried for more Cooper pictures.

They got them. Cooper and Clara co-starred in two sensational films, *It* and *Children of Divorce.*

Paramount offered him a new contract of $600 a week. He turned it down and went off fishing in Montana and Idaho. When he came back, the studio had upped the ante to $1,750 a week.

When he did the classic Owen Wister story *The Virginian,* Cooper emerged as a superstar—which he remained until the day he died.

"When you say that, smile."

That classic western line, delivered with Cooper simplicity, made Coop the top western hero in the movies.

But Paramount worked the ass off him.

"Sometimes I would be making three pictures at once, working twenty hours a day. I once worked solid for five years without a day off."

Cooper was in big demand and he knew it so he asked for two pictures a year, script approval, a percentage of the gross, and a few other clauses unheard of in 1932.

Adolph Zukor balked. He even brought in a New York and English vaudevillian by the name of Archie Leach as a threat to Cooper. Even when they changed Archie's name to Cary

Grant, Cooper still held his ground.

Finally, he and the Countess Dorothy di Frasso, one of the wealthiest women in the world at that time, took off for six months of hunting and giggling in Africa. When Cooper returned home, there was much publicity about this great white hunter. All was forgiven at the studio, and Cooper, thirty years ahead of his time, got what superstars have been getting in recent years.

The stubborn Cooper had beat the big studio system by just being himself.

"I didn't give a damn whether I came back to acting or not. I had the money to live on a ranch the rest of my life."

Cooper had a basic rule on scripts.

"I'm an average guy. If the script excited me, then I figured it would excite the public. And make sure at least one western every two years."

Coop had another torrid romance with the extroverted Lupe Velez, who delighted in extolling Coop's bedroom antics to columnists. This didn't hurt Coop's appeal to women.

Jack Oakie once summed up Coop's appeal beautifully.

"Half the women in the audience want to mother him. The other half wants to fuck him."

Countess di Frasso was the one who introduced Coop to international society. No one could wear white tie and tails better than Coop—not even Fred Astaire.

Poet Carl Sandburg once described Cooper's appeal:

"A traditional while he's living—something of a clean sport—a lack of the phony."

My last memory of Cooper—long after his death—was visiting the Movieland Wax Museum in nearby Buena Park. There they have a remarkable likeness of Coop in his *High Noon* outfit.

Sitting in front of the wax figure was a woman in her nineties. An employee of the museum told me she came over there once or twice a month and sat for hours in front of the Cooper wax figure.

The little old lady was Gary's mother.

I Thought I Was Getting Better

Often on TV or radio talk shows I'm asked if I have ever withheld stories. I always answer: "Yes, and I'm glad."

Most famous example came one day when a nurse in St. John's Hospital called and told me that Betty Grable, suffering from terminal cancer, would never leave the hospital alive. That she had three months at most. The tip was good because I knew the nurse and her husband. I didn't print it. Mostly because Betty and I were old and dear friends and I felt very bad about it.

A few days later Joyce Haber, then writing for the Los Angeles *Times*, printed the same story, probably from the same source. The story was accurate because Betty was gone within three months.

But the day after Joyce's story appeared, I got a call from Betty from her hospital bed. She was in tears.

"I actually thought I was getting better until I read that story."

There wasn't much I could say, just try to cheer her up as best I could.

Ringo Starr: My Favorite Beatle

Of all the Beatles, Ringo Starr is the only one I have gotten to know real well, although occasionally I will have a drink with George Harrison or John Lennon. I have met Paul McCartney but you don't see much of him on the Hollywood scene.

I first saw the Beatles in London around about 1960 when they first came down from Liverpool. Walter Shenson, a London producer who had once been a Hollywood press agent, recommended that I catch them at some club. I saw them and was not impressed. Told Walter their hair was too long and that their music would never make it. Give me Rudy Vallee and his Connecticut Yankees.

Well, Walter was impressed and immediately signed them for all their movies. Even after *A Hard Day's Night* Walter could have retired but he made a few more with them. There will be no benefits played for Walter.

I could have been in on the ground floor, too, but I'm the guy who wrote the song "Bon Voyage, Titanic."

But Ringo's okay in my book because he once made me feel what it's like to be an instant celebrity.

A lot of people will tell you that Ringo and the Beatles are Britain's revenge for the War of 1812. I never bought that.

My memorable experience with Ringo and the other Beatles took place in 1964 at Los Angeles International Airport, when their trans-polar flight made a refueling stop en route to San Francisco.

Thousands of young girls, who had gotten wind of their flight plan, jammed the TWA lobby. Only the press were allowed planeside. The army of teenyboppers were held back in the lobby by scores of police. It was really pandemonium. As soon as the famous four came down the gangplank, girls started swooning by the dozens in the lobby as they pressed their faces against the big windows.

All of the Beatles, despite their long flight, were affable, none more so than Ringo. It was their first visit to the West Coast and a planeside press conference seemed the thing to do.

Some TV reporter asked Ringo how he found America:

"Very easy. First you go to Greenland and then make a left turn."

Then a sob sister asked about a purported romance with Ann-Margret.

"That's a lot of roobish," said Ringo in his best Liverpool accent.

Finally, I asked the first intelligent question of the day. Something like, "Who has first rights on your overflow of women?" Ringo liked that and put his arm around my shoulder as we talked. I thought of it as nothing more than a friendly gesture from a likable fellow.

They got back into their plane and it taxied off.

I walked up the ramp to the lobby. There, massed in front of me, were hundreds of teenagers looking like lions ready to devour gazelles in the African bush.

I unconsciously turned around to see what was the attraction. I found it was me—or is it I?

The girls all seemed to scream in unison: "Ringo touched him."

One girl asked for the sleeve of my jacket. Another for my tie. I gave up the tie but I wasn't about to give up the sleeve. It went with the coat.

Then the girls lined up one by one to touch my shoulder. As they touched the shoulder where once dwelt Ringo's arm, they all shrieked. One girl noted some papers in my hand.

"Is that what they said?" she screamed.

Before I could tell her they were not notes, just scrap pieces of paper with nothing on them, she grabbed them from my hand. She was in ecstasy, but not for long. About fifty girls pounced on her and soon the notepaper was shredded to bits.

Then the girls, all frustrated at not getting the Beatles, asked for my autograph. Enjoying it all immensely, I signed their little autograph books; when they shrieked, I yelled: "Yeah! Yeah! Yeah!"

At heart I was an aging Beatle.

I signed autographs for about five minutes and then one of the girls yelled that the Beatles' plane had taxied to the runway.

I was left barefaced with pen in hand. The girls, hundreds of them, fled en masse like a lynch mob to the other side of the lobby. Three Marines sauntered lazily out of a bar just as the screaming exodus began. All three were knocked on their chevrons—and their asses.

If you think I'm making all this up, you have never seen teenyboppers behave around the Beatles when they were in their prime. It was like a banzai attack on Iwo Jima. Ask those three Marines.

I went home shaken but exhilarated by the experience. More was yet to come. Ringo's hand around my shoulder was on every channel for the six-o'clock news. Soon all the teeny-boppers in the neighborhood knocked on my door. The same touch on the shoulder. The same shriek.

Then the next morning Paul Harvey, the ABC radio network newscaster, quoted me by name on a line I had put in my story about the Beatles—that they are the only entertainers in the history of show business who make a million dollars a year by letting the audience entertain them.

Then for days afterwards, the phone calls came from the teenyboppers. All, judging from their voices, were in the eight-to-fourteen year group.

"Is Paul McCartney really that cute?"

"Is John Lennon really married?"

"Does Ringo really look that sad?"

"Is George Harrison funny?"

By this time, I was really with it. In a rock 'n' roll beat. I shrieked the same answer to each question:

"Yeah! Yeah! Yeah!"

Over the years, I must have told that story a half dozen times to Ringo. He always comments:

"My pleasure, mate."

When the Beatles returned to Los Angeles for their first stay I accidentally and inadvertently did them a disservice. A huge reception was held for them at a Bel-Air home one afternoon. Capitol Records tossed a party for them in the garden and the receiving line to meet them was blocks long. I didn't even bother to get in it.

Finally, I felt a tug on my sleeve. It was Gary Lewis, Jerry's oldest son. His younger brother Ron was with him.

"Gee, Mr. Bacon," Gary pleaded, "you know the Beatles and we haven't got a chance to meet them. Can you get us in that line near the front?"

I took the two boys and we all crawled under the rope where Ringo was standing. The cops were about to kick us out but Ringo said I was a friend of his. I introduced the Lewis boys to each of the Beatles. They were thrilled.

Six months later, Gary, financed by his mother Patti, cut his first recording with his rock group, called Gary Lewis and the Playboys. Gary's first record knocked the Beatles off the top of the charts.

Ringo is still going strong, very serious about his acting career. Over several bottles of wine at the Polo Lounge one day, I asked him if he planned to study acting seriously.

"No, no," he said. "You do what you do and people say it's great and you say, all right, I wasn't doing anything. They say, that's what we want, don't do anything.

"I never really fought to be a big success as a Beatle. I just met them, played with them and joined them, and then we were a fucking revolution.

"I still think there was a force pushing us, pushing me."

The public at large still doesn't realize that Ringo was not the original drummer for the Beatles. The other guy quit and Ringo took his place.

Wonder what ever happened to that drummer? He must have kicked his ass to Liverpool and back a dozen times.

Ringo's success never has affected him. During World War II he was bombed as a child almost to eternity. He spent much of his youth in hospitals.

What the hell are a couple thousand bobbysoxers grabbing at you, compared with a buzz-bomb attack?

Reflected Fame

Everybody knows the star but how many know the guy who is always around him?

You seldom see Frank Sinatra without Jilly Rizzo. Or Dean Martin without Mack Grey. Or Milton Berle without eighty-six-year-old Lou Jackson. Or Bing Crosby without Leo Lynn. Or Jerry Lewis without Irving Kaye.

Grey has had a remarkable career. He has spent an adult lifetime in Hollywood working for only two stars. The first was George Raft. For years, the press hung a hoodlum label, unjustly deserved, on Mack because of his association with Raft. Most of the time he was referred to as Killer Grey.

Actually, he got that name from Carole Lombard. He once came on the set where Raft and Miss Lombard were working. Mack complained of a hernia and used the Yiddish word for it—a word that sounds like "killer." From that time on, he was Killer Grey to Carole and the name spread.

George, who committed crimes only on screen, was a friend of some of the most notorious mobsters in history—Ownie Madden, Al Capone, Lucky Luciano, Bugsy Siegel, and a few others.

But George was basically a dancer. He may have helped move a little bootleg booze during Prohibition, but who didn't?

Mack's job with George was friend and companion. It must have been one of the best jobs in Hollywood history. That's because George Raft only had one hobby in his life—broads.

George, now eighty, once told me:

"I never played golf. I didn't like cards. All I did was fuck some broad in the afternoon and then turn to Mack and say who have we got for tonight?"

Over the years George had some lasting alliances—Betty Grable, Norma Shearer, and some other big names. Mack has his romances, too—one with the young Lucille Ball when she first got started in the movies.

Mack had more in common with Raft than with Dean Martin because they both liked girls. Dean Martin likes golf, booze, girls, but not necessarily in that order. Mack doesn't drink or play golf so he functions mostly as a music coordinator for Dean.

He has never married. Why buy a cow when milk is so cheap?

Once Mack got very serious with a sexy young starlet under contract to Paramount. Her name was Valerie Allen and her mother was a Ziegfeld Girl so you know Valerie was beautiful.

We were all up at the Sands one night when Martin and Lewis were still together and performing in the Las Vegas hotel. Now Valerie was a fun-loving girl and Vegas is a fun-loving city. She and I proceeded to get smashed in front of the nondrinking Mack. He took an extremely dim view, especially when I started promising Valerie that I could get her a better contract at Warners.

She was impressed, especially the next day when I called Jack L. Warner and said: "J. L., I got a little smashed in Vegas last night and signed a beautiful young actress to a Warners contract."

J. L. never hesitated a minute.

"If you signed her, she's signed."

I told Valerie about it but she apologized.

"Mack is furious at you. He will never let me leave Paramount."

Maybe if she had gone over to Warners, she might not be working for RCA in New York now.

Those were the days.

Jilly Rizzo is Frank Sinatra's best friend, and vice versa.

When the two first met, Jilly was a successful restaurant owner in New York—still is. The two hit it off at once and Frank made Jilly's one of the most "in" places in the big city.

Jilly is one of the great characters around town. He's strictly out of Damon Runyon, as is Frank himself. That may be the reason the two of them get along so well.

Jilly spends little time in New York. He's an absentee restaurant owner. He gave up his New York way of life to move out to Palm Springs, where he has a house across the Tamarisk country club from Frank's massive compound.

To give you an insight into Jilly's Runyonesque qualities, I once asked how a Sicilian ever got into the Chinese restaurant business. (Jilly's in Manhattan serves excellent Chinese food.)

"Well, one day I put an ad in the paper for a cook," explains Jilly, "and the first guy what answers the ad is a Chinaman."

Sometimes Jilly is mistakenly referred to as Sinatra's bodyguard. He's not, although he has been known on occasion to disperse crowds for Frank and function on a bodyguard level.

"One night Frank and I are drinking up at Lake Tahoe and

this big Indian, who's gotta be six feet six, sits down with us at the bar. He's drunk and he starts bugging Frank.

"Frank whispers to me, 'Get rid of this guy.'

"Now this guy is so big that there ain't no way you gonna get rid of him. Not even if you're Muhammad Ali.

"So I put a cherry bomb in his coat pocket and before long they picked him out of the snow, not knowing what hit him.

"But he didn't bug Frank no more."

Milton Berle first met Lou Jackson back in 1933 in Chicago, when Milton, along with Sally Rand, was the hit of the Chicago World's Fair.

Milton—and this is not generally known—is a frustrated boxer. He spent all his time around the Chicago gyms in those days working out. Lou was big in the fight game in Chicago and that's how he and Milton met. He's been with him ever since as a major domo.

Lou is postcard happy. No matter where Milton is playing, I always get a postcard from Lou telling me how Milton is doing.

Irving Kaye started with Jerry Lewis thirty-six years ago. At the time Irving was the entertainment director for Brown's hotel in the Borscht Belt. Jerry was a busboy who kept dropping dishes and pestering Irving for a chance to get into show business.

Irving figured it was cheaper to put Jerry into the act than to buy new dishes all the time. So the two of them went on the road with a comedy act. Irving was the comic, and Jerry mouthed words to records.

"It was an $85 a week act at best," recalls Irving.

One night in Buffalo, in their rooming house, Jerry wrote on a slip of paper his appreciation for all that Irving had done for him. The note read:

"When I start making $1,000 a week, I will give Irving Kaye half for the rest of my life."

Irving took one look at the signed note and tore it up. It was not many years after that that Jerry was making $4 million a year.

Jerry, however, has always taken care of Irving. He's on an

annuity and has a charge account at Dunhill's, where he can get all the expensive cigars he can smoke. To Irving, that's living.

Leo Lynn was a classmate of Bing's at Gonzaga University in their native Spokane, Washington. As soon as Bing got rich and famous, he hired Leo, who has been the Old Groaner's right-hand man ever since.

He's chauffeur, road manager, what have you. Bing couldn't function without Leo—and neither could the Crosby family.

Not all people around the stars are there out of pure friendship. There is something about the mind of the comic that requires he have a stooge or two in the entourage. Abbott and Costello used to have a guy named Bobby with them on all their pictures and personal appearances. It was like Ted Healy and the Three Stooges. You would be eating lunch with Lou Costello and Bud Abbott and Bobby would sit with you for a cup of coffee. The routine never varied. Abbott, the straight man, would say: "Bobby, there's that friend of yours over there."

Bobby would look all over the restaurant while Costello the comic would empty the salt shaker in his coffee. Then we would all watch Bobby drink the coffee and spit it out. Bobby would call Abbott and Costello bastards and then laugh with the rest of us.

If you read my last book, you know that the biggest cock in the history of Hollywood was owned by an extra named O.K. Freddy. Like Bobby, he worked on every Abbott and Costello picture. His right name was Freddy Woltman or something like that. Lou Costello gave him the name O.K. Freddy.

As soon as a visiting dignitary would come on the set (mostly male, but I have seen it happen with women visitors), Lou would yell, "Okay, Freddy." At that command, Freddy would start unwinding that gigantic cock, whick looked like it belonged on a Texaco gas pump.

Jerry Lewis used to pull stooge tricks on his benefactor Irving Kaye.

Once the two were on a sleeper train en route from an engagement in Pittsburgh to one in Montreal. About three o'-clock in the morning, the train stopped at Altoona, Pennsylvania, to switch cars and crews. Jerry got out of his berth, put on his clothes, and then went to the sleeping Irving and shook him.

"Get the hell up, Irving. We're in Montreal."

Irving dressed in a big hurry, grabbed his bag, and jumped off the train as it started to move.

"All of a sudden, I am standing on this platform all alone at three o'clock in the morning and the train is pulling out with a crazy kid on the back platform laughing his ass off at me.

"I had to sleep on a bench in the station until I could get another train to Montreal. Just barely made the show that night."

If you don't think an entourage for a star isn't expensive, Jerry in his prime once had an $8,000-a-week payroll for guys to be around him, some of whom functioned in important jobs—but not all.

The comedian must have an audience. No columnist travels with Bob Hope as much as I—from Alaska to Vietnam to Wilkes-Barre, Pennsylvania to New Orleans—you name it.

It finally hit me one morning at breakfast in the suite Bob and I were sharing at the Royal Sonesta hotel in New Orleans. As he sat there eating breakfast with his agents, musicians, and writers, he did a twenty-minute monologue on what I had done the night before.

A hundred other breakfasts just like it all came back to me. I was as important to Hope's breakfast as the prunes he eats every morning.

I guess you could call me a syndicated stooge.

Jimmy Cagney Imitated Too Well

Somehow the phone call from Jimmy Cagney struck me

funny. Here was the most imitated of all stars asking me to write something about a guy who was imitating him too well. (There's a fellow who resembles Cagney somewhat who goes about the country posing as Jimmy.)

"This guy sells phony real estate and generally hoodwinks the public all in my name," said Jimmy.

I've run into the guy myself once. He was just leaving the Bistro when I came in. One of the waiters said: "You just missed Jimmy Cagney."

"That's not Jimmy Cagney," I said. "Hope you got cash for the tab."

Cagney has been retired for years and it's easy to see how this guy fools the people. No one except close friends has seen Cagney since his retirement a decade or more ago. So he makes a prime target for impostors.

Once the phony Cagney showed up in Las Vegas and Barbra Streisand introduced him from the stage. The guy got a standing ovation, which gives you an idea of what the public thinks of Cagney.

I usually see Jimmy once or twice a year when he leaves his farm in upstate New York to spend the winter in his Beverly Hills home.

Producers send him scripts every week but when Jimmy got out of the business, he got out of it. He's not interested.

There are many who think that Cagney is the greatest of all movie actors. Cagney is not one of them.

"I'm a song-and-dance man," he says.

But study *Public Enemy*, which came out in 1931. Cagney's performance in that picture would win critical acclaim today despite the radical changes in acting styles since that time. Cagney was years ahead of his time.

The late Rosalind Russell, one of the screen's best actresses, said the one great disappointment of her career was that she never got the chance to work with Jimmy.

"He's a superb actor," said Roz.

It's interesting to note that the two most simplistic of all acting lessons should come from two members of Hollywood's Irish Mafia of the Golden Era.

Spencer Tracy once said: "Learn your lines and don't bump into the furniture."

Cagney says: "Move into a scene, plant yourself, and then open your face. And when you do, look the other guy straight in the eye and tell the truth."

Jimmy came off the streets of New York around the turn of the century but he is basically a farmer. However, he can't escape his movie past. Once Rollins College in Florida awarded Jimmy an honorary doctorate for his work in soil conservation.

"Here I was in my cap and gown making this speech on what I thought was an important aspect of soil conservation and some guy in the front row nudges his neighbor and in a stage whisper says: 'What the hell is this guy talking about? We came here to hear about Mae West.'"

Cagney is a simple man. He's the only famous movie star I know who drives his car across country each year. There's a reason. He doesn't like the way airlines cage his dog, so Jimmy and his dog take off by themselves in his car. He has a whole list of motels across the country that will harbor him and his dog.

A final note. If some guy claiming to be Jimmy Cagney tries to sell you a lot in a Florida swamp, beware.

P.S. That most famous of all Hollywood scenes, when Jimmy pushed a grapefruit in Mae Clarke's face in *Public Enemy,* was adlibbed.

"It seemed a good way of telling the truth in the scene."

It sure shocked the hell out of Mae. Her reaction was Academy Award stuff.

Marlon's Strange Effect on Women

You hear more about Marlon Brando and Indians these days than you do about Marlon and women—but it was not always so. It used to be fun to see how women behaved around Marlon.

When Marlon married his first wife—Anna Kashfi—she was the most placid individual I had ever met. She had been born in Darjeeling, India, of Irish parents but she looked Indian and she had all the serenity of the Orient about her.

A few years with Marlon and she turned into a wildcat.

Marlon changed, too. He thought he was marrying an East Indian. Then out of Wales came the story that Anna was in reality Joan O'Callaghan, daughter of an Irish factory worker.

Marlon felt he had been deceived because in those days he was into his Oriental period.

Once Anna threw a water bottle at Marlon and another time she broke into his house and bit him three times. Their court battles over the custody of Christian, their son, were like Muhammad Ali title fights.

And then Marlon took up with Rita Moreno, who had come to Hollywood as the original cha-cha girl. She was Puerto Rican. Going with Marlon turned her into an Oriental.

Once, when Rita was the girl friend of Geordie Hormel of the meat-packing family, an official police report listed her as "100 pounds of snarling wildcat." She thought the cops were prowlers.

With Marlon, she went exactly the opposite. She dressed in Oriental slit skirts and her eyes were made up in an Oriental slant. She was docile and behaved like a Japanese wife of the old school.

Once she showed up at a play with Marlon and columnists thought she was another of Marlon's girl friends, the Oriental actress France Nuyen.

France at the time was on Broadway, 3,000 miles away, starring in the hit play *The World of Suzie Wong*.

And Marlon had a strange effect on France. Her change took the most unusual form for an actress. The shapely Indonesian first came to town to do *South Pacific*. She was ambitious, as are most actresses. Career took precedence over romance—until she started going out with Marlon.

Her career blossomed. A major break was *Suzie* on Broadway, and then she got the movie version. After $800,000 worth of footage had been shot on the picture with Bill Holden, France was dismissed and replaced by Nancy Kwan. The reason she lost the best movie role ever offered an Oriental actress was Marlon. Marlon so frustrated her that she went on a calorie binge, eating candy by the box, and got too fat for the part.

Haven't heard much from Anna in recent years. Rita forgot the Orient and became Puerto Rican again. It won her an Oscar for *West Side Story* and she was a big hit last year in *The Ritz.*

She's all cha cha now.

Last time I saw France, she had slimmed down to her old ravishing self. Marlon was long forgotten.

Strange, isn't it?

My Friend Bogie

When I toured last summer for *Hollywood is a Four Letter Town,* one of the most often asked questions was: "How come you didn't write more about your pal Bogie?"

Betty Bacall had told me shortly before I wrote the book that she thought Bogie had been done to death. She was particularly incensed at one writer who had practically made a career out of writing about Humphrey Bogart.

"It's ghoulish," said his widow.

I have since talked with her and even she is convinced that she was married to a Hollywood legend who will never die.

Bogart fans fit no particular age group. The kids know more about him than their elders. And the old-timers have always revered him.

Casablanca is one of the two best movies ever made—*Gone With the Wind* is the other.

There will always be a Bogart cult.

Bogart was my first close brush with cancer, and the way he handled his illness can be an inspiration to others, even those doomed like he knew he was.

Doomed, but damn optimistic just the same.

I saw Bogie a day or two before he had the eight-hour operation to remove that malignant growth on his esophagus—the pipe that connects the throat and the stomach.

He was a healthy man when I saw him before the operation. He was death warmed over the next time I saw him, during his recuperation at Frank Sinatra's home in Palm Springs.

Bogie told me the growth was cancerous without my having to ask him.

The poor guy looked horrible—and he was no Cary Grant to start with. His face was so drawn that his eyeballs almost popped out of their sockets, like those victims of overactive thyroid glands. But he was still the old Bogie when he saw the stunned look on my face.

"What the hell do you expect after the Big Casino? Some goddamn All-American tackle from Notre Dame?"

He poured me a scotch and he had a hefty one himself. His old needle just came out of a thinner frame. We had a few drinks and I left.

"See you in Romanoff's," he said. And he did, a few weeks later, looking a hell of a lot better. I told him so and he was optimistic.

"I'm lucky that my cancer was slight and contained. It didn't spread like Babe Didrikson's. That went in every direction and no one can stop it."

The Babe was dead by this time—1956—but Bogie didn't let it bother him. We each had about four or five scotches at Bogie's favorite table at Romanoff's.

Mike Romanoff, with great tact, joined us and said:

"Well, you know if Bogie wasn't going to make it, you'd hear it from him first."

Bogie looked at him and laughed.

"Leave it to the Little Prince to cheer you up when you need it."

Bogie really did look better, although his weight was down

thirty-five pounds. He had had about seven weeks of daily 3,000,000-volt radiation treatment at the Los Angeles Tumor Institute.

"That's where my fucking weight went—not the cancer," he said. "And that's why I'm weak. Hell, I wasn't no Duke Wayne to start with and taking thirty-five pounds off me is like taking thirty-five pounds off Sinatra."

Frank was thin in those days.

"If Sinatra lost thirty-five pounds he would have to put steel mesh over the bathroom drain."

He had gained back five of the thirty-five pounds and I, for one, was cheered by that news.

Bogie during this luncheon talked openly about his illness.

"Why shouldn't I speak openly about it?" he said. "It's a respectable illness. It's not like getting a dose of clap. I'm not ashamed of it. It's no worse than gallstones or appendicitis.

"They'll all kill you if you don't catch them soon enough. I caught mine."

He talked about the marathon session on the operating table.

"Every time they cut out a cancerous piece of tissue, they put it under the microscope for study. That's how you keep it from spreading.

"I can drink, smoke, and fuck as much as I ever did," he said. "The only thing I can't do—that I could do before—is swing a golf club. They took out a few ribs. I went out in the back yard the other day and tried a backswing. It damned near killed me.

"I was always better at indoor sports like fucking anyway."

There were other encouraging signs about Bogie. First was the voice. It was the same old lispy bark that with a curl of the upper lip could persuade the toughest screen hoodlum to drop the gun. Damon Runyon and other victims of throat cancers always had preceded their end with a hoarseness, then a whisper, and then no voice at all. But here was Bogie, still smoking, and no loss of voice timbre.

Bogie, in his prime, would knock off four to five packs of Chesterfields a day. Duke Wayne, before his lung cancer, would go six packs of Camels a day.

All of Bogie's friends were optimistic, mostly because Bogie made them feel that way. He never changed his lifestyle. He never felt sorry for himself. He tried, as long as he was able, not to be a burden to his family.

"That Betty is one great woman," he told me one day. "Those three weeks in the hospital she was never away from my side for more than an hour at a time and then only to look at the kids. And she turned down some damn good movie roles. That's how you separate the ladies from the broads in this business."

Until the night he died, Bogie never varied his lifestyle. At the end, he made the cocktail hour only with the help of a dumbwaiter that lowered him into the den, but he still made it. Hours before his death he had a drink with pals like Spencer Tracy and Katharine Hepburn.

All during his illness, he was up eating breakfast at 8 A.M., reading the morning paper.

"Then I get on the phone and start lousing up people around town," he said.

Bogie loved nothing better than starting a fight between two guys. Once Duke Wayne threw a big party at the old California Racquet Club for some occasion or another. All of a sudden there was a terrific fist fight going on in the middle of the bar area between Wild Bill Wellman and Paul Mantz, the famous stunt flier. Everybody was stunned because these two guys were known as the best of friends.

I was there and I watched Bogie start the whole thing. First he went up to Wellman, the director of *Wings*, who prided himself on his World War I combat flying record.

"Wellman," said Bogie, "Mantz says all that stuff about you being in the Lafayette Escadrille is a crock of shit. He says you never got out of flying school in the United States."

Then he went over to Mantz and said:

"Wellman says you can't fly now and you never could fly.

He said you wouldn't have lasted overnight with him in World War I."

This went on for about five minutes with similar barbs, until the two friends started slugging at each other. Of course, a lot of booze had flown over the bar.

But Duke pulled them apart and no one was hurt. It was Bogie at his devilish best. Bogie in his whole life never fought with anyone but Mayo Methot, his wife before Betty Bacall.

That marriage was one long battle.

"I never asked anyone to visit me for fear they would get cut by flying glass."

During his illness, Bogie tried his damnedest to start fights over the telephone.

"That's doing it the hard way, though," he said. "You need a bar to lean on to start a really good fight."

Bogie never lost his sense of humor—except once.

Dorothy Kilgallen, the New York gossip columnist, had printed an item to the effect that Bogie had suffered a relapse and had been spirited away to the eighth floor of the Los Angeles Memorial Hospital. He called me to come up to the house the day the item appeared in the New York *Journal-American*. He was furious when I got there.

"The fact that there is no such hospital as Los Angeles Memorial (there never has been) didn't bother me as much as that goddamn eighth-floor shit.

"That's pretty damn ominous-sounding, isn't it? Like Ward A—or wherever in the hell they strap the psychos and winos. It's a hell of a thing to read that you are spirited away to the eighth floor of a nonexistent hospital when all the time you're home feeling pretty good. No wonder Sinatra hates that broad."

He asked my help in composing an answer to Dorothy, who was known to be careless with her facts. Finally, he called in his secretary and dictated what we had composed. It read:

"Unless you start checking your facts, you're apt to wind up on the nineteenth floor of Bellevue Hospital, and that's a hell of a lot worse than the eighth floor of Los Angeles Memorial."

Concise and to the point.

I had never seen him so pissed off as he was on that eighth-floor mention. He was boiling, because the item caused concern among his New York pals.

Ben Hecht wired him: "Is there anybody you want bumped off?"

Hecht was one of the few who contacted Bogie direct about the item. All the others, believing the item, had called Betty first.

"I guess they all thought I was already laid out in the parlor," said Bogie.

Boiling Bogie by this time had already downed three scotches. He ordered another one and asked the butler to serve us lunch in the den.

"Hell, I'm as good a man as I ever was," he said over chopped chicken livers and crackers. As he sipped his fourth scotch of the morning, I could only comment that I agreed with him.

Bogie always was a light eater and he never did gain his weight back.

When he made *The African Queen* in the African jungle, everybody got sick except Bogie. He ate little but always managed to get in at least a dozen scotches a day.

"Those fucking bugs used to take one bite out of me and drop dead."

And then when he made *The Barefoot Contessa* in Rome, he lived on scotch and minestrone.

"Those dagos throw everything but Mussolini in that soup. You don't need to eat anything else."

And once again Bogie didn't get sick, even though the rest of the cast all came down with the *turista*.

But he couldn't outdrink his cancer—but God he tried.

Bogie was his own best press agent. He always had a syndicated columnist with lots of circulation for a pal. That's how I got in so solid with him. That, and the same capacity for scotch.

There was one New York writer whom Bogie liked but didn't trust.

"I can never trust a guy who doesn't drink," he said of the writer.

To show you how savvy he was about publicity, we were all at a party one night when a writer from a small upstate New York newspaper came up and introduced himself to me and said he would give anything in the world if I would introduce him to Bogie. I introduced the guy and Bogie was Bogie. He talked with the guy for about fifteen minutes and then asked him how big' his paper was. The reporter, as I recall, said about 50,000 circulation.

Bogie turned and yelled at me across the room:

"Bacon, you son of a bitch, how come you let me waste my time with a guy who's only got 50,000 circulation?"

Then he walked away.

In 1952, when Bogie won his Oscar for *The African Queen*, he knew he had tough competition—Marlon Brando in *A Streetcar Named Desire*. Bogie came up with a classic publicity campaign to win the Oscar. He knocked hell out of the whole Academy voting procedure.

"How in the hell can you judge one actor over another?" he said to me one day. "The only way to judge fairly is to let each nominee do *Hamlet*."

He attacked the Oscars so much that the voters were made to look bad if they voted against him. He won and it was the most popular win in Oscar history because he had deserved to win in 1943 for *Casablanca*.

Bogie had another vote-getting trick. He would go to a party and grab an Academy member by the lapel and in best Bogart gangster style say:

"Listen, you cocksucker, you better vote for me or else."

Brando never had a chance.

Bogie knew he had to do something drastic to win his one and only Oscar. Like Cary Grant, Bogie had made it all look too easy. He knew he had to hit the voters over the head to tell them he was acting out there on the screen. It worked.

By the way, here's a tip on how Bogie discovered he had cancer.

"My morning orange juice started tasting bitter. When I put

sugar in it, it still tasted bitter. That's when I went to the doctor."

People are always asking me to explain the Bogart cult among today's younger people. It's easy to answer. Bogie was the most honest man I've ever known. There wasn't a phony bone in his body. The kids today sense that. That honesty showed in his acting, his offstage demeanor, everything about the man.

About the only dishonest thing about Bogie was his manner of speech. He talked like a gangster, even in person, but he was anything but. He was Park Avenue born, the son of a noted surgeon and Maude Humphrey, one of the nation's most famous magazine illustrators at the turn of the century.

Bogie was born Christmas Day, 1900, and while still a baby posed for one of his mother's soap ads. I think he was known as the Sweetheart soap baby and that may have been why he talked tough the rest of his life.

His family was rich enough to send him to Andover, one of the nation's famous prep schools. He left for service in the U.S. Navy in World War I. The Navy has a way of altering one's speech, too.

He early drifted into the Broadway theater and once was married to Helen Mencken, one of the noted actresses of the day. It's hard to believe, but Bogie, in one of his Broadway plays, originated the line, "Tennis, anyone?" He started out in some drawing-room drama as a patent-leather-haired juvenile with blue blazer and white flannel trousers. He bounced out on the stage, tennis racket in hand, and uttered the famous line.

"I looked like a goddamned faggot," he once recalled.

But to his dying day, he carried Alexander Woollcott's review of that performance. Only an honest actor would carry a bad notice all those years. Woollcott's review read:

"The performance of Humphrey Bogart could be described mercifully as inadequate."

Bogie loved it.

Perhaps his greatest Broadway performance was as the killer

Duke Mantee in *The Petrified Forest*. He did it on the stage with Leslie Howard, with whom he formed a lasting friendship. When Jack L. Warner signed Howard to recreate his starring role in the movies, Warners wanted to put its own contract killer in the Mantee role—either Edward G. Robinson or Jimmy Cagney. Howard insisted on Bogie.

"No Bogart, no me," he told J. L.

So J. L. reluctantly signed Bogie to a Warner contract and thus was born one of the greatest stars in Hollywood's history. Bogie was an instant sensation in the movie version of *The Petrified Forest*.

When Bogie's daughter was born, he named her Leslie after the pal who had stood up for him.

Bogie, despite his gruff exterior and all his needling, was a softie at heart. He was a man of great gentleness. I remember once during his illness when he said:

"The only tough thing about this fucking cancer is that I won't see my kids grow up."

He had his children late in life, and although he didn't quite know how to cope with the situation, he was a kind and loving father.

Bogie used to have one favorite story he gave me every year. It started out by saying that fifty percent of all movie broads had no sex appeal. He would up the figure by five percent each year. In 1957, when he died, he had it up to ninety-five percent.

I once asked him what effect it had on him and his relationship with the Hollywood queens.

"Every time I make that statement my wife Betty has to take a golf club with her to parties to beat off those broads. Else they would fall all over me.

"Every one of them is trying to prove she's in the five percent category. I think the next time we do that story, we'll up it to 100 percent. It won't make no difference. All those broads will be trying to prove me wrong."

Bogie really did think that most Hollywood actresses lacked sex appeal.

"Look at all those dames MGM has under contract. I can't tell one from the other. I call them all Debbie. If I can't tell them apart, how can the public?"

A lot of people want to know what Bogie considered his best picture, *Casablanca* or *The African Queen*. Neither.

Bogie's favorite was *Beat the Devil,* which most people hated when it first came out, especially the critics.

"Wait and see," said Bogie once. "They will all come around to that picture. It's twenty years ahead of its time."

Apparently he was right because it has become somewhat of a cult film for critics, even those who didn't like it the first time out. Once more, it was the Huston-Bogart magic at work, just as in *The Maltese Falcon.*

An amusing incident happened on *Beat the Devil.* The company was shooting in Rome and one night, John Huston, Bogie, and Peter Lorre got drunk in a restaurant. Peter recalls that they saw the young Larry Harvey sitting in the restaurant, so they invited him to get drunk with them. Soon a woman fan came up and asked for an autograph. Bogie decided to give her a kiss instead for a few lire. Then the whole table started selling kisses to fans. "Everything was going fine," Peter recalled, "until I felt a tongue going down my mouth. I looked up and it was Larry Harvey doing the French kissing.

"I told Bogie what happened. He took Larry, drunker than a skunk, and dumped him head down in a big urn and left him there until some waiters pulled him out.

"Bogie said it didn't show good manners on Larry's part."

As the end neared on Bogie, the rumors about his condition became more morbid by the hour. They all filtered back to Bogie. So he called me up to the house one day to give me a statement, which read:

"I have heard that both my lungs were removed and replaced by a pump salvaged from a defunct Standard Oil station. I have practically been on the way to every cemetery in town, including several where I am certain they only accept dogs."

As he handed it to me, he said: "The bastards."
Then he said, "See you next week."
I did—in a coffin.
What Hollywood needs today are more Bogies. The town might be a better place to live in.

Mitchum and the Other Tyrone

One of my favorite stars over the years—and the most under-rated actor I know—is Robert Mitchum. Mitch and I got involved early in his career when he made page one around the world for his arrest at a marijuana party in 1948.

Today a marijuana bust wouldn't make the page before the classified ads, but in that puritanical era, it was a major story. Mitch got a bum rap on that one. There are many publicity-seeking cops in the police force, as my friend Joe Wambaugh has often pointed out. I am convinced that Mitch was set up for that arrest because of his publicity value. No other reason.

"Hell," said Mitch, "I got arrested for going to a wild Hollywood party—and I didn't even get in the front door."

It's true. Mitch, who had been a hit in *The Story of G.I. Joe*, was a natural for the set-up.

Before *G.I. Joe*, he had worked mostly in Hopalong Cassidy westerns as one of the bad guys.

"Those were happy days," Mitch recalls today. "A hundred dollars a week and all the horseshit I could carry home."

At the time of his arrest in the fall of 1948, Roberto was under contract to Howard Hughes at RKO. Hughes figured that a lengthy trial would hurt the box-office chances of a big budget movie called *Rachel and the Stranger*, starring Mitch, Bill Holden, and Loretta Young. So Hughes hired the famed criminal lawyer Jerry Giesler to defend Mitchum. Giesler promptly pleaded Mitch guilty and he got sixty days at the sheriff's honor farm. No messy trial. Had there been a trial, a guy fresh out of law school would have gotten Mitchum acquitted, but the headlines would have dragged on.

Big-studio thinking in those days was to minimize the publicity. It was a shortsighted policy because there is nothing like page-one headlines to make an ordinary actor into a box-office star.

Mitchum was practically in tears when I went up to the honor farm to talk with him.

"My career is ruined. I've got small kids and a wife to support. What the hell am I going to do?"

In a rare moment of profundity, I said:

"As long as you don't get picked up for molesting small boys like Bill Tilden, you can't beat front-page publicity. This is your image. Your career will zoom."

It was one of my better prophecies. All of a sudden, *Rachel*, which hadn't been doing all that well, had lines around the block waiting to buy tickets. And *The Story of G.I. Joe* was being replayed all over the country. Mitchum became a major star and has been one ever since.

Mitch was a natural hell raiser, always has been. No one knew this better than Howard Hughes, who assigned a bodyguard named Tyrone to Mitchum. There was only one drawback. Tyrone made Mitchum look like Little Lord Fauntleroy.

But all of a sudden, it was Mitchum keeping Tyrone out of trouble.

Mitchum and I used to frequent a bar called The Coach and Horses on Sunset Boulevard in the low-rent district. Dick Martin, later to become famous as part of Rowan and Martin of *Laugh-In* fame, was the bartender.

To give you an idea how crazy this bar was, there used to be a guy who would drive his big Harley-Davidson motorcycle through the swinging doors, rev it up inside the place, and then park it along the bar. He always ordered Chivas Regal with ginger ale, a horrible thing to do to good scotch.

First time this ever happened when Mitch and I were there, Dick Martin never batted an eye. The guy had a couple drinks, revved up his Harley, and zoomed out through the swinging doors into the sunshine.

Mitchum, with his typical underplaying, turned to Dick and said: "Isn't that kind of unusual?"

"Yeh," said Dick, "he's the only customer I got who orders Chivas and ginger ale."

This was Tyrone's type of bar.

One day Mitch and a bunch of us were sitting in a booth and Tyrone was up at the bar trying to make out with a beautiful chick. After about twenty minutes, we were treated to an amazing sight. Tyrone was down on his knees going down—or up—on the broad, who was enjoying it immensely. Then after some minutes, he stopped and ordered another drink, which Dick immediately supplied. And then came another amazing sight: Tyrone took the girl's drink and stirred it with his cock—all in pure sight of all the patrons in the pub.

Funniest part of all was a middle-aged couple who had come into the place to eat dinner.

"They were either old-age pensioners who lived in the neighborhood or else tourists from Iowa, you know the type. I was watching them more than Tyrone," Mitch recalls. "They never missed a bite of food. They'd take a forkful, glance over at Tyrone and the broad and keep right on eating just as unconcerned as anyone could be."

Needless to say, Hughes got another bodyguard for Mitch.

Mitch loves to shock people. In the aforementioned *Rachel and the Stranger*, the director was Norman Foster, who was married to Loretta Young's sister, Sally Blane.

Loretta, very religious, used to have a profanity box on all her sets. If someone in the cast or crew said "damn" or "hell," it cost him twenty-five cents. Taking God's name in vain cost as high as a dollar. Loretta gave all the money she collected to her favorite charity, St. Anne's Home for Unwed Mothers.

Well, one night on location Mitch overheard Loretta and Norman outlining the scenes for the next day's shooting.

"I suddenly realized that Loretta was actually directing the picture and I was being fucked.

"So I walked into her room and dropped $5 in her profanity box and said 'Is that enough for saying fuck you?'"

There used to be a very good United Press Hollywood reporter by name of Aline Mosby. I think she still writes for UPI in Paris or Moscow or some other farflung place.

Aline was a very nice girl and she told me that she had always wanted to meet Mitchum. One day I'm sitting in Mitch's dressing room at 20th Century-Fox when Aline walked by. I yelled at her to come in. Somehow the talk got around to wartime service. To make conversation, Aline asked Mitch what he did in the war.

"I was an asshole inspector," said Mitch without stopping for a breath. "I worked in the medical corps and whenever a soldier came in to see the doctor, I first looked up his asshole.

"I got so goddamn expert at it that I could tell with one look up a guy's asshole what was wrong with him, no matter what part of the body the ailment was in."

Then he stood up and said to Aline:

"Have you had a physical examination lately? I can tell you in a minute what's wrong with you."

Aline fled out that door like a four-minute miler.

Another time Mitch was on location for a western in Colorado when a young girl from the local newspaper interviewed him. She asked him all the usual questions, including "What is your favorite hobby?"

"Well," said Mitch, "when I'm in wild country like Colorado, my hobby is hunting."

"What do you hunt?" asked the girl reporter.

"Poon tang," said Mitchum.

In case you don't know, *poon tang* is another word for pussy.

Well, the punch line is that the story came out in the local paper with the news that Robert Mitchum's favorite game is poon tang.

Back in those days, it was Hollywood slang, probably invented by Mitchum, but the word hadn't gotten to Colorado yet.

Mitchum is a two-fisted drinker. You can sometimes get into trouble with him.

There used to be a wonderful restaurant across the street from Paramount and RKO called Lucy's. It served good food and drinks. You could also get anything else you wanted in there from broads to narcotics. It was a favorite hangout of visiting firemen from Chicago, Detroit, Cleveland, and other syndicated cities.

I dropped in for lunch one day and there was Mitchum sitting with a young girl reporter and an RKO press agent, Nat James.

It was an interview, and this girl was a new addition to the UP Hollywood staff. I was with AP but it meant nothing to Mitch that we were competitors.

Well, as often happens with Mitch and Nat James, now gone from this earth, lunch dragged into dinner and finally to the 2 A.M. closing time.

I drove home and opened the garage door. Then I proceeded to go right through the back of the garage into the bedroom where my wife was sleeping. It didn't help matters that I was driving a car at the time.

"Where have you been?" she stormed.

"I had lunch with Bob Mitchum and Teddy Roosevelt's granddaughter."

It was three o'clock in the morning, but I told the truth. The young girl reporter was Edith Kermit Roosevelt, who was indeed the daughter of Kermit Roosevelt and granddaughter of Teddy.

As I said, Mitchum likes to shock people.

Charles Laughton, who was a flaming fag, and producer Paul Gregory, now married to Janet Gaynor, had a movie property called *Night of the Hunter,* which Laughton directed and Gregory produced. Mitchum gave a superb acting performance in it.

But in the pre-production days, all three met at Mitchum's house for dinner and the drinks flowed, mostly in Mitch's direction. Finally, Mitchum took his cock out and placed it on a serving plate, poured catsup over it, and turned to his shocked guests and said:

"Which one of you wants to eat this first?"

Gregory later told me of the incident and also the fact that Mitchum went out and pissed all over Gregory's Cadillac. It was a hilarious story, actually. I laughed but there was nothing I could do about it until now.

By coincidence, I kidded Mitchum about it. He admitted it was all true. And then *Confidential* magazine came out with an even funnier story, which told about Mitchum going to a Hollywood costume party stark naked, walking in the door and pouring catsup over his head, calling himself a hamburger rare.

It was pure falsehood, of course, but Gregory in telling the story around had given some writer inspiration.

For years, Mitch always thought I wrote the story and he would greet me every time he saw me: "Hey, Jim, you still writing for *Confidential?*"

I never wrote a line for *Confidential*, Mitch, although now that I read my books, I should have.

Mitch has mellowed in recent years and he retires after every picture he makes. One of these days, he will win an Oscar that is long overdue.

He is certainly one of the few colorful stars we have left. He once asked me what to buy his wife, Dorothy, for a wedding anniversary present.

"How about a Purple Heart?" I advised him.

Over in Ireland, where Mitchum made two pictures, *A Terrible Beauty* and *Ryan's Daughter*, they are still talking about Mitchum. The Irish consider him the American Brendan Behan.

Once in a pub, after far too many drinks, a little Irishman asked Mitch for his autograph. He asked the guy's name, which was something like Paddy.

Mitch, in a shocking mood, wrote: "Fuck you, Paddy."

The Irishman, who was sober and probably wasn't Irish at all, took a poke at Mitchum and knocked him off the stool and on his ass. Shows how important the element of surprise is in barroom brawls.

Raymond Stross, the English producer who made *A Terrible Beauty,* sums it all up.

"I really like Bob Mitchum, even though he gave me the only ulcer I ever had."

During the making of the picture, Mitchum, with a few belts in him slipped a noose around Stross's ankle and hoisted him over a lamppost and let him hang down for a few minutes until the blood all rushed to his head.

"I do that to all my producers," said Mitch. "It's just playful. And playful pictures make good pictures."

But Mitch met his drinking match in Dingle, a tiny village with ninety pubs. The challenger was Archie Campbell of Dublin's Abbey theater.

"Archie was barred from every pub and the post office in Dingle because of his drinking," Mitch told me.

"Why the post office?" I asked like a straight man.

"They caught the son of a bitch drinking the ink," said Mitch.

The Princess's Gold Record

In 1958, a bunch of us were invited to Monaco as the guests of Princess Grace and Prince Rainier. Our leader was Frank Sinatra, who was entertaining at a gala for the Princess's favorite charity, the International Red Cross.

About 100 members of the press descended on Monaco for the big event, but none were invited to the palace except for me. As Hedda Hopper, who was furious, commented:

"You were the only one who came bearing gifts."

Before I left Los Angeles, Cary Grant had dropped by the house one night to give me a special gift for Grace and Rainier to be delivered personally. Believe it or not, it was a ouija board—a big favorite in the palace.

I left for New York and the charter flight to Nice. On the way, I took a side trip to Philadelphia to buy some Lebanon bologna, Philadelphia scrapple, and some choice Pennsylvania sausage. Being a Pennsylvanian myself, I knew what a Pennsylvania girl misses most when she's far from home.

I got off the plane in Nice carrying the only greasy carry-on luggage but it paid off. I got invited up to the palace.

Grace and Rainier were gracious hosts as they led a tour of the 900-room palace. We didn't hit every room but we saw a lot.

The tour ended in the Rainiers' private apartments, in a paneled den and bar, much like a suburbanite might fix up for his tract house in the San Fernando valley. As I recall, the Prince had hung up a sign over the bar, which read: "In God we trust, all others pay cash." Corny but homey.

All of a sudden, Sinatra nudged me. "Look at that hanging on the wall."

It was a gold record awarded to Grace for her duet with Bing Crosby, "True Love" from *High Society*, in which Frank also starred.

"I'll be a son of a bitch," said Frank. "She makes one record and sells a million. I've made hundreds and I haven't got one yet."

And at that time he hadn't.

Tony Quinn the Irishman

Somehow you don't think of Anthony Quinn as half-Irish, even though Quinn is his real name. But he is.

Amazingly, Tony has more believers in Ireland than he does south of the border.

"I once went over to Cork to visit my grandfather's birthplace and I was received royally as an Irishman. I also found out I looked Irish. There's lots of Irishmen who look like me."

There's a historic reason for that. When the English fleet sunk the Spanish Armada back in the time of Queen Elizabeth, the Spanish sailors who escaped to the Irish shore were hid by the Catholic Irish. Eventually they married the Celtic colleens and that's why you have Spanish-sounding names in the West of Ireland (Costello is a prime example). It's also the origin of the term Black Irish.

In Mexico, the land of his birth, Tony always got the *pocho* treatment, the derogatory term for Mexicans who are gringo-ized.

"When I made a picture down in Durango, the people accused me of being born in America—and called me a phony Mexican. Finally, the governor of Chihuahua happened to visit the set. He said he always admired me on the screen and asked if there was anything he could do for me.

"I said: 'Yes, for God's sake, get me a birth certificate.' I was born in Chihuahua during the Revolution and no one had time for recording births in those days.

"The governor went back home and talked with people who remembered my Mexican mother and my Irish father and when I was born.

"So at age fifty-one, I was issued a birth certificate. If he hadn't gotten it for me, I know I could have gotten one in Cork that would have made me Irish."

Tony is the hardest-working actor I know. He's always working, so much so that he often is in competition with himself on the screen. He's also one of the best. He holds the record for winning an Oscar for the smallest role—little more than a bit part. In *Lust for Life,* the story of Vincent Van Gogh, Tony was only on the screen for seven minutes, but he made that brief stint pay off with an Academy Award for best supporting actor.

No one gets deeper in a part than Tony. We have been friends for thirty years, but when I visited him in Rome during *Shoes of the Fisherman,* in which he played the Pope, he kept calling me "My son," even in his dressing room.

I'll never forget the first day I walked on that set at Cinecittà studios outside Rome. It was a replica of the Pope's balcony in the Vatican and Tony was imparting a pontifical blessing on the imaginary throng below in St. Peter's piazza.

Except for one thing—the people below were Italian grips and studio laborers on the soundstage. Tony was so convincing that the devout among them were crossing themselves, forgetting they were looking at a Mexican-Irish actor and not Pope John.

Few people know that Tony was a special protégé of John Barrymore in that great actor's last days in Hollywood. Tony was so impressed with Barrymore that he once tried to match him drink for drink one night.

If you think that the Barrymore-Quinn relationship is something dreamed up by me, read Gene Fowler's classic, *The Minutes of the Last Meeting*, and you'll find Tony's name in there with Barrymore, W. C. Fields, and the rest.

"I was only nineteen at the time and I survived because of my youth," says Tony.

Despite Barrymore's keen perception of Tony's talent, he played mostly Indians or Latin gigolos in his early days. Even the fact that he was Cecil B. DeMille's son-in-law then didn't help matters much. C. B. cast him as an Indian in *The Plainsman*.

Tony was bursting with pride and ambition in those days. One day on location during the lunch break, C. B. invited his son-in-law to lunch with him privately in the great director's tent.

The next day, a columnist wrote: "Anthony Quinn is too big to eat with the other actors on the location of *The Plainsman*, he eats his meals with C. B. DeMille himself."

For some strange reason this item upset Tony enormously. He began avoiding DeMille and eventually it led to an estrangement between the actor and his father-in-law.

Worse, in the early days of television, during the heyday of Hopalong Cassidy and Davy Crockett, Tony was offered a $1 million dollar contract to do an Indian series on TV. He could have used the money but he turned it down.

"The sons of bitches wanted me to play a Mohawk and keep my head permanently shaved, Mohawk-style. Worse, the contract stipulated that I could never appear in public unless me, my wife, and children appeared as the last of the Mohicans."

That offer, from a breakfast cereal company, drove Tony to Europe, where he became one of the all-time great actors.

Tony is the only person I know who has his footprints in the forecourt of Grauman's Chinese theater—the same theater where once he was turned down for a job as usher.

"The guy who was hiring ushers said I looked too Mexican to work in a Chinese theater."

Who Says There Aren't Any More Colorful Stars?

Someone was moaning the other day that Hollywood no longer has the colorful stars it used to—like Errol Flynn, Humphrey Bogart, W. C. Fields, and the like.

True, the American stars are pretty dull. They're more interested in their percentage of the gross than in having fun.

But thank God for the British and the Irish. What would a columnist do without people like Richard Harris, Oliver Reed, Peter O'Toole, and Richard Burton?

Burton will kill me if I group him with the British. Once I was in his dressing room at Warners when an RAF colonel was introduced to him. The colonel, to make conversation, said:

"How nice to meet a fellow countryman."

Burton stood up and politely but firmly said:

"My good man, I am not your fellow countryman. You are English and I am Welsh."

Richard Harris, the wild Irishman from Limerick, and I first met when he made *Mutiny on the Bounty;* later we frequented the same pub in County Clare next to Bunratty Castle.

For 500 years the pub had been known as Ryan's. Richard

changed all that. To him, it was always Durty Nellie's. And about five or six years ago, the pub's name was officially changed to Durty Nellie's.

Richard is the only actor I've ever known who is barred from the Chateau Marmont, a hotel patronized by actors for years. There's a good reason for this. During *Mutiny* Richard got kicked out of a Hollywood pub at 2 A.M. and immediately started looking for something exciting to occupy the rest of the night. He went back to the Chateau Marmont and pounded on every door in the hotel, screaming:

"They've dropped the bloody bomb."

The hotel emptied in minutes. One gorgeous actress came out nude and got as far as the lobby before she realized it. She went back for her mink coat.

I once visited with Richard in his Belgravia apartment in London. He introduced me to a handsome young Irishman thusly:

"This is my brother Dermot, I think."

When I queried him on the "I think" remark, Richard told me this history:

"I came from a large family of brothers and sisters in Limerick, but I left for London to study acting before some of them were out of diapers.

"One day about two years ago, this chap knocked on my door and said: 'I'm Dermot.' I said, 'Yes, Dermot who?' He said, 'Your baby brother Dermot.'

"So what the hell else could I do? I couldn't ask my own brother for his birth certificate, now could I? I invited him in and he's been living with me ever since."

Dermot is now a fixture of the Harris household.

Richard is possessed of superior talent. Like a Bogie or a Barrymore, he works hard but he also plays hard.

Once when he did a solo tour de force on the London stage in *The Diary of a Madman*, every critic in London gave him superior raves except one—the late Bernard Levin.

The management of the theater wanted to blow up all the raves and display them out front. Richard would have none of it. He had Levin's solo bad review blown fourteen feet high. It was the only review in the lobby.

This puzzled Levin no end. Finally the critic asked Richard why.

"I just want the audience to see it when they walk out of the theater so they will ask, 'What the fuck does that guy know?'

For years Richard used to travel around with his personal bartender, Malachy McCourt, also from Limerick. Malachy, even wilder than Richard, used to own a saloon in New York called Himself.

Then Richard went to Hazleton, Pennsylvania, to make *The Molly Maguires,* a movie about labor trouble in the early days of coal mining in Pennsylvania. Malachy had planned to take a day off just to visit Richard, but Richard got him a one-line bit in the movie. Somehow with all the drinking, Malachy's one line lasted for five months of location shooting.

Malachy is the highest-paid one-line actor in Hollywood history. Of course, it cost him his saloon. Last I heard Malachy was a popular radio performer in New York City with his own program.

He always lived with Richard whenever he came to Hollywood. Richard, as befits his stature, usually rented a mansion in Bel-Air or Beverly Hills.

Once Richard came to New York just as Malachy was leaving for Beverly Hills. It was summer and hot in California. Richard told him to be sure and use his house and pool.

"It was so damn hot when I got out there, I didn't even try the front door of the house. I just went down to the pool house, took of my clothes, and jumped in the pool bare-ass naked.

"I was having a marvelous time until the cops came. That son of a bitch Harris no longer rented the house. His lease had expired and some new tenants had moved in. When they saw a naked Irishman splashing around in their pool, they called the cops. I had a hell of a time getting myself out of that jam. Just one of Richard's little practical jokes."

Malachy was brought up on the dole in Limerick by his widowed mother, who fed a family of five on about $5 a week.

"As a kid I used to see Richard Harris ride by in his father's chauffeured Rolls-Royce. The Harrises were very rich. His father owned a grain mill."

That explains why Richard is so elegant and charming. He has all of the social graces. Denise Minnelli Hale, one of Beverly Hills and San Francisco's top social arbiters, once told me that Richard is the only male star who properly knows how, to throw a dinner party.

"His taste in food, wines, and guests is faultless," said Denise.

One other story about Malachy. He's the guy who once gave himself a month's holiday and with $10,000 decided to buy a drink in every pub in Ireland.

"I started out strong," Malachy, "but I only was able to hit about 1200 in one month. I gave up when I hit a village in Connemara which had 400 people and 80 pubs."

Oliver Reed and Harris have been carrying on a much-publicized feud for years although the two have never met. It all started when a London interviewer once suggested to Harris that Reed was a bigger star than he.

"Yes," said Richard, "about fifty pounds bigger."

It's too bad the two have never met because they would like each other inmensely. They're two of a kind.

I almost pulled off a meeting and reconciliation. For years Oliver and I had talked with each other over the phone but had never met. Often I would get a call from a London pub. Oliver, in his cups, would chat for what seemed hours over the transatlantic phone.

Then once in London he invited me to come down in the country to see him at his manor house. I went down but no one, including his brothers, could find Oliver. I later found out he had walked off into the sunset and was taken suddenly drunk.

Finally, he came to Beverly Hills and was ensconced in the Beverly Wilshire. He invited me over for breakfast.

"That way we'll be sure to meet," he said.

Promptly at 10 A.M., I showed up and Oliver was feeling no pain. He was drinking tumblers of vodka and crème de menthe. It seemed an odd drink for such an internationally famous drinker.

"I brushed my teeth this morning with a mint toothpaste," he explained. "And I want to preserve the aroma."

Even at that hour of the morning it made complete sense.

In the course of breakfast, which proceeded past the lunch hour with no sign of food, I convinced Oliver that he should meet with Harris.

"I guarantee you two will become the best of friends," I assured him. Oliver gave the go-ahead to call Harris, who also was in town.

I got Richard on the phone in his producer's office at 20th Century-Fox and told him I was lunching with Oliver Reed and I would like the two of them to meet.

"It's not another of your delicatessens, is it now? said Richard. I assured him it wasn't.

He was referring to the time I drove him up Pico Boulevard near Fox looking for a place to eat. I saw a huge sign for a delicatessen in the distance.

"Richard," I said, "there's a great delicatessen here. The food is great."

We drove in and the delicatessen wasn't built yet. All that was there was the huge sign and the concrete block shell of the building. Harris has never forgotten my recommending the food in a restaurant as yet unbuilt.

"Okay," said Richard, "hold Reed there and I'll come over as soon as I finish up here."

Richard didn't sound like he was drinking. I told Oliver that Richard was on his way and would be there within the hour.

Then a strange thing happened. Oliver disappeared. The others at the table couldn't understand what had happened. We checked the men's room, his own suite, and the doorman—who gave us a clue. Oliver, mysteriously, had taken a cab. I say mysteriously because he had a chauffeured limousine waiting by at $30 an hour.

I figured that the shock of meeting Richard Harris was just too much, so he forgot about the reconciliation attempt. When Richard showed up, I would explain what happened.

Within the hour Oliver showed up with his arms full of packages. He had found a shop in Beverly Hills that featured Irish imports.

There were gorgeous Irish linen handkerchiefs, Irish shamrock cuff links, cravats, an Irish cottage-made hat from Connemara, and even a beautiful shillelagh that must have cost a fortune.

It really was a nice thing Oliver did.

We kept drinking. Soon the El Padrino room of the Beverly Wilshire smelled like one big mint julep from that concoction Oliver had been drinking since breakfast.

Still no food and no Richard. Oliver got up at 4 P.M. and announced that he had an important appointment he could not break, Richard or no. He left.

I stayed around a half hour or so but I finally left. Just as I got to the carriage-way entrance, Richard's limousine drove up.

The chauffeur opened the back door and Richard rolled out like a rubber ball. Even had Richard shown up an hour early, it was obvious he wouldn't have been able to see Oliver, let alone reconcile with him.

I'll get the two together one of these days but we'll have to start before breakfast.

Peter O'Toole is a star I have talked with and met many times over the years but he was always drunk. We were always the best of buddies at these sessions as drinking buddies often are.

Finally one day I met him in some Etruscan fields near Rome where he was shooting *Man from La Mancha* and he was sober. So was I. It was as if we were meeting for the first time.

A common trait among drunks is telephonitis. One night

the transatlantic operator got me on the phone and said Mr. Peter O'Toole was calling from London.

Soon that beautiful voice got on the phone and asked:

"Jim, is that you?"

I assured him it was. Then he said:

"Fuck you."

I said: "Peter, do you mean to say that you called all the way from London just to say 'Fuck you?'"

Peter then said: "I had a compulsion to call someone in America and say 'Fuck you.' And then he added: 'Fuck you again, Jim,' and hung up.

Another time en route to London's Heathrow Airport, I stopped in Guinea, a great pub off Berkeley Square. Peter was in there drinking in mid-afternoon.

I said to him, "Aren't you opening in *Hamlet?*"

"Yes," he said, "but that's not for several hours."

I left after a while and flew the Atlantic. At my hotel in New York, I picked up a copy of the New York *Times* to read before I slept.

There in the theatrical section was a story from London quoting the various London critics, all of whom raved about O'Toole's *Hamlet*. One called it the most brilliant in English theater since Sir John Gielgud's.

Yet I had left Peter flying in the Guinea just a few hours from curtain time. How do the British, Welsh, and Irish actors do it?

Richard Burton once drank a quart of brandy during his performance of *Hamlet* on Broadway. The only visible effect was that he played the last two acts as a homosexual.

"I found the play rather lends itself to that interpretation," said Richard. "Fortunately, we had a theater party of hair stylists there that night and they loved it. Even gave me a standing ovation."

O'Toole and Burton are great friends, but O'Toole is envious of Burton's capacity for the sauce.

"He takes it as a national insult upon the Irish that I, a Welshman, can outdrink him," says Richard.

So that means that O'Toole is constantly challenging Richard to drinking contests. Once during *Becket*, Richard and Elizabeth Taylor came into a pub near the studio. Peter, at the bar, challenged Richard to a contest right out of the bottle. Richard, no dummy, invited Peter to go first.

O'Toole put a bottle of Irish to his lips and downed a healthy portion of it in one gulp. It's a wonder such a swallow of the lethal stuff didn't kill him. He turned around to Richard and said: "Your turn, my dear Richard."

Before Richard could get the bottle up to his lips, Peter had fallen flat on his face, completely out.

"Another win by default," said Richard, who stepped over Peter and resumed drinking by the glass with Elizabeth.

I landed in Dublin one night at the Shelbourne Hotel and got a call from O'Toole, who wanted me to visit his set the next morning at Bray, not far from Dublin. Told him I would be there.

Peter sounded fine so I went into the Shelbourne bar and confirmed something that I have always known—that an Irishman will take any side of an argument. Ran into the brilliant comedic actor, Gene Wilder, in the bar and insisted that he try my favorite Irish whiskey—Paddy's. In ordering, I made the comment loud enough for others at the bar to hear that Paddy's is the best Irish whiskey.

A well-dressed, obviously well-heeled Irishman said he begged to differ with me. "Power's is the best Irish whiskey."

He ordered a round of Power's for all of us. And then I ordered a round of Paddy's for his group. And so it went the rest of the night.

Finally, the Irishman, a charming fellow, departed. The bartender turned to me and said: "Do ye know who that Corkman was who was extollin' the virtues of Power's?"

I said no.

"Well, he was havin' fun with ye. He's one of the owners of Paddy's."

On that note, departed the next morning for Ardmore studios in Bray, where Peter and Susannah York were making *Country Dance*, later changed to *Brotherly Love*. First person I ran into was J. Lee Thompson, the director, who used to drink himself and knows a thing or two about drinking actors.

"I don't know what the hell happened to Peter. He didn't show up this morning and his hotel said he didn't come in all night."

Lee was very philosophical about it.

"Never in all my years have I seen such creativity in an actor as I have in Peter. When you are that brilliant, you have to go on an occasional binge. He'll show up bye and bye and we'll continue."

That night in the Dublin papers, Peter's mysterious disappearance was explained. There in headlines it told how Peter had tried to open a Dublin pub at 4 A.M. All pubs in Ireland close at 11 P.M. in self-defense.

There was an unusual heat wave on in Ireland then, with the temperatures and humidity around ninety. Peter undoubtedly felt the need of a cool pint and pounded on the door of the pub. The owner not only fought O'Toole but sicked his German shepherd on the wild Irishman. To Peter's credit, he took on both man and beast and would have licked them both if the cops had not arrived.

They hauled Peter off to jail where his lawyer got him sprung for about thirty pounds. The lawyer explained that Peter, who lives in England, was unfamiliar with Ireland's closing laws.

Peter is very professional, but all that emotion must burst out sometime in the making of a movie. For instance, in *The Lion in Winter*, I thought Peter stole the picture from Katharine Hepburn, who got an Oscar for best acting. Joe Levine, the producer, told me Peter only got drunk once on that picture.

"He came down in the hotel lobby and pissed in the fountain. It really didn't matter because it was a light day and he only had a scene or two. His piss may have cost me $10,000 but the rest of the stuff he put there on the screen is worth millions.

"So what the fuck is one little piss? I know it upset Kate, but hell, what doesn't?"

In all the years I have known Richard Burton and have

drunk with him—starting in 1949—I never saw him piss in a fountain. Richard can outdrink anyone but Elizabeth Taylor. I have always thought that is why the marriage broke up. Who wants to be a legendary drinker married to a wife who can drink you under the table?

Drinking is what attracted Richard to Elizabeth and also to his current wife Susan Hunt. I don't know how he met Sybil, but she's Welsh too—so that explains a lot.

The first five months Richard worked on *Cleopatra,* he didn't get a call. Elizabeth was doing all her scenes with Caesar, played by Rex Harrison.

"I was in a villa outside Rome waiting for the phone to ring, so there was nothing else to do but get drunk. And when the call came to work, I was nursing the worst hangover of my career.

"As Elizabeth and I met, I was so trembling from the night before I could not hold a coffee cup. Suddenly, Elizabeth saw my difficulty and held the cup for me like a mother would for a baby. And I just as suddenly realized this beautiful creature was human after all."

The first time he ever saw the beautiful, blonde Susan was in the Alps in Gstaad at Christmastime.

"I thought she was drunk at lunchtime. How delightful. A girl after my own heart. I helped her along, but she wasn't sloshed. She was teetering because she had lost her contact lens."

The break from Elizabeth—or rather breaks—stem from two distinct incidents, one of which involved me.

I had a falling out with Elizabeth, once a dearest friend, over Henry Wynberg, her used-car consort during one of the separations from Richard.

Bill Shiffrin, a co-producer of *The Klansman,* had promised me a part in the movie starring Richard and Lee Marvin. Also I had been invited up to the location in Oroville, California (population 8,000) in my regular capacity as a columnist.

First the movie's publicist called apologetically and said that Elizabeth, who was up there, had a big fight with Richard over me. She wanted me barred from the set although she didn't have a goddamn thing to do with the movie. Richard insisted that I be welcomed with open arms. Elizabeth, in the presence of the publicist, had called me an evil companion for Richard. Can you imagine anyone at this point being an evil companion for Richard Burton?

At the same time, Bill Shiffrin sadly told me that my part in the picture was out, too, for the same reason.

This created quite a bit of sympathy for me among some of the members of the crew and as it turned out, I got all the good stories out of Oroville without once ever having set foot in the town.

I also predicted to the publicist that the Burton marriage was in trouble because the minute Elizabeth started acting like a wife and dictating on who could or could not visit her husband, evil companions or not, Richard would tell her to go fuck herself.

And he could do it with that cathedral he carries around in his tonsils. Apparently that is what he did, because Elizabeth only lasted a day or two in Oroville after the fight over me. She came back down to Beverly Hills and took up with Wynberg again. Richard went on the most monumental binge in the history of moviemaking.

I doubt today if he remembers making *The Klansman* but he will always be remembered in Oroville. Richard was knocking off three bottles a day during the film. Even Lee Marvin was impressed.

One day he bought a $450 bauble in a jewelry store for an eighteen-year-old waitress but that was nothing—just a mere whim.

His real love in Oroville—and one that almost got him shot—was one Ann DeAngelo, a thirty-three-year-old mother of three and wife of the school janitor. Lady Ann, as Richard called her, was an extra in the movie and had a dark-eyed beauty somewhat reminiscent of Elizabeth's.

Who can fault Lady Ann for taking off with Richard? Here she was, a housewife and mother in a small town, and all of a

sudden one of the world's great lovers was asking her to re-
place Elizabeth Taylor. It's enough to turn any girl's head.

But there was an irate Sicilian husband to reckon with.
Richard was too drunk to realize the seriousness of that involvement.

He soon found out. Richard had to take a day off to fly to
Beverly Hills to narrate an album. Lady Ann, Richard's dog,
and Richard were being driven to the Oroville airport. All of a
sudden, Richard's driver spotted a pursuing Tony DeAngelo
in the rear-view mirror. Immediately, visions of a gun popped
into Burton's mind.

The driver, fortunately, had some stunt training. He took
off through Oroville like a Steve McQueen movie chase. Poor
Tony, not realizing his wife and Richard were en route to the
airport, got lost. No mayhem.

This rather unnerved Richard, so when he landed at Los
Angeles International, he sent Lady Ann and the dog back to
Oroville without him. He stayed in town alone to narrate the
album.

The husband, justly so, was fuming. Worse, co-producer
Bill Alexander tried to talk with him.

"He was a violent man but I assured him that Richard
would no longer see his wife."

That calmed the husband somewhat, but getting the word
to Richard was another matter, especially when he had two
bottles of vodka in him.

So back in Oroville a few nights later, Richard shows up in
the bar of the Prospector's Village in Oroville with Lady Ann
and a pretty airline stewardess from Munich named Karen.
Co-producer Alexander was also in the bar trembling. He had
heart failure when he looked up and saw Tony the husband
come in. Fortunately, by this time the hotel had employed a
moonlighting deputy sheriff as bouncer. He intercepted Tony
and made sure there would be no trouble.

At any rate, Tony came to the Burton table and asked his
wife to dance. She did. At this, Burton, despite a snootful of
vodka, decided it would be a good time to flee with Karen the
stewardess, who was a beauty.

Ann, out on the dance floor, spotted the exodus and left her husband standing out there while she fled frantically down the hall yelling Richard's name.

In writing about all this, I said: "Producer William Alexander, fearing that World War III was going to erupt, turned white."

I had never met Alexander or even heard of him before this picture. The day after the column appeared, Vincent Tubbs, a publicist who once went to college with Martin Luther King, Jr., called and asked:

"Can you fix that statement in your column? Alexander is a black man. He didn't like it when you said he turned white."

It was an honest mistake. I apologized in print the next day and Alexander and I became friends, especially when it turned out that I was the only member of the press who liked *The Klansman*.

Why not? I was the only columnist who had fun making it.

Not long after that, Bob Wilson, Richard's longtime aide de camp, came in with a doctor's report on his alcohol consumption.

"Richard," said Bob, "you've got about two weeks to live unless you get in a hospital soon."

Fortunately, Richard was through with the movie and he flew immediately to St. John's Hospital in Santa Monica, where they had to beat his liver into submission with a baseball bat. While Richard was drying out in a private hospital room, his Lady Ann sat dejectedly alone in the lobby. She never was summoned to his room.

Sober lovers are often forgetful. Finally, she went back to Oroville. Her Sicilian husband forgave her. She's back being a housewife and mother but she often thinks of Richard.

No question about it. She had one hell of a fling with Richard and no other housewife in northern California can say that.

After Richard dried out and mellowed, Elizabeth took him back after a while.

But there were some months in between where he had a beautiful idyll with one of the prettiest and most cuddly black girls you have ever seen by name of Jeannie Bell.

How Jeannie wound up with Richard in his villa in Geneva, Switzerland, is quite a story in itself.

Richard made a deal to work for a married producer who had Jeannie as a mistress. Richard, separated from Elizabeth at the time, often took Jeannie out dining, setting the paparazzi wild. Richard was, in effect, acting as a beard—a cover-up—for his producer friend, whose wife would never have approved of Miss Bell, even as a protége.

Then there came a big hassle over money. Richard got peeved at the producer and stopped acting as a beard. In fact, he got Jeannie to move in with him as sort of a ransom.

"I loved the idea," Jeannie once told me, "because the producer was married and Richard was not."

It soon developed into a love affair. Jeannie was a good influence on Richard and got him off the sauce.

"Even Elizabeth Taylor, who used to call every night, told me how much she appreciated what I was doing for Richard," said Jeannie.

But Richard sober started appealing to Elizabeth again. Before long she came over to Switzerland and Jeannie came back to the United States to pursue her acting career.

I met her the first night she came home and offered to take her out to dinner at the Bistro or Chasen's. She preferred to go to a place on La Cienega called Fatburger. She had gotten tired of all that French cuisine and wanted a delicious hamburger with the works, including onions.

She gave me a scoop that night—that Elizabeth and Richard would soon remarry. Sure enough, they did, in that quaint tribal bush ritual in Africa with all the rhinos and bull elephants watching.

"Romantic, I suppose," said Richard some months later, "but not realistic."

Then Richard came to New York to rehearse for his brilliant thirteen weeks in *Equus* on Broadway. He met Suzy Hunt again. She had separated by this time from James Hunt, the famous British car-racing star.

Soon gossip columnists were reporting that Richard and Suzy were hitting the spots around New York. Elizabeth, in the meantime, got picked up in a Swiss bar by a Maltese advertising man.

How come I never see girls like Elizabeth Taylor in bars?

The British press was filled with her five-day fling with the advertising man in Gstaad.

Then she came to New York for the opening of *Equus*. One night after a performance, Richard went to Sardi's with Elizabeth and spotted Suzy sitting there. In full view of Elizabeth, Richard kissed Suzy on the mouth.

The London *Sunday Mirror* printed an amazing page-one picture of the incident of Richard kissing while Elizabeth, looking unamused, watched.

Is it arrogance or guts to kiss your mistress warmly in front of your wife in a public place?

But isn't it better than *Mary Hartman, Mary Hartman?*

I Ain't Never Heard No Horses Singing

The most overworked word in show business is "genius." In my thirty years in the business, I have met only one authentic genius—Louis Armstrong. And to the day he died, he didn't know he was one. Satchmo is up in heaven playing duets with the Archangel Gabriel, the only horn player who can match him on the high notes.

Jazz is the only culture America has given to the world, and Louis was—and still is—its greatest purveyor. Bing Crosby, an old friend of Armstrong's, says: "Satchmo is the only musician since Beethoven who can't be replaced by somebody."

And it was Bing who came up with a quick $10,000 so that Louie's statue could be finished and displayed on a flatbed truck on July 4, 1976, on national television—the 200th anniversary of our country's birth and the seventy-sixth anniversary of Louie's.

How fitting! How appropriate! How so beautifully American!

Considering his beginnings, he should have been a lifer in a penitentiary or under a headstone behind a honky-tonk saloon with a knife wound in his heart.

But Louie became the American dream personified.

I was just a kid the first time I ever heard Louie hit those beautiful notes. He was playing cornet in those days with Fletcher Henderson's Hot Six, and like all bands of the twenties, they hit the small-town Pennsylvania dance-hall circuit.

It was music from heaven when Louie took those solos. No one before or since ever blew a horn like he did.

Louie suffered all the indignities of his race during those years—and even after he became world-renowned.

I first met him years later when I did a story on him in the early fifties when he was teamed at the Sands Hotel in Las Vegas with—of all people—the great Metropolitan Opera star Robert Merrill. Jack Entratter was the impresario at the Sands and I naively asked Jack for Louie's room number because I wanted to call him for an interview. Entratter, a wonderful man, said:

"Louie can't stay at this hotel. He would if I could lick Las Vegas all by myself but Louie has to stay in a motel that will take blacks."

But I found him and met one of the great heroes of my life.

And for twenty-five years after that, Louie and I had annual reunions.

Happily, in his later years, he could stay in the swank Strip hotels where he starred.

Each time we met, he gave me a packet of his physic. Over the years he had concocted a laxative mixture that was about as close to liquid dynamite as you can get.

And each time, Maury Foladare, his press agent for forty years, would tell me:

"Don't touch that stuff. It will blow you apart."

But Louie swore by it.

"Man, it purifies me. You got to get all that soul food and booze out of your system so you can start over again tomorrow."

Louie would polish off brandy like a nursing baby takes to mother's milk.

One night I was at a party the legendary Bricktop gave for Louie at her apartment. After much booze had been consumed, Bricktop suggested that she and Louie should sing a duet. But there wasn't one piano player in the house and the duet was never sung.

It wasn't long after that Louie died and Bricktop called me to say:

"We should have sung that night without music because that's one duet that's never going to be sung again."

The two were going to harmonize on "Miss Otis Regrets," the song that Cole Porter had written especially for Bricktop when her place in Paris was the favorite hangout of Porter, F. Scott Fitzgerald, Ernest Hemingway, Picasso, and all the other greats of that long-ago era.

It's one of the great regrets of my life that it never took place.

Louie's fabulous horn was idolized by everyone from royalty to African tribesmen. Louie once told me about the time he visited Africa with his longtime manager Joe Glaser. As the plane circled for a landing, Louie looked down on a sea of blacks. Tribesmen had assembled for days to welcome Louie Armstrong. Joe said there were at least 100,000 gathered at the airport.

Louie's comment, made with no disrespect intended for his race but with typical modesty, was:

"What the hell are all those niggers doing down there?"

Black people often use that derogatory word in talking about each other but they don't like it coming from whites. I only repeat it because it was Louie's abject humility that prompted him to say it.

Glaser, a white man, handled more black artists than any other manager in show business history but to the day he died was mystified how people in the African bush could have heard about Louie Armstrong.

"They not only knew of him but they idolized him," said Joe, who added:

"But nothing ever surprises me about Louie Armstrong except the simplicity of the man himself."

When Prince Philip of England visited Beverly Hills in 1966, I attended a party given in Philip's honor. Every major star in the business was there but the Prince monopolized Louie.

"My whole family digs you," said Queen Elizabeth's husband in Louie's own language.

"And I dig you," said Louie, who was used to being around royalty.

At the same party, a rather pompous Britisher asked Louie if he were going to change his style to folk music, then very much in vogue.

"Man," said Louie, "all music's folk music. Nobody but folks listens or plays music. I ain't never heard no horses singing."

Louie was always about twenty years ahead of his time with music. When Dizzy Gillespie popularized bop and with it the beginnings of modern jazz, Louie one day up in his suite at the Ambassador Hotel in Los Angeles recalled how the legendary King Oliver in New Orleans had told Louie to play the lead.

"People will know what you are doing," said Oliver.

At that time, Louie said, he had been doing variations exactly like Gillespie's bop—and this was right after World War I.

"There ain't nothing new in music. People think jazz originated in New Orleans. It did, but I can't remember it being called that until I got to Chicago. When I started, it was called ragtime, but before my time it was called levee camp music. Most of the time it was gospel music that swung."

Maybe it was because we were vulgar young boys, but in the twenties, the word "jazz" was considered a derivation of *jism,* a common obscenity for semen in those days. In Chicago, where the syncopated music flourished in the Capone gin mills of Prohibition, it seemed logical to associate the new music with fucking, a lot of which was going on in Chicago and other cities in those times.

You will never find that origin of the word in Webster, but who knows what devilment evil minds can conjure?

Louie's unique charm—and it never left him—is that he never saw himself as a genius. True, he took raw jazz out of the New Orleans whorehouses and quite unknowingly refined it into a culture that is studied and revered around the world.

Jazz buffs the world over analyze and dissect Armstrong's music note by note even though he has been dead for six years.

"Some of these cats know more about my music than I do," Louie once told me. "I just go out there and blow that goddamn horn and get in a few licks with the chops.

"I never worry about a black cow giving white milk. I just drink the milk."

King Oliver's advice to Louie back in the early days stuck with him all his life. It used to horrify modern musicians when he would say that his favorite band was Guy Lombardo.

"I dig Guy. Always have, ever since they started in Al Quodback's Granada Cafe in Chicago. That band plays the tune. They give the melody first and it's beautiful. That's my style, too."

Louie may have had something there. The Lombardos have been going strong for more than fifty years, while some of their musical critics are parking cars or spitting out tacks on an assembly line.

I used to love to hear Louie talk about the legendary Bessie Smith, the all-time Queen of the Blues. Louie played cornet on many of the race records that Bessie made in her career.

"That woman never trusted banks. She used to wear a carpenter's apron under her dress. Whenever I wanted change for a hundred-dollar bill, I didn't have to go to no bank. Bessie would just pull up her dress and make change like a teller in a bank."

Louie had class about him without trying. He proved that class is something you're born with no matter how humble your beginnings.

Louie was born in a red-light district of New Orleans and

spent his childhood hauling coal for the whores in their cribs.

"I used to help those chicks start their fires and get a little peek in at the same time."

By the time he was twelve, he could play the slide whistle and he used to make a dollar a night entertaining the whores and their pimps in Storyville.

"I took it home to my mother, who used to feed us by washing clothes for white folks on Canal Street."

Then one New Year's Eve, Louie took a .38 pistol from one of a succession of stepfathers and went out to celebrate by shooting blanks just like the big folks. It was about the time of the beginning of World War I in Europe.

But the police took a dim view of Louie's celebrating and he wound up in the Waif's Home. His only crime was using a pistol loaded with blanks like other kids of that time would use a firecracker on the Fourth of July. Louie was known as a street kid from a broken home. He never had a chance when he found himself before a juvenile judge.

But it was the best thing that ever happened for him—and the world—because an unsung hero by the name of Peter Davis asked Louie if he would like to play in the reform school's band.

"Mr. Davis tried me on the tambourine and then the snare drum. Finally one day he handed me a bugle and taught me how to play 'Home Sweet Home.'"

Thank God for Peter Davis. Thank God for Louie Armstrong.

Just hours before his death in 1971— on the last birthday of his life—he was visited by famed trombonist Tyree Glenn in the Armstrong home in Queens. The two old friends talked of old times, then out came the trombone and the trumpet. Before long there was "Sleepy Time Down South." Louie took a solo and the notes came loud and clear as always.

He put down his horn for the last time.

How the Press Saved Jimmy Stewart's Career

Forty-three years ago this fall, a gangling, hesitant-talking

Pennsylvanian came to Hollywood to be met at the train by a Broadway pal, Henry Fonda.

And after all those years, what is the most vivid memory of all for Jimmy Stewart?

"Well, I'll tell you," drawls Jimmy in a perfect imitation of Rich Little doing Jimmy Stewart, "it was a few years after I came back from the war—the big war—and I had a couple of pictures that didn't do too well. I was quite surprised when a magazine writer said he had an assignment to do a story on me.

"As I say, I was quite surprised after those flops but I did manage to ask him what the story was about. " 'The Rise and Fall of Jimmy Stewart,' said the writer.

"Boy, did that shake me up? Right away I called my agent and said, 'Get me a western, quick.' "

Since that time Stewart, now pushing seventy, has appeared in dozens of westerns and is still one of our more durable superstars. That article never was written—and never will be.

Stewart's decision to go western was a big career boost for him. Pre-war, he had been one of the industry's biggest stars but, despite an heroic combat record, he was like many a returning star—forgotten for the good scripts.

Harry Cohn said there is no such word as gratitude in the Hollywood language. And he was right.

Jimmy had been in only one western pre-war—*Destry Rides Again*. Acting on his request, Lew Wasserman, the agent, got Jimmy *Winchester 73*, a picture that saved Universal, which Wasserman now heads.

In those days, Bill Goetz was head of the studio and it was in financial trouble. There were no star names on the roster, just $75-a-week contract players like Rock Hudson and Shelley Winters. Goetz cast Rock and Shelley in the movie but needed a star name to sell the picture. Wasserman sensed this and demanded—and got—a fabulous deal for Stewart that netted him fifty percent of the profits.

The movie was a blockbuster at the box office. Jimmy got rich. Goetz got blasted by all the other studio heads for ruining the industry. Percentage deals for stars were practically unheard of in those days.

Jimmy made millions off the deal. He occasionally works for Wasserman.

"He still drives a hard bargain. He's not my agent anymore. He's the boss. He wants to pay a flat salary."

More Adventures with Errol Flynn

One day in Paris I walked into a little mom-and-pop bistro near the studio de Boulogne. I think the bistro was called Le Cadran Bleu. I had just left Brigitte Bardot in her dressing room at the studio, where we shared a couple of bottles of champagne and some words of endearment.

And who should I meet in the bistro but Errol Flynn with fifteen-year-old Beverly Aadland, his beloved then and until the day he died a few years later. I didn't spot him at first but soon I heard that familiar greeting: "Hey, Sport."

It was Errol, all right. I had come in for a bite to eat but Errol would have none of that. He wanted me to try a new Russian vodka he had discovered. It was potent but good.

Errol introduced Beverly as "the coming Marie Wilson," whatever that meant. Then he made the suggestion, since he had a few days off from *The Roots of Heaven,* that he and I and Beverly all visit the Brussels World Fair the following week.

"I'm not crossing any state lines with that child," I told Errol. He laughed and suggested that we go out on the town that night in Paris. That was okay.

We were all staying at the George V so naturally we met next door that evening in the bar of the Prinze deGaulles.

"I prefer that bar because all the hookers are allowed in there. The George V is much too stuffy and kicks them all out," Errol explained.

Drinks came by the jars, as always with Errol. Soon we were joined by one of England's legendary drinkers, Trevor Howard, who also was in the Darryl Zanuck-John Huston picture.

All of a sudden, Errol had an amazing idea. It seemed years

ago when he was married to the French actress Lili Damita, he had visited a lesbian nightclub on the Left Bank. It had been more than twenty years since he had been there but he remembered the name and the address.

Before long we were at a table overlooking the dance floor at this gay spot. The dance floor was filled with bull dykes dancing with young girls. There were a few other males in the place but mostly there were lesbians.

Surprisingly, the presence of Flynn and Howard had little effect on the crowd, but Beverly was something else. Although Beverly had been around the track once or twice at age fifteen, her youth gave her a virginal look.

The bull dykes focused their collective eyes on her and before long one of them came to the table and asked her to dance. Beverly looked at Errol. He said why not? And soon Beverly was out on the dance floor.

At first Errol thought it was fun but then he started getting jealous of the way the bull was dancing cheek-to-cheek with his concubine.

Suddenly, he got up and strode out on the dance floor like Captain Blood. He wrenched Beverly from the arms of the lesbian and started pulling her off the floor. About that time, the bull dyke with whom Beverly was dancing hauled off and let Errol have a right to the jaw that sent him reeling. Two or three others of these Amazons started pelting him, and soon Errol Flynn, who had conquered Burma single-handedly for Warner Bros., was flat on his ass on the dance floor.

Stunned into disbelief, all he could say was: "You cunts."

Then he looked over at me for help. Trevor by this time was too far gone to be of any help.

I said: "Errol, let's get the hell out of here. These dames will kill us."

I, for one, was not about to tangle with these broads, some of whom looked like linebackers for the Los Angeles Rams. We all fled amid a torrent of French cusswords.

Outside on the street, Errol turned on that famous charm and pleaded:

"Sport, don't ever print anything about this. It would ruin

the Errol Flynn image if word ever got out that three lesbian cunts tossed me on my ass."

I gave him my promise. A promise which I have kept until now when it doesn't matter anymore.

Needless to say, we hit no more lesbian joints that night although we hit plenty of joints.

Around about 5 A.M., it became increasingly difficult to load Trevor in and out of taxicabs so we headed back to the George V.

At that hour of the morning, that swank hotel was treated to a strange sight. There was I holding up Trevor's head and Errol his feet as we transported the brilliant English actor across the lobby to the elevator.

To our credit, we only dropped him once before we finally got him in bed.

Errol then said:

"Both of us have a nine o'clock call at Fontainebleu. This poor bastard will never make it but I will. See you in a couple hours."

At seven A.M., we met in the lobby for the long ride out to Fontainebleu. It must have been forty or fifty miles at least.

On the way out, Errol was nursing a monumental hangover. He usually had cocaine to get him over these sieges but today he had none. He was dying.

Both of us had given up on Trevor. He had been horizontal most of the time since midnight and no doubt was horizontal yet.

When we reached the set, which bore a remarkable resemblance to the African veldt, we were greeted by an amazing sight—a chipper, sober, and alert Trevor Howard.

As Huston rehearsed the scene in the French woodlands, Howard was letter-perfect in his lines. Flynn couldn't remember a damn thing and was stumbling all over the place.

But Huston decided to shoot the scene anyway and ordered that a wild hyena be loosed from its cage. Flynn took a snarling look at the snarling beast and asked Huston:

"Where's the trainer?"

Huston explained there was none. Hyenas are so wild that no one has ever trained one.

"You just remember your lines, Errol," Huston told him. "I'll handle the beast."

Errol looked at me with those listless hangover eyes and said, "Let's go back to the hotel, Sport. I need a drink."

And we did. The scene was shot another day.

PART II: SEX IN AND OUT OF HOLLYWOOD

Beauty, romance, hookers, the mile-high club, and
crepes Suzette

The Beautiful Grand Prix Driver
and the Chef

Strange adventures have a way of finding me when I travel around the world. One cocktail hour I found myself drinking martinis with the beautiful Jacqueline Bisset at a little hotel in Avignon in the south of France, the same place where the Popes lived in exile from Rome during the Middle Ages. Came dinner time and Jackie suggested Baumaniere, a three-star Michelin hotel, which translated means that it has one of the twelve best restaurants in all of France.

I didn't know at the time that Baumaniere was up a mountain as rugged as any in Arizona. In fact, it was near a vast bauxite canyon that Dante used as a model for Hell in his *Inferno*. Baumaniere is located at Les Baux and once was a monastery—and has the wine cellar to prove it.

I once went around the course at Riverside Raceway with Bob Bondurant, the onetime Grand Prix race driver. Even at 180 miles down the straightaway and 80 to 90 miles around the figure-eight curves, I was not as scared as I was with Jackie Bisset driving her little sports car up to Baumaniere.

The mountain road was all hairpin curves and Jackie took them all at 100 mph plus. Sometimes we spun completely around like a movie stunt driver.

"Do you always ride gripping your seat in such terror?" she asked me once as we missed a curve. Then she calmed me by adding:

"Actually I'm very nearsighted and I don't see those bloody turns until we're right on them."

Fortunately I had had about three martinis else I would have jumped out of the car and rolled down the mountains. But suddenly we pulled into the parking lot at Baumaniere. I said a couple of Hail Marys and relaxed.

The dinner was everything it was touted to be. I remember I ordered lamb, which I hate, because I feel that it is the only way to test a good restaurant. Order something you don't like.

113

It was the only time in my life I ever enjoyed lamb. Baumaniere deserved its three stars.

At the end of the dinner, served with a superb house white wine, Jackie suggested we go down the mountain to Avignon. She was staying in the hotel there where we had met. I had not checked in and my bags were in her car.

To give you an idea of how scary that ride up the mountain was, I had my choice of going back to Avignon with one of the most beautiful women in the world—or else checking into a room at Baumaniere.

I chose the latter. Can you imagine going down that mountain with a frustrated Grand Prix driver at the wheel? And with a few martinis and some wine inside her?

I slept like a baby in a charming room in the quaint inn. In the morning I was awakened by a knock on the door. It was the head chef.

"Monsieur Bacon," he said warmly, "are you the same James Bacon who was a friend of Henri Charpentier?"

I told him I was indeed. The Baumaniere's chef had apprenticed under the famous Charpentier, the inventor of crepes Suzette.

By way of background, Charpentier was a chef who studied under Escoffier, who was his cousin. He worked with Escoffier at the Savoy Hotel in London and then came to the U.S.A., where he worked in various New York restaurants until he opened his own place on Long Island. It was a famous restaurant in the thirties.

His later years were spent in a little house in Redondo Beach near Los Angeles where every night he and his assistants cooked a meal for ten or twelve people that required reservations a year, sometimes two years, in advance. It was a memorable dining experience.

I had written about him often. Sadly, it was I who wrote his obituary, which the chef at Baumaniere had clipped out of the Nice *Matin*. He showed it to me.

But Henri invented crepes Suzette long before he became a famous chef. As a boy of ten, he went to work at the old Café de Paris in Monte Carlo, not to be confused with the Hotel de

Paris. In Victorian days, it was the favorite restaurant in the south of France for the Russian Grand Dukes and English royalty, including Queen Victoria herself.

Henri's first job at the Café de Paris was to put a pillow under Queen Victoria's feet as she dined. The famous Queen took a particular liking to the young French boy and always requested that he attend her when she dined.

Needless to say, promotions came rapidly for the youngster with that kind of patronage.

By age sixteen, Henri was the youngest captain of waiters in the Café de Paris, serving such as the Prince of Wales, later to become Edward VII, King of England.

As his mother before him had given her name to the Victorian Age, Fat Eddie was to give his to the Edwardian Age. But the night Henri invented crepes Suzette, Edward was still the swinging Prince of Wales.

I loved to hear Henri tell the story of that night. It's really quite romantic.

"Ah, monsieur," he would say, "the Prince came in with a beautiful French girl, no older than I. She was so beautiful that I can dream about her and see her face now even in my eighties.

"The Prince asked for crepes for dessert. Monsieur, we have had crepes—or pancakes—since the Romans but until this night not the way I fixed them. I mixed cordials and poured them on the crepes and was about to serve them to his Royal Highness. And then, quite by accident, I brushed over a candle, which fell on the crepes. Immediately there was flame.

"But, monsieur, I was only sixteen and had all the brashness of youth and acted as if nothing had happened. I was too embarrassed to admit that I had set afire the crepes by accident. So I served the crepes still flaming to the Prince.

"He was astonished but he tasted them. My heart stopped beating for a second. Then he turned to me and said: 'Henri, this dessert is superb. What do you call it?

"Your royal highness, it is something that I created just for you. I call it crepes Prinze de Gaulle.

"At that the Prince looked at this beautiful dinner

companion—Mon Dieu, she was so beautiful—and said:
'Henri, we shall call this marvelous dessert crepes Suzette.' "

I told the story to the chef at Baumaniere, who said he had
heard the same story as a boy. Now there are as many chefs
who claimed to have invented crepes Suzette as there were passengers on the Mayflower.

When I wrote the story first, I got a nice letter from Lucius
Beebe in Virginia City, Nevada, who said that of all the ver-
sions he heard, he would henceforth take mine as gospel.

Anyway the chef at Baumaniere thought the whole thing
called for a special celebration. He took me down in the wine
cellar, where I saw the most fabulous collection of wines I
have ever seen—before or since—Chateau Lafite from the 1870s
and priceless vintages of the great wines of France.

Then we stopped before an ancient bin.

"Here are wines from the time of Napoleon—rich reds of
1803 and 1804."

I stood in awe and then he calmly took an 1803, uncorked
it, and drained the sediment and poured us each a glass. The
wine was still excellent. I have no idea what a wine like that
would bring at an auction. I'd guess several thousands of dollars at the very least.

But it made that harrowing trip up the mountain with the
world's most beautiful Grand Prix driver all worth while.

An Obscene Call on a Telethon — a First

I am the only so-called celebrity—certainly the only male one—
that I know of who ever got an obscene phone call on a national telethon.

I forget the disease but it could not have been too serious an
ailment, as there was no comedian sponsoring it. Dennis
James, the game-show host, was the master of ceremonies.

After I did my little bit at the microphone I went over to the
telephone bank, as is the custom, and started answering calls.

First caller—I swear—was a fag who made an indecent
proposal right then and there. Even gave me his apartment

number and phone number in Hollywood. Where else? He was watching me as he talked. Once he asked me to wave to him. Like a horse's ass, I did. I never felt so silly in my life but it's an automatic reflex on TV.

As luck would have it, Dennis decided to switch over to the telephone callers. First place he stopped was my place.

"Jim, have you had any interesting calls?"

In front of all those millions watching, I couldn't very well repeat what had just been said to me so I stole one of Red Buttons' routines.

"Yes," I said, "Red Buttons, in honor of the Bicentennial, has just pledged a big amount in honor of his ancestor, Solomon Schwartz."

"Yes," said Dennis, still holding the mike on me.

"Solomon Schwartz," I said, "was the only Jew with George Washington when he crossed the Delaware."

I could see Dennis was believing me so I continued.

"It was Solomon Schwartz who said: 'General, how come everybody else spends the winter in Miami Beach? And we gotta spend it in Trenton.'"

Dennis still held the microphone on me. He was nodding in agreement and not laughing. Could it be possible he was believing me? So I added:

"Solomon Schwartz also said to Thomas and Mrs. Jefferson: 'Watch my word, someday the Jeffersons will be on television.'"

Dennis, still unsmiling, said: "That was Jim Bacon telling you about Red Buttons' ancestor, Solomon Schwartz."

Surprisingly, several other people later commented to me how interesting it was to hear me talk about Red's ancestor. They took it seriously too.

Funny, when Red tells it, he gets big laughs.

Must be the delivery.

How I saved Julie Newmar's Life

I guess there is no man alive who wouldn't agree that Julie

Newmar is the most beautifully put together big girl the movies have ever produced.

Julie, who has never married and still looks sensational, always has liked short guys.

"They do everything twice," she says with some logic.

But one day in 1953, when Julie was just sixteen years old, she almost let—or rather Columbia Pictures almost let—that gorgeous body depart this earth.

Sam Katzman produced a movie called *Serpent of the Nile,* which was the story of Cleopatra low-budget.

Julie, a luscious dancer, was signed to do a serpent dance as a theme for the title of the movie. The makeup department had painted her body from head to toe with gold paint.

Press agents Bob Yeager and Milt Stein introduced me to Julie just as she left the makeup room. Even all gold, she was the most gorgeous thing I had seen that year outside of Elizabeth Taylor.

Miltie and Bob left the two of us alone and we talked. The more we talked, the dizzier she became. It could have been tossed off as excitement—as it was her first movie and first interview—but it was obvious something horrible was happening to this girl.

I told her to lie down on the couch and I immediately summoned Katzman and some makeup people and told them they had painted this girl with some kind of nonporous paint that was shutting off all her circulation.

Within a matter of minutes, they had cleaned off the paint. And Julie, who had completely passed out, started coming to life again.

They must have painted her with regular paint because her body stopped breathing for a minute or two.

Now, wasn't that a good deed?

Lady Trisha in the Nude

A manager called one day and said: "How about having lunch

at the Polo Lounge with Lady Trisha Pelham, who is an actress and the daughter of the Duke and Duchess of Newcastle?"

Well, my mind immediately conjured a vision of someone like Dame May Whitty. Imagine my surprise when Lady Trisha turned out to be twenty-four years old and quite beautiful. And her ancestors once employed Robin Hood, the real one, not Errol Flynn.

But biggest shocker of the lunch was the news that Lady Trisha had made her American movie debut in *Linda Lovelace for President*. And also, her ladyship had done a nude scene while playing an American college cheerleader.

"I even went to see the Rams play the San Diego Chargers to research my role," she said.

What did her father the Duke think about her playing in a movie with the Queen of Pornography?

"He had absolutely no idea who Linda Lovelace was. When I told him, all he said was 'That's quite nice.' "

But more important was the family's connection with Robin Hood.

"My father's ancestral holdings include Sherwood Forest and the village of Nottingham. Robin worked as forester for one of the Dukes of Newcastle. Of course, that was some time ago and before he took up robbing the rich to give to the poor."

She said she had come to America because she met a fellow in London whose family had invented the ice cream cone. He was an American.

"We got married and moved here. I love Southern California. We're divorced now but he's still my best friend. I intend to stay here and become a serious actress."

She said her title has proven somewhat of a handicap in snobbish Beverly Hills and Bel-Air.

"Everyone I meet wants to socialize, not talk business," she said.

"I never really took the title all that serious as a child in England but apparently it becomes a big thing with some Americans."

When I finished the interview, I thought the whole thing was too preposterous to be true but I checked with several high-placed British friends. Everything she said was true.

Hope she gets a chance to play Maid Marian in a remake of *Robin Hood* someday.

That would be nice.

The World's Most Universal Profession

For some strange reason, Jews in Beverly Hills will never believe there are hookers in Israel. Just like the Irish always resented Joyce for writing about the hookers in Dublin.

Once in the town of Nahariya near the Lebanese border, I was approached in a bar by a very sexy Israeli girl. She gave that old familiar smile and handed me a gold card, beautifully engraved. It read:

"If you want to make love with me in your hotel room, the price is $50. If not, please return the card as it is expensive."

Even the Iron Curtain has them. In Zagreb, Yugoslavia, the hookers came out in droves around the Intercontinental Hotel (where I was staying) as soon as it got dark. I commented to the desk clerk, who spoke excellent English:

"How come a communist country allows prostitutes to operate? It's against the core of Marxist philosophy—the exploitation of the masses."

The clerk shrugged:

"We do it only for the Italians who come over here from Milan."

My favorite hooker story concerns Jim Backus, the actor-comedian. He stayed once at the Hotel Excelsior on Rome's Via Veneto. Impatient for his wife Henny to get dressed, he strolled out on the famous boulevard alone. A streetwalker approached him, and once again, the $50 price. Jim, kiddingly, said he never paid over $5 in the U.S.A. and walked back to the hotel.

A few minutes later Jim and his wife strolled up the same street. The same hooker idled alongside Jim and whispered:

"See what you get for five dollars?"

Down in Mexico in a small village where Darryl Zanuck was shooting *The Sun Also Rises,* the cast and crew were severely depressed. There was not one hooker to be found in town. Only one thing could be worse for a movie company on location—no saloon.

Fortunately, Darryl had cast Errol Flynn in the movie in what turned out to be one of the finest acting jobs of Errol's career.

The company had been in Mexico for about a month and was becoming mutinous. Then Errol showed up for his stint. First night in the village, Errol found a young and beautiful cocksucker. Everybody was happy again. Errol, with his built-in radar, had saved the day. Th company made a hero out of Errol but Flynn pooh-poohed his status.

"Unlike Babe Ruth," said Errol, "I've never struck out once."

Back in the days when *Life* magazine was an important force in Hollywood journalism, one of the *Life* staffers in the Los Angeles bureau called Harry Brand in desperation. Harry in those days was director of publicity at 20th Century-Fox and a man who could do anything.

It seems that one of the big *Life* executives from the New York headquarters was coming out here for a few days without his wife. He had expressed a desire to date a starlet while he was here. Could Harry fix him up with one of the Fox contract girls?

Harry was not about to pimp for any of the studio's starlets, but he did the next best thing. He called up a particularly sexy $100-a-night call girl and bought her off for the three nights the executive was in town. Then Harry had one of his boys dummy up a studio biography on the girl and give her a few credits in movies. Then she showed up at the executive's hotel suite for drinks.

The executive, an Ivy Leaguer from the word boola boola,

was thrilled. He took her to dinner at Chasen's, went night-clubbing at Ciro's, and really had a nice friendly three nights on the town with her. She was a looker, too.

The executive went back to New York and called Harry to thank him. And then almost casually, he admitted to Harry:

"I wish I could have had more time out there. I think I could have fucked her if I had tried."

Once a Madam, Always a Madam

One of my favorite people is the mayor of Sausalito, California. That's because Sally Stanford was San Francisco's most famous madam before she moved across the bay and became a restaurant owner and politician.

Sally Stanford wasn't her real name. She was due in court on a prostitution charge and had so many arrests under her other name, she decided to change it fast. It was after the weekend of the Big Game. When you say Big Game in San Francisco, it means only one thing—the football game between Stanford and California.

"I decided to take the name of the winner, which happened to be Stanford that year. It could just as easily have been Sally California," she recalls.

But Sally Stanford it was. And Stanford is one of the big society names in Northern California because of Leland Stanford, founder of the university that bears his name.

Society, however, wanted no part of Sally—at least the women members. Then a strange thing happened. Sally married one of her customers—a Gump. Now the Gump family owns the biggest department store in San Francisco. And here was Sally the madam holding forth in the Gump mansion on Nob Hill.

That's what started Sally on the road to respectability. She is not ashamed of her past. In fact, she talks freely about it.

"I had a lot of Hollywood customers. The worst was Humphrey Bogart, who was always getting drunk and starting fights in my place. It was embarrassing with the police, who had always been so kind to me. My favorite was Errol Flynn. He liked his booze but he liked his women better."

Once Hollywood hired Sally to be a technical adviser on a movie called *Sylvia,* starring Carroll Baker as a hooker. Accordingly, Paramount sent me up to Sausalito to do a story on Sally for the Associated Press.

I went across the bay to her Valhalla restaurant, one of the finest up there. I introduced myself to the maitre d' and he said that Miss Stanford was expecting me. He ushered me into a waiting room that looked for all the world like Sally's old place. After waiting a few minutes, Sally came in with a parrot on her shoulder and gave that madam smile and asked:

"Which one is the gentleman from Hollywood?"

I stood up and Sally and I went to a table. She did all the ordering. The wines were fabulous—a Pouilly Fuisse, a Chateau Lafite Rothschild, and of course the champagne was Dom Perignon. Chateaubriand was the entry, Maryland cracked crab the appetizer along with caviar and Polish vodka. After dinner there was the finest brandy and Monte Cristo Cuban cigars—very hard to find since Castro took over, but Sally had them.

And then the pièce de résistance—the check. It came close to $150 for the both of us and it was handed to me.

That came as a shock but, what the hell, I paid it. Then I commented to Sally:

"You know, my dear, that I often dine with Dave Chasen or Mike Romanoff in their own restaurants and they would never dream of giving me a check."

Sally's face lit up. She gave me that madam's smile and answered:

"Once a madam, always a madam. We always get paid."

Mr. Perkins, World's Greatest Latin Lover

"Zsa Zsa Gabor is the only television star who has made marriage into a series" (Bob Hope, 1976).

After seven marriages, Zsa Zsa buys rice by the case lots.

She finally got smart with her seventh husband, Michael O'Hara. He's a divorce lawyer.

But before Michael, Zsa Zsa always said the two men she loved the most were the ones who treated her the worst— George Sanders and Porfirio Rubirosa.

Sanders was such a tight bastard that when Zsa Zsa would ask him for a cigarette, Sanders would charge her three cents. And that was in the days when cigarettes were twenty cents a pack and Zsa Zsa was buying all of them.

It was Sanders who was responsible for Zsa Zsa's going on television. In the early days of Los Angeles TV, columnist Paul Coates came up with a clever idea called *Bachelor's Haven*. It was a crazy advice-to-the-lovelorn show.

Zsa Zsa, then on her third marriage to Sanders, was asked to be a panelist. She asked George for his advice.

"You're too stupid to go on television," said George.

Naturally, Zsa Zsa went on.

"And proved it," said George.

Actually, Zsa Zsa was a hit. One viewer wrote in and asked her what to do with a husband who travels with other women.

"Shoot him in the leg," said Zsa Zsa on the live show.

Within three days, there was a case on the Los Angeles police blotter of a wife shooting a philandering husband in the leg.

George once told me that married life with Zsa Zsa was like living on the slopes of a volcano.

"Very pleasant between eruptions."

Zsa Zsa, despite George's meanness, always said, "He is the only man I ever loved."

Unfortunately for the marriage, Rubirosa came along about the same time.

On Christmas Day, 1953, George called me at home and said he had just broken into his wife's bedroom and found Zsa Zsa in bed with Rubirosa. With that beautiful voice, he went into elaborate detail of how he had taken a ladder out of the garage and climbed to the second-floor bedroom of the Bel-Air home Conrad Hilton had given Zsa Zsa in a divorce settlement.

I asked why he didn't go through the front door since he had a key.

"I was overtaken by the Christmas spirit and wanted to play Santa Claus. Unfortunately, I was too rotund for the chimney."

Then in classic understatement, he said:

"You can print that our marriage is ended."

I called Zsa Zsa and she was hilarious in describing the scene.

"When George went out the front door I screamed at him, 'George, dollink, I have a present for you under the tree.' I thought that would bring the cheap son of a bitch back but it didn't."

While all this was going on, Rubirosa vanished under the bed or more probably down the ladder and down the driveway.

George filed for divorce and Zsa Zsa counterfiled. On their fifth wedding anniversary the following April, 1954, the divorce was granted.

Zsa Zsa, typically, celebrated the divorce with a costume party. Everybody was to come as his favorite character. Since I had been having a lot of fun with Howard Hughes for a few weeks, I didn't shave for a few days, wore a crumpled suit and tennis shoes. I also wore a slouch felt hat.

Zsa Zsa met me at the door and said:

"Dollink, why didn't you come in costume?"

One of the guests at the party was Nicky Hilton, who once had been Zsa Zsa's stepson. He came as John Wayne with real guns.

We didn't find that out until Nicky got loaded and started shooting them. When the bullets smashed a mirror or two, he was disarmed.

Then Nicky tried to lure the always-gorgeous Zsa Zsa to bed.

"Dollink," said Zsa Zsa, "I don't do incest."

Marion Davies came as General Douglas MacArthur, her idol. It was Larry Harvey's first Hollywood party and he came straight from the set of *King Richard and the Crusades,* his first Hollywood movie. He wore a jump suit and his hair long. Remember this was long before the hippie era. Marion thought Larry had come as Christ. She asked me to introduce her. Larry, always the perfect gentleman, stood up.

Captain Horace Brown, Marion's husband, told him to sit down.

"General MacArthur doesn't outrank Christ," said Brown.

It was a great party but Zsa Zsa was feeling low. She had lost a husband and the word had just come out that day that her lover Rubirosa was going to marry Barbara Hutton, the Woolworth heiress and one of the few women alive who could afford Ruby.

Ruby, had he lived, would have been in that chapter in my last book with Milton Berle, Forrest Tucker, and O. K. Freddy.

But the party buoyed Zsa Zsa's spirits somewhat and the next day she was leaving for Phoenix to be in a Martin and Lewis movie called *Three Ring Circus.* By coincidence, I was cast in the same movie as a clown. I think Zsa Zsa played the daring young girl on the flying trapeze.

Hal Wallis had said he thought I was one hell of an actor but he was lying.

It was to be the last picture Dean and Jerry would ever make together and Wallis had some misgivings that the feuding comics wouldn't get through this one. Jack Keller, press agent for the pair, had suggested to Wallis that the two wouldn't split as long as a columnist was on the scene. Keller was my agent for the part—although I didn't know it.

The movie was finished but it was like working in a saloon fight. Not only were the comics at each other's throats but so were their wives.

My big scene in the movie was the famous little car stunt. About twenty clowns were piled like cordwood in an Austin with Dean as a driver. The temperature was over a hundred in Phoenix and we lay there suffocating.

Then Dean's weird sense of humor took over. He farted. In retrospect, it's funny but it was hell at the bottom of that little car.

One other memory of that movie. One of the clowns, now grown up, was the kid to whom Al Jolson sang "Sonny Boy" in his second talkie, *The Singing Fool.* The guy still had his mother on the set with him.

But back to Zsa Zsa. Her best friend in Phoenix was Mary Lou Hosford, a pretty blonde who is married to Cornelius Vanderbilt Whitney, known around Belmont Park as Sonny.

Everytime I see Mary Lou, I always ask her about Mr. Perkins. Sonny thinks I'm a little odd.

But Rubirosa did marry Barbara Hutton, who gave him a $250,000 plane with pilot and co-pilot as a wedding present. Ruby used it on his wedding night to fly from Palm Beach to Phoenix to see Zsa Zsa.

Mary Lou registered Ruby as Mr. Perkins at the same hotel where Zsa Zsa was staying. I think he signed in as Bill Perkins.

Barbara Hutton, minus the groom in her bed, sent two platoons of private detectives to Phoenix. It wasn't hard to guess where Ruby had vanished.

From then on, the whole thing became a Keystone Kops chase. Zsa Zsa and Mary Lou spirited Mr. Perkins to a private home in the mountains. Then Zsa Zsa, Mary Lou, and Arthur Wilde of Paramount led the detectives on a wild goose chase to all the Phoenix pubs and nightclubs.

Finally, at 2 A.M., the pubs closed and the cops gave up. Ruby meanwhile was back at the ranch getting drunker by the minute. He wanted to take a poke at Wilde, who after all had been only acting as a Good Samaritan in getting the cops off his tail.

He took a poke at Zsa Zsa but was so drunk he missed.

Ruby got so disgusted, he flew back to Palm Beach the next morning and told Barbara he had flown down to the Dominican Republic where he once was married to the dictator Trujillo's daughter.

Barbara believed him because the detectives reported back

that they couldn't find him in Phoenix. In fact, they couldn't even find the airplane, which had been landed at a hidden airstrip.

Zsa Zsa once told me that Ruby was insanely jealous. Once I greeted her and kissed her on the cheek as I always do.

She told me later that Ruby smacked her across the face as soon as they were in private.

"But there is something I will always love about Rubirosa," says Zsa Zsa.

Maybe I should have put him in that long-dong chapter post-humously.

Hollywood's Greatest Womanizer

People always ask me to name Hollywood's greatest cocksman. Naturally, they expect me to say Errol Flynn, Richard Burton, Warren Beatty, or someone like that.

I never do.

The greatest offstage lover in Hollywood history—and I believe my old friend Humphrey Bogart as my source—was Leslie Howard.

"Leslie fucked more women in this town than any one man—and he did it the hard way while staying married to the same wife and being blind as a bat," said Bogie.

I remember one night in Bogie's den when he was extolling Leslie's prowess with the broads. It was like a great football coach talking about an O. J. Simpson.

"You would introduce Leslie to a dame—she could be a movie star or a socialite—and within ten minutes, he was banging her in his dressing room or the back seat of his car. And I don't mean tramps—although he had plenty of them too. He did it with some of the biggest names in this town.

"He had that soulful look that women go wild about. One big star said fucking Leslie was like fucking a priest—something forbidden. It turned them all on. Some even thought he was a fag and they wanted to find out for sure.

Christ, he made Errol Flynn look like a fag."

I never knew Leslie. He was killed in World War II. Bogie said he always traveled with a phony secretary who was one of the legendary blow jobs in Hollywood.

"If Leslie's wife ever came on the set, this dame would pick up a notebook and look for all the world like a secretary. Leslie's wife never got wise," said Bogie.

"You know Leslie went down in a plane during the war. The Nazis thought Winston Churchill was on the plane. I often wonder if Leslie had his phony secretary with him on that last trip."

About the time Bogie was rhapsodizing about Howard, Richard Burton had just come on the scene and was knocking leading ladies off right and left.

"Christ," said Bogie, "Burton may have done all right with leading ladies but that fucking Howard was so damn nearsighted, he was knocking off every waitress in the commissary and half the cleaning women on the lot."

No wonder Scarlett O'Hara loved him more than Rhett Butler.

Land of the Midnight Sin

No country can top Sweden for beautiful women, and a lot of young Swedish girls come to Hollywood and take jobs as maids because that is the only way they can get into this country.

One gorgeous twenty-two-year-old whom we will call Ingrid came here and immediately got a job in the home of a famed automobile designer.

I'm not mentioning any names here because our divorce courts are already jammed.

The automobile designer entertained a lot and when Ingrid passed the soup and salad around, some of the biggest names in the country flipped for her.

Before long she was the Beverly Hills girl friend of one of

Detroit's biggest automobile names, a major league slugger, and two of the nation's top TV stars.

Her boss, faced with so many nocturnal demands on her time, hired another maid and installed a private telephone for Ingrid.

Needless to say, Ingrid, from the Land of the Midnight Sin, fucked as well as she looked.

That's how she became the first Beverly Hills maid ever to have her own maid.

I Shook Hands with Mandy Rice-Davies

When I met Mandy Rice-Davies over a drink at the Polo Lounge one night, that's all that happened. When we parted, I didn't even kiss her on the cheek. Just shook hands with her.

How many people do you know who have had a rendezvous with the girl who helped rock the British Empire with her sexual favors—and then parted shaking hands?

When I met her, Mandy was a different girl—a wife and mother—from what she had been in 1963 when she and her roommate Christine Keeler were the star performers in the Profumo sex scandal.

I remember talking with the late Louis (Doc) Shurr, Bob Hope's longtime agent, the day Mandy's name broke in the scandal that caused one suicide and forced the resignation of British War Minister John Profumo from the cabinet of Prime Minister Harold Macmillan.

"You know," said Doc, "I took that girl out four nights in a row the last time I was in London. I thought she was Grace Kelly. I never laid a glove on her."

When I first met Mandy some years later, I reminded her of that remark.

"Yes," she said, "if I had listened to Doc, none of that scandal would surround my name today. He wanted to take me to Hollywood and get me a movie contract. He kept calling me the Grace Kelly type. Unfortunately for Her Majesty's Government, I didn't take him up on the offer."

When I met her, she was twenty-five. She had only been eighteen when she rocked the Empire.

Doc told me he could have made her a star. And he, of all people, could have. It was Doc who first discovered Kim Novak and let her wear his mink coat.

Doc owned a couple of beautiful mink coats. Whenever he would discover a luscious new talent, he would give her the mink coat to wear to a party or premiere. The girls always had to return it after the ball was over. But Doc felt it was easier to sell a girl as a potential star if she looked like one. It paid off.

Mandy looked the part. There is nothing so sexy on screen as an exploding iceberg. Alfred Hitchcock once said that of Princess Grace.

Mandy, besides having that cool, blonde beauty, had acting experience. She told me of one play she had done where she played a sixteen-year-old virgin.

I commented that she had a good memory. She gave me a nasty look so I hastily added:

"For studying lines."

That's when I decided it was best to shake hands and leave.

Banana Split at MGM

The late Arthur Freed produced some of the most memorable musicals in Hollywood history—*Meet Me in St. Louis, Strike Up the Band, Easter Parade, On the Town, Annie Get Your Gun, Showboat,* and *An American in Paris,* to name just a fraction.

It's sad, then, that he should be best remembered in Hollywood history for a cocksucking incident. And the reason he is remembered is because he always told the story on himself. I heard him repeat it a dozen times.

As you all know, the casting couch has always been with us in Hollywood—and always will be. The biggest break for any young and beautiful contract actress on the MGM lot was to be in an Arthur Freed musical. And the girls all knew that the surest way to get in an Arthur Freed musical was via a superior blowjob.

Now there was one particularly beautiful young girl in those days who was later to become one of the most beautiful stars of the screen.

Cocksucking was a repugnant art to her but she knew it was either that or wind up in a low-budget western.

At the appropriate point in the audition, Arthur whipped out his cock behind his big desk in the Thalberg Building.

Our young actress screamed:

"Oh, I couldn't do that plain. Do you have any chocolate syrup? I just love chocolate syrup."

Arthur put in a hurry-up call to the commissary and soon a busboy showed up with a pint container of chocolate syrup.

"It took her a half hour to lick all that syrup," Arthur used to recall with a happy smile on his face. Then came the punch line: "I supplied the whipped cream and nuts."

Once I asked Arthur:

"What would you have done if she had said she wanted hot fudge?"

He Only Lost 1,500 Feet

One cannot write a book with fornication as a theme without mentioning the remarkable feat of Hollywood stunt flier Paul Mantz.

Mantz, until the day of his fatal crash on *The Flight of the Phoenix,* had performed some of the most remarkable flying stunts in movie history. The crash in which he lost his life was something he had done a thousand times before with his left hand.

Paul, as was his wont, had been drinking until 6 A.M. the day he was asked to dip his wing on the ground for the opening shot, which unfortunately for Paul took place at 8 A.M.

But his greatest feat came, he once told me, when he took a busty young starlet up on a flight on a movie location in a single engine plane with only one cockpit.

Holding the joystick in his left hand, he somehow managed to bang the starlet at about 15,000 feet in altitude.

"It was an adventure," he recalled, "because I had one eye on the instrument panel and one eye on this gorgeous girl.

"I only lost 1,500 feet altitude."

That's how the expression "mile-high club" originated. Only before and probably since Paul, it was always done with a stewardess on red-eye flights in the passenger compartment with someone else flying the plane.

How Do You Like It on Top of the Table, Anatole?

Everyone has heard the famous Hollywood story about director Anatole Litvak going down on a famous movie queen of the Golden Era under a table at Ciro's. But no one has ever heard the famous punch line to the whole incident delivered by Elsa Lanchester.

In case you haven't heard the Litvak story, it goes like this. Anatole and the movie queen, who is still very much alive and dangerous, got smashing drunk at Ciro's, the legendary Sunset Strip nightclub of those days. Herman Hover, the owner, was horrified at what the two called dancing. Had the music stopped, it would have been called fucking on the dance floor.

With that tact that nightclub owners possess, Herman maneuvered Anatole and the beauteous movie star to a table in the corner. Herman heaved a huge sigh of relief but not for long. With practically the whole nightclub audience watching, Anatole went under the table and started sneezing in her lettuce, if you know what I mean.

Years pass, and I am cast in a circus picture with Martin and Lewis along with Elsa, who played the bearded lady. Title of the picture, for you movie buffs, was *Three Ring Circus.*

Elsa and I decided to have lunch together in the Paramount commissary—she with her full beard and I with my clown getup.

We were carrying on an animated conversation about her husband, Charles Laughton, when Anatole walked by the table.

Without missing a beat in the conversation, Elsa stroked her beard and yelled:

"Hey, Anatole, how do you like it on *top* of the table?"

It's a classic ad-lib one-liner, and Elsa to this day is very proud of having said it.

Anatole turned, scowled at her, and yelled back: "Fuck you, Elsa," and stormed past.

A modern-day version in reverse of the same type of incident took place recently at Studio One, a gay nightclub in Hollywood.

A star of one of television's top-rated series—this time a girl—stopped dancing and suddenly got down on her knees and calmly sucked the cock of her dancing partner while about thirty people watched.

A girl I know who witnessed the whole episode said:

"When I saw her drop on her knees, I thought at first she had fainted but she hadn't. She obviously was high on something. I don't think it was booze."

The rest of the people kept on dancing around the two— dancing and watching.

There never has been any publicity about this because Studio One is such a weird place that it probably wasn't noticed.

But my informant was a nurse who had just come to town from Oklahoma. She noticed.

The Last of the Great Courtesans

Linda Christian in her prime was one of the great beauties of the world. She still is a knockout.

She also was a very talented actress. Take a look at her sometime in a movie called *The Happy Time,* in which she plays the sexy maid who seduces the young boy in a French-Canadian family.

But Linda's talent lay in other things. From the time she was discovered as a ravishing beauty of seventeen swimming near Errol Flynn's yacht in Mexican waters, Linda has been the lover of crowned heads and tycoons the world over.

I run into her all over the world. She is always with an oil-rich sheik or a French industrialist.

She was born two centuries too late. Had she lived in those days, she would have been Madame DuBarry.

When I first met her she was married to Tyrone Power, one of the most handsome and most gentlemanly of Hollywood stars. She had won Ty in a typical Linda Christian way. At the time, Lana Turner thought she was going to marry Ty but something funny happened on the way to the wedding. Ty married Linda instead.

Then Ty and Linda broke up. She kept the house on Copa de Ora Road in Bel-Air. I used to see her there often. Once she greeted me at the door wrapped only in a towel. She was unbelievably beautiful and sexy. I could only say one thing:

"Linda," I said, "I can give you an experience that you have never had before."

Her fabulous green eyes sparkled as she said: "What?"

"Fucking a poor Irishman," said I.

Linda laughed. She always had a great sense of humor, and let me in the house.

Linda knew everything sexual about everyone in the movie colony. At one time, one of the top actresses of the screen, married to a virile he-man star, was banging everybody in sight—from leading men to grips. I asked Linda why. She held her thumb and forefinger about two inches apart.

"She was only a child when she fell in love with him. The size of his penis meant nothing to her at that age. I think she was fifteen.

"Now that she has gone to bed with large men, she asks herself 'How long has this been going on?' "

Before too many more months the actress, one of the finest

the screen has ever produced, left the so-called he-man star for another. The star himself is now an old queen. What other way could he go with an infantile cock?

Linda said she would have reconciled with Ty, except for one thing. She mentioned a particularly beautiful, big-busted European actress whom most everyone in town had laid. It was common knowledge that Ty had had a long fling with her while he was married to Linda.

"I would have forgiven him even for that. Ty, after all, was a man.

"But once, on a lark, Howard Hughes took Ty and this woman up in his plane. (Howard was flying a Constellation in those days.) She and Ty had intercourse right on the floor of the airplane. And Howard took pictures of everything.

"When Ty and I fought, he showed me the pictures to humiliate me.

"I was furious, of course, but when I quieted down, I asked him to destroy the pictures. He refused. That's one of the main reasons we split. He absolutely refused to destroy those pictures. If he had, I would have forgiven him, I think."

Linda once had a big affair with Brazilian Billionaire Baby Pignatari, which turned into an international incident when Baby hired pickets and posted huge signs that read, "Linda, Go Home."

But one of the funniest involved Glenn Ford. Glenn promises to marry every girl he goes to bed with—even hookers. Sometimes it gets him into trouble.

Like one early morning with Linda. The proposal came at the moment of truth. As he said he wanted to marry her, Linda was dialing the home phone number of Harrison Carroll, then the columnist for the old *Herald-Express*. She got Harrison on the phone and said: "Harrison, Glenn has something he wants to tell you."

Linda handed the phone to Glenn. Remember now, it was at the exact moment of truth so Glenn repeated to Harrison that he wanted to marry Linda. The phone was hung up and the night was lived happily ever after.

Next morning the *Herald-Express* bannered on page one that Glenn Ford and Linda Christian were going to get married. The AP called me at home and asked that I get confirmation from Glenn.

This was about 6 A.M. I called Glenn at home.

A voice out of an alcoholic haze answered the phone. I read him the *Herald* story.

"My God, did I say that? It wasn't me talking. It was Jack Daniels."

Then came pleading: "Jim, you have got to get me off the hook on this one. I don't want to get married now. Linda is a great girl and it's nothing personal. I just don't want to get married. Help me."

All men are beasts so I got him off the hook as graciously as one can in such a circumstance. He's been grateful ever since. In fact, when my first book, *Hollywood is a Four Letter Town*, came out, Glenn read it and commented: "You should have put that story about Linda and me in there."

Well, here it is now, Glenn. Sorry, Linda.

He Should Be in a Jar at Harvard

Every time I go on a talk show, I am invariably asked about Warren Beatty's sex life. I have a stock answer:

"He should be in a jar at the Harvard Medical School."

When an Irish friend of mine, Malachy McCourt, decided to make that pilgrimage to all the pubs in Ireland in one month, he only made about 1200 of the 15,000 pubs. Warren, who doesn't drink, is batting much better with the beautiful women he meets.

He is remarkable. Besides that, he is reasonably young, a millionaire, a movie star, and (most important) a bachelor. What is even more amazing, he seems to run up the numbers while ostensibly anchored to a permanent base like Julie Christie or Michelle Phillips.

Once he carried on a torrid romance with Natalie Wood, with whom he co-starred in his first movie, *Splendor in the Grass*. He took her dining at Chasen's one night and as he entered the famous restaurant, he spotted a particularly beautiful hat-check girl who happens to be a friend of mine.

In the course of the dinner with the beautiful Natalie, he excused himself for a moment and struck up a conversation with the hat-check girl. In a matter of minutes, he completely charmed the hat-check girl into quitting her job on the spot, and she and Warren took off for three days.

Poor Natalie, stuck with the check, will know now what happened to Warren that night.

What more can you say—without envy—to a guy like that?

PART III: THE TYCOONS

From movie bosses to feared heads of the Soviet Union, plus a President of the United States or two—and even Las Vegas's highest roller. How would you like to walk out of a casino with $1 million in a paper sack?

Hollywood First in Space?

One of the worst propaganda defeats ever suffered by the United States happened on October 4, 1957, when the Russians and their Sputnik were first into space. Not until the Americans landed on the moon was that Russian propaganda victory erased by the U. S.

But we could have been first into space, financed by Hollywood—and it would have been a victory for free enterprise. And a savings to the taxpayers of $5 million.

Here's an amazing story that producer-director Andrew Stone told me the day Sputnik zoomed into outer space. It was confirmed by the Caltech Jet Propulsion Laboratory and by Lt. Gen. James M. Gavin, retired U. S. Army chief of research and development.

'Back in April, 1957," Stone said, "MGM asked me to do a movie called *Guided Missile,* all about our space program. We got secret clearance, which allowed us to do research on missile programs at Redstone Arsenal and White Sands.

"The more we got into it, the more we got interested in a space satellite. Inevitably, our research took us to Dr. William H. Pickering, head of Caltech's Jet Propulsion Lab, the nation's top expert on rocketry."

Stone said he found Dr. Pickering very depressed because the Russians were going to beat us into space. And it was all so unnecessary.

"Dr. Pickering told me that the United States could be in space in ninety days—probably in July—but that rivalry among the various services was preventing it. All that was needed was a carrier, but the Navy, Army, and Air Force, through jealousy, were bickering and the program was hopelessly mired in the Pentagon. (This was in the days before the space program was centralized in NASA.)

"I asked Dr. Pickering again how soon we could be in space if the go-ahead were given. He said ninety days at most, maybe within two months if all went well and speedy. He knew that the Russians were close and that it would be a tremendous loss in world prestige if they beat us up there.

"Being a publicity-minded producer, I next asked him what it would cost to launch a satellite. Dr. Pickering said the job could be done for $5 million.

"I proposed—almost as a comic thought at first—that MGM finance it. I knew they would go for the publicity value alone. I saw it as a third-act curtain to the movie."

Pickering took the producer seriously and, in fact, became enthusiastic. The scientist urged Stone to take it up with the Pentagon brass.

MGM okayed the extra $5 million budget immediately.

"We could even have done it for $1 million, provided we could use the Jupiter C, a vehicle which was then being tested," said Stone.

Pickering confirmed that with free use of the Jupiter C, the launching could have been staged for $1 million or less. That was peanuts by government standards of spending—and even peanuts for MGM.

"Pickering told me that perhaps the Russians had a better satellite at the moment but the important thing was to get up there first."

Stone, known for the documentary realism of his films, next tackled Washington, which is like a rookie linebacker going after O. J. Simpson.

"I began one of the most frustrating experiences of my life in Washington at the Pentagon and the White House. I had the money but there was no way you could go ahead without government approval.

"I had meetings with generals, defense department executives, and third assistants in the White House that got nowhere. I got exasperated.

"Finally, I told one top executive in the Department of Defense to tell me either yes or no. I could take no more stalling. He said no.

"It was such a devastating experience that *Guided Missile* was not made and the Russians beat us into space. I took $1 million and sank the Ile de France for *The Last Voyage,*

another project I had in the works. I said to hell with the
U. S. space program."

I asked him why he didn't take his plan directly to President Eisenhower in the White House.

"We thought about it as we were driving to the airport but
my wife said—and she was right—"We couldn't have even gotten in to see him. Ike would have kissed us off as a couple of
screwballs from Hollywood."

Stone could have launched his rocket in July, beating the
Russians by three months.

"And I wasn't going to save it for release of the picture. I
wanted to beat the Russians as much as Dr. Pickering did."

Did *Laugh-In* Nix Hubert out of the White House?

In 1968, Richard Nixon made president by one of the closest
votes in history and it's interesting to conjecture how many
votes his appearance on *Rowan and Martin's Laugh-In* got
him.

I personally thought it humanized Nixon's then Jack Armstrong All-American-Boy image and probably won him thousands of borderline votes.

After the election, Lena Horne, a rabid Democrat, told Dan
Rowan: "Well, you guys elected him. I hope you're satisfied
with what you have done."

Dan reminded her that the same opportunity was handed to
Hubert H. Humphrey, then the Vice-President under LBJ.

HHH refused.

"As you recall," Dan told me, "Nixon did a one-second ca-
meo in which he said, 'Sock it to me.' Our plans called for
Humphrey to follow and say only 'Yes?'

"We were quite stunned when Humphrey's television man
turned us down because the whole thing seemed quiet innocuous.

"Later, after there had been much favorable comments on

Nixon's appearance, the Democratic TV man said he was still glad he refused.

"He said he didn't want me and Dick Martin throwing a pail of water on the Vice-President of the United States."

Dan was appalled at this.

"Did you think for one moment we would have done a thing like that to the Vice-President? Where did you hear such a thing?"

Turned out it was a casual remark someone had made because the water throwing was a regular routine with Judy Carne on the show.

Nixon made a solo appearance and it's significant that when he became President, Paul Keyes, producer of *Laugh-In*, became one of the White House inner circle of Nixon buddies.

Just think, maybe *Laugh-In* is responsible for Watergate.

Adolphe Menjou—He Thought the John Birch Society Much Too Far to the Left

Hollywood always has been a town marked by extremism in political thinking. You have John Wayne and Ronald Reagan on the right—and Jane Fonda on the left.

But there never was anyone like the late Adolphe Menjou. On screen, he was the supreme master of suave sophistication, a superb actor and one who enhanced any movie he was ever in. He was a master of comedy timing in the same league with Cary Grant.

And he could be just as adept at the heavy dramatics.

But, man, was he far to the right in his politics.

One day I got a call from him to join him for lunch in his dressing room at RKO, where he was making a movie for Howard Hughes. He told me to pick up a sandwich for myself on the way. Adolphe was not one of the big spenders.

I found him in his dressing room eating his lunch out of a lunch bucket—the same kind that construction workers use.

His butler had packed it for him that morning.

"I've got a story for you. Eisenhower's a communist."

"Adolphe," I said, "how can you call our President a communist?"

This was during Ike's first term in the White House and no one had ever accused him of being to the left. No one. Not even Duke Wayne.

"That son of a bitch appointed Paul Hoffman to the United Nations. If that isn't communism, what the hell is?"

I told Adolphe that I had known Hoffman since my days in South Bend, Indiana, and if there's one thing Paul Hoffman isn't, it's a communist.

Adolphe then went into a tirade about Hoffman. He almost got into a rage.

I kept my cool and calmly explained that when I knew Hoffman, he was chairman of the board of the Studebaker corporation and was the biggest capitalist I had ever known. I described the house he lived in, the number of servants, and so forth. Still Adolphe was not impressed.

"Well, goddammit, do you want this exclusive or not?"

I told him no and started walking out.

"I'll tell you something else. I sent in my resignation to the John Birch Society. They're a bunch of pinkos."

I'm sure that Adolphe is the only rightist who ever thought the John Birchers were too far to the left. They probably were, for him.

But I did write a story about Adolphe that got wide play.

I happened to be driving by the Hollywood unemployment office one day as Adolphe drove up in his chauffered Rolls-Royce and stood in line with all the other unemployed actors to collect his $70.

That kind of socialism was okay in Adolphe's book.

The Henpecked Tyrant

When he was premier of the Soviet Union, Nikita Khrushchev

was the most feared man in the world. He made everybody tremble.

Except his wife. My experience with the Russian leader made that indelible impression on me.

It has never really come out in the open, but what inspired Nikita's famous blast at the United States as a land of gangsters was our refusal to let him visit Disneyland.

A bunch of us were whooping it up at the movie industry luncheon for the touring Khrushchev at 20th Century-Fox. I had a ringside seat at the same table with Mrs. Khrushchev, their son-in-law the editor of *Pravda*, David Niven, Frank Sinatra, Shirley MacLaine, and a few others.

One amusing incident. I introduced Lionel Crane, a friend of mine who worked for the London *Daily Mirror*, to the editor of *Pravda*, whose name I can neither spell nor remember.

The Pravda editor belligerently demanded of Crane: "How dare the London *Mirror* boast the largest circulation of any newspaper in the world when we have a million more than you?"

Crane very calmly replied: "But my good man, ours is voluntary."

Touché!

In the midst of Khrushchev's tirade at the United States during the luncheon, Mrs. Khrushchev, who spoke good English, mentioned to Sinatra and Niven how disappointed she was that the Russian party could not tour Disneyland because of security.

Sinatra and Niven were amazed.

"It's the safest place in the world," said Frank. "We'll take you there ourselves."

Mrs. Khrushchev immediately wrote a note, which was delivered by an aide to the Premier in the middle of his speech. He stopped, read the note, and then launched into his famous tirade about being barred from Disneyland.

The next day press agents from every amusement park in the country were called on the carpet and asked why they hadn't gotten their parks on page one banners across the world.

With Ingrid Bergman and Director Mark Robson on location in North Wales for *Inn of the Sixth Happiness.*

You want laughs? Lunch at NBC Burbank with, left to right around the table: Steve Allen, Harry Ritz, Marty Allen, Bacon, Alan King, Milton Frome, Milton Berle. Jack Carter is hidden, which makes this picture a collector's item.

Greg Peck as MacArthur with Vice-Admiral Bacon on deck of U.S.S. Missouri for reenactment of the surrender of Japan.

One of the most remarkable photos ever taken, at what was supposed to be Sophia Loren's first Hollywood party. Even she was impressed at Jayne Mansfield's decolletage.

Playing a Georgia redneck with Leslie Uggams and Dub Taylor on location in rural Georgia for *Poor Pretty Eddie.*

Redd Foxx and I on Diego Garcia, a flyspeck in the Indian Ocean halfway between Mozambique and Pert, Australia. We were there entertaining the Seabees on Christmas Day, 1972—Bob Hope's last Christmas show.

Bob Hope and I in Vietnam in 1971.

A whole history of the movies. That's Jackie Coogan, the Kid, with Duke Wayne in the center. I just got through asking Coogan whatever happened to that guy with the baggy pants and cane he used to work with. Jackie was working with Duke down in Durango, Mexico.

Jim Bishop presenting me with the Al Freeman award in Las Vegas. Or is it the other way around? That's Jim Brann of the Union Plaza Hotel on the left.

(Above) With Lee Tracy in his later years. He wasn't bitter that ten seconds spelled the end of a brilliant career in the movies. *(Below)* With Mike Curtiz, the debonair Hungarian director who gave us *Casablanca* and some sexy lunch hours with sexy extra girls.

(Above) Anna Kashfi, the most docile of women until Marlon Brando turned her into a wildcat. (Below) With Ara Parseghian, then coach of Notre Dame, and Bob Hope at Notre Dame field house in Notre Dame, Indiana. This was the time that Hope mentioned me on his TV special—and not the Gipper.

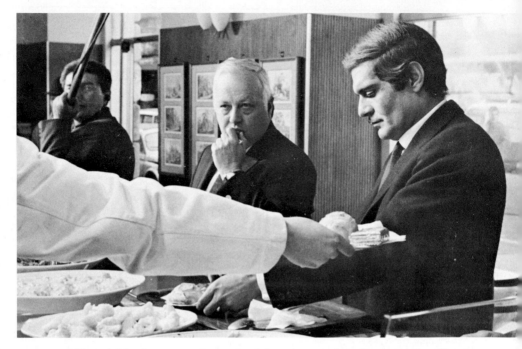

(Above) My famous role as lead tray in a cafeteria scene for *The Appointment,* starring Omar Sharif. The picture was about as good as the food. Sidney Lumet, a director noted for his hits, has me in a movie and gets his first flop. *(Below)* Bacon, who has portrayed four-star generals and admirals in movies, gets between two real ones—General of the Army Omar Bradley (left) and General Jimmy Doolittle (right).

(*Above*) Bacon counting the take for *Hollywood Is a Four Letter Town*. Or how it feels to handle a million bucks. (*Below*) A happy cowboy in *To Hell You Preach*.

(Above) Cantinflas and Bacon in *Pepe*. The beginning of a hilarious scene that was cut from the movie—else Latin America would have had a new Abbott and Costello. (Below) Living it up, from left to right, with Bacon, Doris Bacon, Michael Wayne, Gretchen Wayne, Big Duke, and Red and Alicia Buttons.

Lillian Roth and Susan Hayward tell Santa (me) what they want for Christmas. It was at the Christmas premiere of *I'll Cry Tomorrow*, the movie that won Susan an Oscar for playing Lillian's tragic fight with alcohol.

(Right) Old timer's night. Bacon with Eddie Cantor, legendary star. (Below) Walter Winchell and I in *College Confidential,* or was it *High School Confidential?* Walter and I matched each other scene for scene, word for word, and day for day. I got scale. He got $12,500. Got myself an agent after that.

(Above) Joe Don Baker and Robert Duvall knock off a Mafia bookie joint in *The Outfit.* Thanks to Duvall and his realistic acting, I gave an Oscar performance in this one. *(Below)* Charlton Heston and Bacon the ape in the original *Planet of the Apes.* This is when Heston asked me if I was working in the picture. I told him I had just escaped from the San Diego zoo.

Marty Allen and Bacon do a time step for the photogs.

Traveling on the Super Chief through New Mexico with Gloria Swanson, who had just made a movie called *Three for Bedroom C*. This was right after her smash performance in *Sunset Boulevard*.

(Above) Playing *bocce* with Tony Quinn and Sophia Loren. It's sort of bowling, Italian style. *(Below)* With Maurice Chevalier, one of the legendary names in show business.

(*Above*) Another legendary star, Mary Pickford. This was long before Mary shut herself in her bedroom at Pickfair. (*Below*) With Zsa Zsa Gabor at one of her weddings. Zsa Zsa gets married so often she only buys Minute Rice.

The next example of Mrs. Khrushchev's sphere of influence came after the luncheon when we all went to the soundstage where they were shooting the big musical *Can-Can,* starring Sinatra, Miss MacLaine, and leggy Juliet Prowse—her first movie.

Only one scene from the movie was shown the visiting Russians—the sexy and thrilling can-can dance number. I was sitting fifteen feet away from Khrushchev and his wife. No man enjoyed that dance more than he, especially when the gorgeous gams of Juliet Prowse went up in the air or when the beautiful dancers exposed their derrières. He was laughing, clapping like a big butter-and-egg man seeing his first Ziegfeld Follies.

Mrs. Khrushchev, in contrast, was infuriated by the sexy display. Her demeanor was dour. Her embarrassment was obvious.

Khrushchev and his party left smiling, except for Madame, who had been quite congenial and affable at the luncheon table.

The next day, after instructions from Mrs. Khrushchev, no doubt, the Soviet Premier blasted 20th Century-Fox for a tasteless show of immorality.

One other Khrushchev story I could not get on the AP wire (I was always considered too outrageous for such a conservative organization) was the Russian golf course story.

You all remember when an American company of *My Fair Lady* toured Russia in the fifties and scored a tremendous hit. Michael Evans, who played Henry Higgins for more performances than Rex Harrison, became extremely popular in the Soviet Union. When he came back to Hollywood, he told me an amazing story. One of the high officials in the Soviet cultural echelon had given him a peek at a beautiful eighteen-hole golf course built as.a complete surprise for President Eisenhower's visit—which never came off.

Remember how Gary Powers and that U-2 spying incident abruptly cancelled that summit meeting in Russia?

But Evans had been given a tour of the golf course, which Khrushchev had designed and built just for Ike's visit.

"There was only one thing missing," Evans said, "There was not a single golf club or ball in the Soviet Union and Ike surely would not have brought his to a country where golf was unheard of."

When Evans mentioned this to the Soviet official who gave him a preview of the course, it almost threw him into panic. No doubt clubs and balls and all the other golfing accessories were quickly ordered.

I submitted my story to the boss, who was afraid of it. Why I don't know. It certainly was innocuous as far as Soviet-American relations went.

The story was sent to our Washington and Moscow bureaus for checking. Neither one could confirm it. Of course they couldn't. The course was built as a surprise for Ike. And any correspondent in Moscow filed only what he was given to file in that censored news country.

The story went in the wastebasket. Five years later, a Russian correspondent for the Chicago *Daily News* got good play with the story of the unused golf course, later turned into a park, built for Ike and never seen or used by him.

P.S. I don't know whether there was any significance attached to the location, but the golf course was built on a beautiful lake resort—in Siberia.

The Giants: Griffith, DeMille, and Sennett

One of the advantages of being a survivor in Hollywood is that you can say you knew the men who made the town.

There were many, but the three biggest were D.W. Griffith, who was the first to give the movies a mirror on life; Cecil B. DeMille, who is responsible for making Hollywood the movie capital of the world instead of Flagstaff, Arizona; and Mack Sennett, the King of Comedy.

Of the three, I knew C.B. the best because he was working until the day he died.

Sadly, when I knew Griffith, he was gulping gin and chasing young girls, which at age seventy-three is somewhat commendable. He had not made a movie since 1931 when I first introduced myself to him, yet to this day no director has ever come up with something on the screen that Griffith hadn't done first.

As DeMille once put it so eloquently:

"Griffith was the first to photograph thought."

By coincidence, I met Griffith and Sennett on the same day—and on the same street, Hollywood Boulevard. Both were strolling down the street—at different times—unrecognized and forgotten by the town they put on the map.

I introduced myself to each of them in a burst of shameless hero-worship. Sennett and I stood on the street and talked for an hour. Griffith and I talked for a few minutes and then went into a bar where the great director made a pass at every girl in the place. It only increased my admiration for the man.

I saw him several times after that. Then one day he died. The year was 1948.

D. W. had made and spent 20 or 30 million of his own fortune since he made *Birth of a Nation* about the year I was born—1914. I think it was released in 1915.

He had little of it left but he felt no bitterness. He lived in the Hollywood Knickerbocker Hotel in the center of Hollywood. He had enough booze and broads, but I felt he would have loved a job better than anything. Men who had been his assistant directors and prop men were running the town now.

Hollywood hasn't changed much. Young directors today, who were never successful as mailroom clerks, are turning out garbage, half of which is not fit for release. Meanwhile the Polo Lounge is filled with the Wylers, the LeRoys, the Capras, and others who don't get scripts anymore. And these are the men who made the movies that they study and restudy in college cinema classes.

Figure that one.

I'm not saying there aren't some real talents among the young directors. There are. But when the name of one of the all-time greats comes up for a movie, some young punk in the front office kisses him off with one line:

"He's an old-fashioned director."

I've heard it a hundred times.

As far as I could judge, Griffith seemed happy enough. He knew what he had done and his attitude was "Fuck'em!"

The only trace of bitterness came when I mentioned that I thought *Citizen Kane* was vastly overrated as a movie. It was heresy in those days—and I knew it.

"Then how can you claim to be a fan of mine?" Griffith laughed. "Orson Welles stole most of it from me."

Which is true, of course.

I still think *Gone with the Wind* is the best movie Holly-wood ever made, although *Citizen Kane* usually rates the top of the polls. And when I made my comment to Griffith, I wasn't working for a Hearst newspaper as I am now.

Sennett lived in an old apartment house up the street from Grauman's Chinese. Last time I looked, the Garden Court apartment house was still standing. I used to see him walk past hundreds of tourists at Grauman's who were all looking at the footprints—and not one recognized the man who had made the world belly-laugh.

But the regulars on the street all knew him. Often he would stroll down Hollywood Boulevard and stop at a bus stop to talk with Percy Kilbride, the droll Pa Kettle. While stars less famous than Percy lived in luxurious mansions in Bel-Air, Percy's hangout was a bench on Hollywood Boulevard.

Mack, who gave Charlie Chaplin his first job, had the same explanation of how to make people laugh as did Chaplin.

"Kick dignity in the ass."

It can't be put any more succinctly than that.

Mack had a favorite joke. He told how he had walked past Grauman's the day after Pearl Harbor, Dec. 8, 1941. By coincidence, Jack Oakie walked by and yelled at Sid Grauman, who was standing in the forecourt.

"Hey, Sid, aren't you glad you didn't call it Grauman's Japanese?"

Said Mack: "That's what makes good comedy—timing."

Mack discovered most of the great comedy stars of the silents from Chaplin to Ben Turpin, but he made a few other important discoveries, too. Carole Lombard was once a Mack Sennett bathing beauty and Bing Crosby made his first appearance on film for Mack.

He was pushing eighty when I knew him but he was as sharp as they come. He said his biggest mistake was that he had Harold Lloyd first and fired him.

"I didn't think any guy who wore glasses was funny."

A few years later, Lloyd's income from comedy was $60,000 a week and not a cent for the IRS.

A few years ago, David Merrick produced *Mack and Mabel*, starring Robert Preston and Bernadette Peters. It was the love story of Mack and his greatest star, Mabel Normand. The love affair ended suddenly one night when Mabel caught Mack in bed with another actress.

Maybe if Merrick had put that scene in his musical, it would have made it on Broadway. I still think it was a good show.

You often hear how Hollywood became the movie capital because of three men—Jesse Lasky, Sam Goldwyn, and Cecil B. DeMille. It's true in a sense, but it was DeMille alone who founded Hollywood.

Goldwyn was a glove salesman, one of the best in the business. Lasky was a vaudeville trumpet player, and DeMille a successful stage director.

Around about 1913 or so, the three got together in New York and decided to get into the infant movie business, just coming out of its nickleodeon phase.

They had a well-known stage property called *The Squaw Man*, which they decided to film out west. Lasky and Goldwyn, the salesmen, stayed in New York and DeMille bought a ticket on the New York Central and Santa Fe to Flagstaff, Arizona, which seemed like a good place to make a feature western movie.

If you have ever been to Flagstaff, you know that when it

rains there, it rains like hell. It's high up in the northern Arizona mountain country. Well, when DeMille's train pulled into Flagstaff, it was a cloudburst. DeMille summoned the conductor and said:

"I'm riding to the end of the line."

The end of the line was Los Angeles. All he had to do to find western scenery was to travel to Hollywood, at the corner of what is now Selma and Vine. And that's where he set up shop.

DeMille, unfamiliar with moviemaking, used stage lighting to shoot *The Squaw Man.*

He sent the print back to Goldwyn in New York, who promptly wired back that the lighting was so dim that the exhibitors weren't buying the picture.

DeMille wired back to tell the exhibitors that the picture was shot in the revolutionary "Rembrandt lighting."

And that's how supersalesman Sam sold it. And it was a box-office smash, the first feature picture ever to carry "Made in Hollywood, California" on the titles.

DeMille was always surrounded by a huge entourage—even an assistant who put a chair under him whenever he felt like sitting down. DeMille never looked, but the chair was always there.

Each day for lunch, he and his entourage occupied the same table in the Paramount commissary. And every Monday for thirty years, Pauline Kessinger, who ran the commissary, served C. B. his customary bean soup. This went on for thirty or forty years.

I happened to be in the commissary when C. B. was making his last picture, *The Ten Commandments.* I found Pauline in panic. The cook who made the soup had gotten drunk the night before. It was Monday and no bean soup. Nothing to do but explain the situation to DeMille.

"Thank God," he said. "I always hated that goddamn soup anyhow."

When *The Ten Commandments* was first previewed at the Paramount studio theater, C. B. and his associate producer,

Henry Wilcoxon, were waiting at the foot of the stairs for my opinion.

"Too Jewish, C. B.," I said.

Whereupon C. B. went into a long discourse about Moses and how, after God himself, Moses had rescued the Jews from slavery. I don't think he appreciated the joke—or even knew it was one.

Wilcoxon had been an actor on the London stage when a Paramount executive tested him and sent the test back to De-Mille, who was looking for a Marc Antony to play opposite Claudette Colbert's Cleopatra.

DeMille and his entourage looked at the test. Never one to give his own opinion first, DeMille turned to his costume designer and asked: "What do you think?"

"My God," she said, "what a head for a helmet!"

Henry got the part and a few more big ones before he became DeMille's production associate.

Henry, after all those years working for C. B., got a little on the pompous side, too. Who wouldn't? So when he went back to Paramount's New York office to promote *The Ten Commandments,* some of the boys back there rigged up an elaborate practical joke on him. They told Henry that the way to get carte blanche for the film in New York was to meet with a certain rabbi, nun, and monsignor.

"If these three approve, you're in like Flynn," they told him.

So accordingly a meeting was arranged in Henry's suite at the Plaza with the holy three. Henry did a great selling job but before the trio could give their okay, they asked if they could go in another room and talk it over privately.

Fine. Henry sat there for a few minutes and out came the three stark naked. Immediately, they proceeded to stage an orgy right in front of the horrified Henry, who fled in terror.

All were hookers hired for the joke. It took some of the pomposity out of Henry.

I always got along fine with C. B. The trick was to treat him like any other god.

I always remembered that the Red Sea had been divided only three times, twice by DeMille.

L. B.'s Logic

Louis B. Mayer was a tyrant, probably the meanest of all Hollywood tycoons, but he often came up with some funny stuff.

Most classic of all is when Herman Mankiewicz took up flying back in the days when it was a perilous thing to do.

Herman, of course, was one of the best of the screenwriters and was in the middle of writing a major MGM epic when L. B. heard about the flying lessons.

Herman was immediately summoned to Mayer's office in the Iron Lung and called on the carpet.

"Herman," said L. B. "What the hell is this nonsense? You're our ace writer and you can get killed up there right in the middle of a picture. I insist that you stop this horseshit immediately."

Mankiewicz refused adamantly.

"You know, Herman, I can fire you and you would be out of a job."

Herman turned for the door and screamed at Mayer: "Not for long, you son of a bitch."

As Herman headed for the door, Mayer got up from his desk and grabbed Herman's arm. As he did so, the big tycoon dropped on one knee, a favorite Mayer pose when he wanted something.

"Herman," pleaded L. B. sobbingly, "Name me one great Jewish flier."

How I Saved Lew Wasserman's Job

The most powerful movie tycoon in Hollywood today is Lew

Wasserman, who runs Universal and a myriad of other MCA enterprises.

But back in March, 1969, he was about to be fired by Dr. Jules Stein, founder and biggest stockholder of MCA. High in his office in the charcoal-gray tower at Universal, Stein said at the time that Wasserman knew nothing about making movies and flatly announced that he was going to fire the man who had spent some forty years building MCA into the number-one entertainment complex in the world.

All Stein had to do was vote his shares at a meeting of the MCA board on March 31, 1969. But I got wind of what he was going to do and wrote a column on the Friday before the board meeting.

Ironically, Lew was to be fired the very day that he returned to his desk after a two week's absence for illness. That and Christmas Eve have always been traditional times for firings in the movie industry.

In my column, I wrote that it was Wasserman's guiding genius of MCA in its talent agency days that boosted Stein from a mere band booker to a multimillionaire tycoon of the entertainment industry.

"But," the column continued, "gratitude is an unknown commodity in the business and entertainment world. You're only as good as your last financial statement, which for MCA was somewhat disappointing."

I cited such box-office disasters as *A Countess from Hong Kong,* with Sophia Loren and Marlon Brando and directed by Charlie Chaplin; *Boom,* starring the Burtons; *Secret Ceremony,* starring Elizabeth Taylor, Robert Mitchum, and Mia Farrow; and the biggest disaster of all, *Loves of Isadora,* with Vanessa Redgrave.

The board meeting coincided with the opening of the Universal Sheraton hotel on the Universal lot and I also wrote:

"Doris Stein (Jules' wife) is much too social to let her husband spoil her parties with nasty business details like firing the guy who built the company."

Doris had invited royal and society guests from all over the world for a gala week at the hotel opening.

The board meeting was held on Monday as scheduled and a few executives who had hoped to get Wasserman's job were disappointed: Jules, instead of firing Wasserman, handed him a new long-term contract.

Since then Lew has had a few pretty successful movies, like the *Airport* series, *The Sting*, and *Jaws*, the most successful picture in the history of the movies. Last I heard it had grossed around $150 million and still counting.

Universal is busier today than any studio ever was, including MGM during the Golden Era. It employs around seven to eight thousand people at all times. It has more hours on national TV than any other studio or independent production company in the business.

And Jules Stein, for not firing Wasserman, is probably $20 or $30 million richer than he was in 1969.

Jules, whom I first met in 1935, never speaks to me anymore, but Lew does.

As late as 1976, *New West* magazine came out with a definitive and exhaustive article on the MCA colossus.

In it, the writer quoted one of the top people in MCA as saying that Wasserman would have been fired if it hadn't been for my column.

Happy to do it, Lew, because you have always been one of my favorite people in town. Lew and I go back to the days when he was Mario Lanza's agent—and that's a book in itself.

As an agent and as a movie and TV tycoon, Lew has always remained a gentleman. And you can't say that about too many tycoons in Hollywood history.

I first met Jules at the Congress Hotel in Chicago the year I was chairman of music for the Notre Dame junior prom.

In those days the college kids had discovered Benny Goodman when he started broadcasting on CBS radio from the Palomar Ballroom in Los Angeles. Now he was playing in his native Chicago so I was sent up to see him.

I had a nice chat with Benny, who loved the idea. His band

had yet to play their first college date and he was thrilled that Notre Dame would be the first.

"Can you wait a few minutes? I'll call my booker to come over and talk with you."

Well, the booker was Jules Stein, who was born in South Bend, Indiana; but he apparently was no Notre Dame fan.

He wanted $3,500 for the Goodman band plus $750 to buy a replacement band for the Congress Hotel for the night of the junior prom. And this in the height of the Depression.

Goodman was disappointed, but not nearly as much as I. It has never been a surprise to me that Jules wound up with $100 million or more.

As I recall, we got Bernie Cummins and his band, very popular then in the midwest; for $750 for the prom.

Jules screwed me once so I was happy to screw him thirty-four years later; but he wound up $20 or $30 million richer because of my screwing.

The New Boy in the Commissary

Mel Brooks makes the funniest comedies on the screen today because he is slightly crazy, but fortunately it is kind of a controlled lunacy.

I first knew Mel when he came out here as a writer on *Pal Joey,* starring Frank Sinatra, Kim Novak, and Rita Hayworth.

Columbia Pictures was the Dachau of the movie studios, but during this picture some levity went on because Sinatra's contract stipulated that shooting didn't begin until noon and ended at 8 P.M.—first time that ever happened in Hollywood in my memory.

Studio working hours usually are from 6 A.M. until 6 P.M. at any studio, and especially one run by Harry Cohn.

But Sinatra was as tough as Cohn and got his way.

Into this situation came Mel, who was immediately taken to an office and watched as his name plate was slid into the slot, pushing out the name plate of a previous occupant, also a famous writer.

"This disturbed me," says Mel. "So during the lunch hour, I took all the name plates off the third-floor offices and reversed them with those on the first floor. Then I mixed up all the names on the second floor."

This was Mel's first day on the lot. I believe it was his first day working in Hollywood ever.

"After lunch, there were 200 executives screaming all over the lot. 'My contract gives me two weeks' notice. Harry Cohn can't do this to me.'"

No one ever knew that Mel had done this. If Cohn had known, Mel would have been blacklisted in every studio in town.

But a lot of horseplay went on in that picture. One night I came on the set to talk with the late Barbara Nichols, a sexily delicious girl in those days. Sinatra came up and offered the use of his trailer dressing room with its well-stocked bar—mostly Jack Daniels. Barbara was a fun-loving girl who liked a drink—as did I.

After an hour or two or three in the dressing room, we emerged and we were completely lost. Sinatra, as a gag, had had a truck tow the trailer a good eight blocks from the studio and park it on a side street.

Barbara and I had a hell of a time finding our way back to the studio. The Jack Daniels didn't help any either.

Those were the only times I ever remember levity on the Columbia lot.

Brooks, finished with *Pal Joey,* next went to work at Paramount for Jerry Lewis. This was in Jerry's zany days when he was making $4 million a year and was the biggest box-office star on the lot. Anything went on a Jerry Lewis set.

But crazy as Jerry was, Mel was even crazier.

One day Mel almost did his name plate changing routine again, but the first name plate he stopped in front of was Y. Frank Freeman, head of the studio. The name plate intrigued him but he thought perhaps it would be more discreet to make a speech instead.

While a bunch of us listened, including Bill Holden, Mel shouted:

"Y. Frank Freeman? I'll tell you Y. Frank Freeman."

Then he went into a long tirade about Freeman's love for the Confederacy, even in 1957.

Freeman was an unreconstructed rebel out of Georgia who had made his money on Coca-Cola and then gone into the picture business. He was the ultimate professional southerner.

Brooks wound up his speech by singing "Marching Through Georgia," the anti-rebel song that glorifies Sherman's devastating march to the sea in which he practically burned down the state of Georgia.

All of a sudden, Freeman's window opened and Y. Frank yelled at Mel:

"Come here, boy," he said. It almost sounded like he said, "Come here, nigger," so redneck was his tone of voice.

"Who are you, boy?" asked Freeman.

"I'm the new boy in the commissary," said Mel. "I just delivered a tuna sandwich on whole wheat."

Y. Frank didn't kick his ass out of there, because Mel had long gone.

You can bet that Freeman called the commissary and told Pauline Kessinger to fire that new kid who had just delivered a tuna sandwich on whole wheat to the executive offices.

Freeman, because of his pomposity, was a favorite target on the lot for the comics. One day Y. Frank was escorting some V.I.P.'s around the lot and impressing them with his importance. He made the mistake of stopping in front of Jerry Lewis's dressing room.

Just as Y. Frank was going to introduce Jerry, the comedian yelled angrily at him:

"Goddamn it, Frank. I thought I told you you're through. Wash up and get your check. I told you, 'The next time I find those toilet bowls dirty, you've had it.'"

Then Jerry stormed into the dressing room while Frank tried to explain that he really wasn't the janitor but the head of the studio and Jerry was only kidding.

Brooks says his happiest writing job—until he started making his own fabulously successful pictures—was with Sid Caesar's *Show of Shows.*

"I loved that show because no matter how crazy I was or how crazy I wrote, it always got on the air the way I wrote it."

That means a lot to a writer, who knows a lot more about humor than the vice-presidents who censor him.

His tries at big-studio writing were frustrating.

"I would write a script on yellow paper and it would come back on green paper with someone else's words."

That explains why Mel made his first movie, *The Producers,* almost single-handedly. He wrote the script, directed it, and composed the theme song, "Springtime for Hitler." He let someone else produce it because Mel doesn't like to fool around with money.

I thought *The Producers* the best picture of the year and plugged single-handedly for its nomination and also an Oscar nomination for best song. Neither made it but Mel won the Oscar for best screenplay.

His household—he's married to Anne Bancroft—is one of the few his-and-hers Oscar homes in the business.

"But neither of us has ours at home. Anne's is on the top of her mother's television set so she can show it to all her Italian old lady friends. Mine's in the same place in mother's apartment so she shows it every day to all the old Jews in the neighborhood."

Mel made *The Producers* for a modest $941,000. It's not kosher to make a successful movie for around $1 million. I once asked a famous producer why.

"Because," he said with dead seriousness, "you can't steal $1 million from a $1-million picture."

I consider that a profound answer.

But that modest movie, a classic in the Marx Brothers tradition, started the Mel Brooks dynasty in Hollywood—*The 12 Chairs, Blazing Saddles, Young Frankenstein,* and *Silent Movie.*

All have been blockbusters. They have all been so successful that even grips who have worked on a Mel Brooks movie are sought by other producers and paid double. Everybody wants success to rub off in Hollywood.

My favorite Mel Brooks story is one he once told me.

"When I was writing *The Show of Shows* for Sid Caesar, we hired a new kid who was known only as Danny Simon's kid brother, Neil.

"He was a nice Jewish kid, a little shy, a little conservative, so on the first day I invited him to lunch. Strictly on impulse, I took a real gun from the prop department. No real bullets but a real gun. We walked through Shubert's alley chatting amiably on our way to Sardi's. Suddenly I pulled the gun on Neil and yelled like a real mugger: 'Your money or your life.'

"Neil didn't know whether I was kidding or not, so I jammed the gun right into his ribs. Oh, did that hurt. So he gave me all his money. I put the gun away and we resumed chatting amiably. Then we had lunch, which didn't cost me a cent although I picked up the tab. Neil never has been quite sure about me."

That little story points up the main theme of all Brooks's works—greed. It's a subject matter that all other producers take very seriously. Remember Erich von Stroheim's twelve-hour silent masterpiece called *Greed?* Irving Thalberg cut about ten hours out of it and it' wasn't so greedy.

But Mel, with that weird sense of humor, gets laughs out of greed. *The Producers* is a case in point. Zero Mostel and Gene Wilder conspire to make the worst flop in the history of the Broadway theater, a Sigmund Romberg-type musical called *Springtime for Hitler.* They sell twenty-five percent shares to dotty old ladies, dozens of them. Object, of course, is for the show to flop so they can keep all the front money. You don't have to return it when the show flops.

Punch line is that the show is so horrendous that the flop turns into a hilarious hit. The greedy producers are devasted.

Mel fought to call the movie *Springtime for Hitler* but Joe Levine, who distributed it, had the final answer.

"Hitler doesn't sell tickets—not even in Germany."

What Are You Doing Down There?

One of my all-time favorites in the movies was the late Michael Curtiz, the Hungarian director who made one of the two best movies ever made—*Casablanca*. The other is *Gone with the Wind*.

I always suspected that most of the so-called Goldwynisms were the result of Sam Goldwyn's press agents following Mike Curtiz around. David Niven used one of Mike's malapropisms for the title of his best-selling book *Bring on the Empty Horses*.

I once did a story with Mike when he was making *The Helen Morgan Story*. At the time, I mentioned that Mike would even settle for an untested singer, if need be, to play the part of the tragic star of the original Ziegfeld *Show Boat*.

As I was working for AP and its 8,000 newspapers around the world, I wasn't too astonished when Mike and I got letters from all over the world—thousands of them. But Mike was overwhelmed. From that day on, whenever Mike tested someone for the role, he called me in for consultation.

Just about this time, *Confidential* magazine came out with a particularly lurid story about how Mike had hired a black couple to make love while he watched in a downtown hotel room. The cops had raided the room but Mike, with a little help from Warners, got off and there was no publicity—except *Confidential*, which undoubtedly was tipped off by someone who saw the police record.

The magazine had barely hit the streets when Mike called me.

"Jeem, can you come with me to the Mocambo tonight? There's a great Irish singer there. Maybe she is our Helen Morgan."

I quickly talked him out of that one. The "Irish" singer at the Mocambo was Ella Fitzgerald.

"Thank God you told me, Jeem," said Mike. "If I hired a black girl, people might get the wrong idea from that goddamn magazine."

Mike was the hardest-working director I have ever known.

He was on the set at 6 A.M., never ate lunch, and was the last to leave at night. Sometimes he would take an aspirin for lunch but mostly he liked to have his cock sucked. Everybody on his crew knew about this latter no-cal diversion.

There was one particularly sexy and voluptuous extra who always had a job on Mike's pictures. She did most of her work during the lunch hour. Usually Mike did this in his office or dressing room, but during one picture—in which, oddly enough, Ronald Reagan was one of the stars—Mike took the girl over to a used interior set on a far corner of the sound-stage.

Now movie sets have no ceilings on them but they do have gangways above them where the grips and electricians work. The crew immediately knew what was going to happen, so the gangways were quickly filled with crew members looking down on Mike sitting on a chair with the sexy extra sucking his cock.

Everything went fine. Mike was enjoying himself and the crew was having a ball plus some envy. Then Mike came, and in ecstasy he pushed his head back and looked skywards. He spotted his crew looking down.

Mike started smacking the girl on the head and screaming:

"What are you doing down there? Get out and let me work."

Biggest High Roller in Las Vegas

There may be bigger gamblers who hit Las Vegas but I doubt if anyone can top Danny Schwartz, Frank Sinatra's friend.

Danny is a fellow who made his first millions building sub-divisions. Since then he has owned a racing stable and a few other profitable investments.

First time I ever met Danny was at a Milton Berle opening at Caesar's Palace. It was after the midnight show and we were all going to have dinner in the Bacchanal Room of the Las Vegas hotel.

Everybody was there except Danny.

His wife, Natalie, was wearing a white faille dress that had real diamonds for buttons. She also had diamond earrings, a diamond necklace, and diamonds on her fingers. She looked like Zsa Zsa Gabor's bank vault. But she was right in style. *Vogue* had just decreed that diamond buttons on dresses were the in thing that season.

Someone said that Danny would be delayed. He was $260,000 in the hole playing blackjack. I noticed that Natalie didn't appear the least bit concerned at the news. I would have cut my throat if it had been me owing that much.

Well, Natalie could have sold that dress and been richer than most of the matrons in Beverly Hills.

Danny plays baccarat with an $8,000 limit per hand. I call him the baccarat king.

But don't feel sorry for Danny. He often wins.

Danny is the only gambler I know who ever walked away from the tables in Las Vegas with $1 million in winnings.

He put the money in brown paper sacks and buddy Sinatra helped him carry it out of the casino.

"That was the night that I gave the biggest tip in the history of Las Vegas," said Danny. "Thirty-six thousand dollars to the dealers. Do you realize how many sons of gamblers I have put through college?"

The Token Democrat

I come from a family that is so democratic that they voted for Thomas Jefferson and Andrew Jackson and voted against Abraham Lincoln. My father, born an Episcopalian, was the only Protestant in Jersey Shore, Pennsylvania, who voted for the Catholic Democrat Al Smith in 1928. My first vote was for Franklin Delano Roosevelt and I was confident that Harry S. Truman would defeat Tom Dewey in 1948, even made money on it. I even voted for McGovern in 1972.

So what the hell was I doing at the inauguration of Richard Nixon in January, 1973?

I had come from an old-fashioned Democratic family, fiercely patriotic but staunchly anti-republican. My Irish Catholic mother never forgot to her dying day that the Republicans regarded the Democrats as the party of "rum, Romanism, and rebellion."

As a child I had fidgeted at Chautauqua through William Jennings Bryan's fiery speechmaking.

In short, I wouldn't vote for a Republican running for sewer commissioner.

But here I was on a chartered 747 at Los Angeles International Airport with a rabid group of Southern California Republicans, including a couple of Nixon's brothers and a whole flock of Pat Nixon's family.

I soon found out that Republicans drink as much as Democrats.

It was a jolly group even before the big jet took off for Washington. The reason for that was that no one had paid for the flight and American Airlines was not about to take off unless they saw the money on the table.

Michael Viner, a record tycoon, came to the rescue. He put the flight on his air-travel credit card—$47,000 worth. And we took off. Viner, an old friend, was, I soon found out, a big man in the second inauguration. He was the producer of all the entertainment galas. He had a Washington background as the son of one of the capital's top public-relations people, Jeanne Viner Bell.

I was impressed with anyone who would pick up a $47,000 tab for politicians, who are notoriously poor pay regardless of party.

On the trip I got very friendly with Donald Nixon, who used to be known as the black sheep of the family.

"I lose money whenever Dick gets elected," he confessed to me as we flew over the Rockies. "Hell, if he hadn't made it, I'd be a millionaire—but when your brother's President of the United States you have to turn down a lot of deals."

Don, an affable guy and full of fun, was a top executive with the Marriott Corporation, in charge of supplying airlines all over the world with food and drink. At one point on the trip, he opened a briefcase that must have held a hundred small bottles of liquor, the size they serve on flights.

"Don't worry about running out of booze," he said. "I got enough to get us across the country."

I had first met Don years before when he ran a drive-in restaurant in Whittier, the Nixons' home town.

That was where the controversial Howard Hughes loans to Don first embarrassed the then Vice-President.

When the Nixons' father was dying at the family home during the Eisenhower administration, I was assigned with other reporters for the death watch at the Nixon home, especially when the Vice-President came out from Washington to visit his ailing father.

Don, who didn't have to do it, fed all the reporters on the house at his restaurant. It was a kind thing to do and I told him so on the flight.

But that still doesn't explain what I, a Democrat, was doing on this flight.

It's all very logical. Bob Hope invited me along, as he had on a hundred other trips. Hope and Frank Sinatra—also a registered Democrat but somewhat fallen away since the Kennedy days—were the big stars of the entertainment galas.

Viner had a major problem on his hands with the shows. Some of the stage managers, all from the Washington area, were overwhelmed by the big names involved. They got so panicky that I even saw one of them cry during a performance.

Fortunately, Viner got hold of Harry Blackstone, Jr., the son of the famous magician and himself a famous magician, and made him stage manager.

Blackstone had just come along for the ride because his son was a member of the Mike Curb Congregation, a rock singing group. But Blackstone knew his way around backstage and was a godsend to Viner.

Even so, there were a few problems.

Pat Henry, Sinatra's favorite comedian, came with Frank,

and Frank wanted him on the show. He never made it because the Secret Service hadn't cleared him. And that was that.

Frank took it all philosophically.

Hope was onstage doing his monologue—his pride and joy—when all of a sudden, the scrim dropped behind him suddenly and Les Brown whispered: "Wind it up, Bob, they want Vikki Carr on right away."

Bob did as he was told but he came off that stage furious. No one had ever cut short a Bob Hope monologue—and he was the President's favorite entertainer and close friend.

In all the years I have known Bob, I had never seen him lose his cool, but he was mad for the first time. He jumped Les, who had been a Hope employee for thirty-five years, and Viner.

After everything calmed down, it turned out that the Secret Service, who know nothing about show business, had ordered Hope's monologue cut short. The President was en route and they gave some lame excuse.

Finally the Presidential party arrived at the gala and Hope was back doing other things in the show. He sang one number that required a momentary bit from a stooge dragging a chaise longue across the stage. Hope decided I should have my moment of glory and asked me to be the stooge, which is like asking Bob Mitchum if he wants a drink.

As I came onstage, Les Brown's band to a man stood up and gave me a standing ovation. We are old friends from the Vietnam tours and dozens of others. Once you become friends with a musician, you are friends. They are a loyal group.

It caused a flurry in the hall, a hell of a lot more than I realized at the time.

The President, I'm sure, recognized me after all the years I had spent covering him in Southern California, from Congress to the Senate, through the "Checkers" speech, the Vice-Presidency, and the Presidency.

But Pat Nixon turned to Dolores Hope, sitting in the presidential box, and said: "Who is that getting such a standing ovation from the band?"

"Why, that's Jim Bacon. I thought everybody knew Jim Bacon."

The Secret Service didn't. Like Pat Henry, I had not been cleared. They were in panic. Soon the walkie-talkies were going like mad and a couple of agents were about to seize me onstage.

Fortunately, my walk-on was so brief that I was offstage before they could muster. Viner then explained to them that I was Hope's friend and that he had asked me to help in the act.

See how easy it is to get thrown into danger as a threat to national security? It was a close call.

The next night Hope and I came together for a Eugene Ormandy concert as part of the inauguration festivities. First person we ran into was Nelson Rockefeller, a friend of Hope's and a friend of mine from the days when I traveled with him in his unsuccessful bid for the Presidency.

Television cameras soon descended on the three of us.

Next morning there were all of us on the *Today* show.

I'm still trying to live that down with my Democratic relatives.

My aunt, Frances Carey, called me from Erie, Pennsylvania.

"Your dear mother must be rolling in her grave and your wonderful Democratic father, too. What were you doing at Nixon's inauguration? Bet you don't go to mass, either."

But to show you how ecumenical politics can be: Michael Viner, the big man at the Nixon inauguration, got me invited to Jimmy Carter's inauguration.

Thanks, Michael. You saved my Democratic soul.

A Presidential Faux Pas

Gene Autry has a telegram from Richard Nixon, when he was President, that is a collector's item.

When Nixon had his winter White House in San Clemente,

he decided to drive over to Anaheim to see the California Angels play ball.

Autry, who owns the Angels and a couple dozen other enterprises, went all out in his hospitality for the presidential party.

The President returned to Washington and soon Gene got a telegram from Nixon thanking him. It ended like this:

"Please give my regards to your wife Dale."

Don't Pee on My Parade

I got to know Lee Tracy very well in his latter days. He hadn't had a drink in years, and he didn't seem too bitter about the ten seconds that ruined his career.

But for those ten seconds, the name Lee Tracy would have gone down in movie history with the Gables, the Coopers, and the other Tracy.

Lee was the original Hildy Johnson in the Broadway hit *The Front Page.*

A superb actor, known for his mile-a-minute style of talking, Lee embarked on a meteoric Hollywood career. In the early days of the talkies, he was one of the biggest stars.

Ironically, he never played Hildy Johnson in the movie version of *The Front Page.* Pat O'Brien did.

But Lee drank and raised hell. He was one wild Irishman. But he was so good, the town put up with his escapades.

Then he went down to Mexico with Howard Hawks to make *Viva Villa* with Wallie Beery playing Pancho Villa. Tracy had the plum role of Floyd Gibbons, the noted war correspondent who always wore a patch over his eye and also talked a mile a minute.

"When MGM gave me Lee to play Gibbons, I was a little more than upset," Hawks recalls today.

"I told Louis B. Mayer: 'If you can't control him in Hollywood, how in the hell do you expect me to down in Mexico?'"

But that was the Golden Era, when the front office dictated casting, even to the director.

Hawks appreciated Lee's talent, but he was so afraid of his drinking that he brought him down to the location days before he needed him.

"Lee wanted to stay in Mexico City but I told him that he drank too much. 'Here I can keep an eye on you. And if you ever come on the set drunk or even with a hangover, I'll bust you in the face.'"

And in those days, the tall, sinewy Hawks could have done it with ease.

"Lee looked at me and said: 'I promise you that will never be necessary.'"

And it wasn't. Hawks said Lee never took a drink until after the picture was finished.

Then he went up to Mexico City and tied on a beaut.

"I told him with the performance he had given, he deserved to go on a binge. I even supplied him with a guard so he couldn't get into any trouble. He slept it off in his hotel room, and when he woke up, he was confused like all drunks are. He mistook the balcony for the bathroom.

"He didn't know the Chapultepec cadets were marching down below in the street in an Independence Day parade. It was all a mistake and Lee was just as shocked as the cadets he peed on.

"The Mexican government took it as a deliberate insult, which it was not. All hell broke loose—in Washington and Hollywood. It became an international uproar.

"Mayer wanted me to say that Lee was intractable so he could fire him from the picture—even though the picture was already finished.

"I refused. Lee, outside of this one unfortunate incident, had behaved beautifully. I was so furious at Mayer that I grabbed him by the throat and backed him against the wall of his office and said: 'You son of a bitch, I'll never work for you again.'"

And for forty-three years, the famous director hasn't worked at MGM.

Mayer scrapped every bit of Tracy's footage from the film and reshot it with another director and another actor—Stu Irwin.

Mayer, then the most powerful man in Hollywood, blacklisted Tracy forever in the movies. He never got work until Mayer was deposed at MGM. He spent his later years doing TV and movie roles in relative obscurity.

He never talked about peeing on the parade except to say it was one huge mistake. Just as Hawks did.

Peeing in the wrong place is one of the hazards of drinking.

A Journalism Lesson

Before I became a Hollywood columnist I was legitimate. In fact, I am the only columnist now writing out of Hollywood who once was a bona fide reporter. That may be what is holding me back. One was president of the Eddie Fisher fan club. Another got her training as a housewife, and so on.

But that's not what this chapter is about.

It's about all the letters I got from journalism students because of *Hollywood Is a Four Letter Town*. In case you don't realize it, journalism is the hot major in colleges today.

As jobs get fewer, journalism students increase. Chalk it up to Robert Redford in *All the President's Men*. He's done more for the craft than Richard Harding Davis.

Even some journalism professors wrote me. One who was writing a textbook wanted to know what I considered the two prime assets of a good reporter. I told him a black suit, preferably English mohair, and a white badge marked "Official." I'm not in the book.

Back in 1953 the Crown Prince of Japan made an official visit to the United States, first member of the Imperial Family to do so since the surrender of Japan after World War II. I was assigned to his Hollywood visit by the Associated Press. The biggest newspapers of the world are in Japan and the whole AP bank account in the Orient rested on my shoulders. I was so told.

Japan was just starting to get on its economic feet after the paternalistic occupation of General Douglas MacArthur. And those eight-million-circulation newspapers in Tokyo were ripe for AP picking—and this was the story that could do it.

On the day of the Crown Prince's visit, I came into the office wearing a black suit. I had to cover a Hollywood funeral first. Our office was in a panic. The boss had just learned that UP, our rival for the Japanese buck, had assigned a reporter who could speak fluent Japanese. All I could say was *"sayonara."*

I didn't like the odds, but what the hell. Things weren't helped any when I heard the UP guy speaking rapid Japanese with the Prince's advance guard.

Security herded all the media—except me—behind a barricade as the Prince's limousine approached. I chalked my exclusion up to the black suit and the grey temples. No one was allowed to approach the Crown Prince.

I didn't have to. When he got out of the car, he approached me. He bowed. I bowed back.

"Thank you so very much for allowing me to visit your studio," the Prince said in perfect English.

We bowed again and I said: "It is truly our honor, Your Imperial Highness." We bowed again. Then I took the Prince by the arm and led him into the soundstage.

The movie being shot was *Executive Suite*, starring Bill Holden, Fredric March, Barbara Stanwyck, and June Allyson. Holden damn near died laughing when he saw me arm in arm with the Prince. Even the stars had been ordered not to approach the Prince unless he approached them.

The Prince and I chatted about movies. He said his favorite star was John Wayne, which was surprising since Big Duke had single-handedly brought about the downfall of Japan at Iwo Jima.

All the time I was chatting with the Prince I could see the UP reporter fifty feet away and behind a rope—cussing me in Japanese and English.

Needless to say, my story got all the play in Japan and the AP made a fortune in selling its service to the Japanese press. Me? I didn't even get a hearty handshake.

But it was the black suit that made it all possible. The Prince thought I owned the studio. The studio people thought I was with the State Department and the Secret Service didn't know who the hell I was but I looked as if I belonged so they didn't do anything.

My first experience with the black suit came in 1952 when Richard Nixon flew back to Los Angeles to make his famous "Checkers" speech and explain how he only bought Pat a Republican cloth coat out of a slush fund.

Guards at the airport were not admitting any press to the plane area—on orders of the Republican National Committee. Nixon was saving all for the telecast.

I retreated and reached in my pocket for a cigar. My hand fell on a white ribbon marked "Official" that had come along with some ticket for some long-forgotten exhibit or show. I pinned it on my lapel, walked through the same guards to Nixon's plane, and chatted with him. Everybody thought I was part of the welcoming committee for the Vice-Presidential candidate.

It enabled the AP to get on the wire with some of the same stuff that Nixon was to reveal hours later on the famous TV speech.

Another place I always wore the black suit was at Cedars of Lebanon Hospital. The Iron Curtain is nothing compared with hospital public relations.

A group of us were gathered in a hospital anteroom waiting for hours while on the fifth floor lay Marilyn Monroe with a mysterious illness. She had entered the hospital after a weekend party where she danced with Clark Gable, who was then unmarried. Was a romance between the King and the Queen of Hollywood in the works?

To heighten the suspense, a huge basket of flowers—red roses—addressed "To Marilyn with love" and signed "Clark" was delivered to the reception desk. Now there were some who said those flowers came from Harry Brand, director of publicity at Marilyn's studio—20th Century-Fox.

Beware of such people for they are troublemakers.

If I could talk to Marilyn, I had the biggest story of the day. It was 1954 and things were quiet in Korea with the war. But the black suit and the official badge wouldn't work with the elderly dame in charge of public relations. She treated reporters and photographers like pupils in her third-grade class.

Then an inspiration walked in—in the person of Tom Towers of the *Examiner* with his arm in a cast, probably from playing tennis. I grabbed Tom and hustled him out of the place. It was morning and Tom's deadline for a morning paper was hours away. The *Examiner* was an AP member to boot.

I explained to Tom what was happening and how he could get—with me—an exclusive interview with Marilyn. One thing he must remember—keep his mouth shut at all times.

Soon the two of us were on a back elevator, used by nurses and interns, on our way to the fifth floor. I handed an intern five bucks and said I wanted to borrow his stethoscope for a few minutes and would leave it with the supervising nurse on the fifth floor. Interns are notoriously underpaid so he complied enthusiastically.

I in my black suit and Tom in his cast got off at the fifth floor and marched down the corridor unmolested. At the nurses' desk, I stopped and said:

"Which is Miss Monroe's room? I'm Doctor Bacon. I was in on her case earlier and since I just happen to be in the hospital with another patient, thought I'd drop in on her and say hello.

It worked beautifully. The supervising nurse herself escorted us to Marilyn's room.

I was Dr. Bacon but Towers was all ham.

"Dr. Bacon," he told the nurse as we walked along, "has just returned from Mozambique, where he single-handedly conquered the tsetse-fly epidemic."

It broke me up—and the nurse too. Our little game was up. "You reporters are terrible," she said.

If I'm ever asked to help write a journalism textbook again, I'm going to add: "Avoid collaborators who overact."

The $240,000 Moving Bill

Rich movie stars aren't the only denizens of Beverly Hills, often called the Golden Ghetto.

Even the multimillionaire movie tycoons were impressed by one Dino Fabra of Milan, Italy, who lived but a short time in Beverly Hills.

A forty-room mansion of Sunset Boulevard lay vacant for some years. I had once been to a party in the house in its gayer days. What impressed me most was that it had a huge ballroom on the top floor in case the owner wanted to toss a New Year's Eve party or a wedding reception.

It saddened me to see it lying empty.

Then one day Dino walked into realtor Mike Silverman's office and asked the price. As Beverly Hills homes go, it was a bargain—$750,000.

"This little guy with the Italian accent never winced, he wrote out a check for the full amount and said 'I'll take it,' " Mike recalls.

Then for a full year a small army of workmen completely refurbished the place. À beautiful new wrought-iron fence surrounded the acreage. Everyone thought the place had to be owned by a rock star or a member of the Mafia. Who else could spend that much?

Especially when Dino brought in paintings and other objects d'art in two chartered 747s at a total cost of $240,000 from Milan and Rome. That and the $1.25 million he spent redoing the place became the talk of the town.

Then sadly, one day even before Dino moved in for good, a "For Sale" sign went up on the front yard.

The price asked—$2.5 million.

Dino had toyed with the idea of doing work in Beverly Hills—like making pictures—but his burgeoning investments in Africa kept him occupied.

Mike says that Dino is an international financier who has made most of his millions in publishing with Milan his base. He doesn't like to stay in hotels so he has homes in Milan, St. Tropez, and Acapulco, all just as lavish.

No one that I know of in Beverly Hills, except Silverman, ever saw him.

Too bad. Anyone who uses chartered 747s instead of a Bekins van to transfer his furniture would have made quite a social stir in Beverly Hills.

PART IV: THOSE LOVABLE COMICS

From the vaudevillian who wound up in the state funny farm wrestling himself, to why W. C. Fields hated Christmas, it's a wacky look at the world of comedy.

Get Me Out of Here! I'm the Guy Who Wrestles Himself

People tend to forget that Cary Grant, the screen's supreme master of urbanity and sophistication, once was a stilt-walker in vaudeville. And, of course, we all know that Milton Berle was spawned in vaudeville.

Well, when these two get together and talk of the old vaudeville days, it's a night to remember.

One night Cary and I went backstage at Caesar's Palace to visit Milton after his closing show at the Las Vegas hotel. The two swapped vaudeville stories that should be incorporated into a book.

The most hilarious came when Cary asked Milton what ever happened to Detzo Ritter, the man who wrestled with himself. All three had shared a bill at Proctor's Newark in the twenties. Milton told a true story about Detzo that had vaudevillian Archie Leach and I rolling on the floor.

"Detzo," Milton recalled with that fabulous memory of his, "got on a train one day at Grand Central Station in New York. There was an empty coach and he sat in it all alone.

"At the next stop, a keeper got on the train with a dozen mental patients. All were on their way to the state funny farm at Mattewan, New York."

It should be explained that Detzo had a fantastic act. He was a contortionist who came onstage, gave himself a couple of airplane spins, a toehold, and a half nelson, and finally pinned himself to the mat for a fantastic finish.

"Detzo rode on the train for several hours with the mental patients. No other passengers were in the coach," Milton went on.

"The train stopped at Mattewan and the keeper gently tapped all his patients to get off, including Detzo. Detzo, who was a German, flew into a rage and started acting like a crazy man. The keeper summoned a couple of strong-arm orderlies who threw a net over him and removed him from the train.

"The last anyone ever saw of Detzo, he was taken from that train shouting: 'I'm Detzo Ritter, the man who wrestles with himself.' "

Can't you imagine that guy in a padded cell at the Mattewan state hospital telling a guy who thinks he's Napoleon that he is Detzo Ritter, the man who wrestles with himself?

That same night, we were all joined by B. S. Pully, the Big Julie of the original *Guys and Dolls*. B. S. is a guy who, if he hadn't been born, Damon Runyon would have invented him.

As Pully came in, Milton whispered to me: "That son of a bitch owes me $200, I'm going to get it from him right now."

Before Milton could open his mouth, B. S. says:

"Milton, I just got through talking with your boy, Billy. That kid is going to be a genius."

Billy was about six at the time. Milton promptly forgot about the $200.

B. S. then produced a check that he had unsuccessfully tried to cash at the Las Vegas horse book.

"Can you imagine," said B. S., "the guy asks me, 'B. S., will this check go the distance?'"

Since B. S. had called Billy Berle a genius, Milton couldn't cash the check fast enough. It was for $100.

The check—and this is a true story—was drawn on the Main Street Blood Bank.

Not long after that, B. S. died. Milton never got his money and couldn't have cared less. B. S. Pully had called his son a genius.

Milton, for all his brash onstage image, is the softest touch in the business. His lawyer finally had to take away all his money.

I've been with him a hundred times when some broken-down acrobat or juggler would approach him and remind him of the time they were on the bill together at Shea's Buffalo or Loew's State. Milton would always pull out a C-note and say: "Take your wife out to dinner tonight."

Jack Oakie tells of the time he and Milton played a split week in Shamokin, Pennsylvania.

"We were stranded there and so hungry and broke that we considered jumping off a bridge into the Susquehanna River. We never did it because we argued over who was going first.

"No vaudevillian ever wants to be an opening act."

No comedian can wear a dress like Milton Berle—not even Flip Wilson. It's not a transvestite thing like it is with one famous Hollywood name. Milton does it strictly for laughs.

But it didn't start that way.

Back in the days when he starred in the Ziegfeld Follies on Broadway, he fell for a luscious showgirl whose mother had let her try Broadway on one condition—that she stay at the Barbizon Plaza Hotel for women. The Barbizon is a famous hotel in New York that does not permit men above the lobby floor.

"I was living at home with my mother and family so I couldn't take her there. Somehow, a motel or hotel rendezvous seemed a little sordid in those days.

"So I had the Follies makeup people and wardrobe people outfit me in a dress, with high heels and lipstick.

"The show over at night, I walked through the Barbizon Plaza Hotel each night with my showgirl—and walked out the next morning.

"My mother was happy. Her mother was happy. And we were happy.

"And I improved my act."

In my last book, *Hollywood Is a Four Letter Town,* I made national folk heroes out of Milton and Forrest Tucker, both of whom are endowed with enormous cocks. Unfortunately for both, it came about twenty years too late.

As soon as the book appeared, I got calls from friends of Harry Ritz of the famous Ritz Brothers. All said I had hurt Harry's feelings. He should have been included.

Which brings up the story of how Milton spent a night in a whorehouse at age sixteen in Pittsburgh.

Milton, a kid vaudeville star, traveled with his mother and his brothers on the road. On a night off in Pittsburgh, Milton wanted to go out on the town with brothers Frank, Phil, and Jack.

Mama said no.

"Milton, don't go out with your brothers. They drink beer.

Why don't you go out with Harry Ritz? He's such a nice boy and he doesn't drink beer."

So Milton called up Harry, who was appearing with his brothers at another theater in Pittsburgh.

Harry didn't take Milton to a beer parlor. He took him to a whorehouse.

"It was much better than beer," recalls Milton.

Milton, who is Jewish, is the most irreverent Jew I know. Once his family moved to the suburbs out of New York City. I recall it was Tarrytown. Anyway, their home was next to the estate of John D. Rockefeller, Sr.

John D., Sr., was famous for his strolls, during which he passed out shiny new dimes to everyone he met. He did it to Milton one day and Milton, ever the comic, told the billionaire:

"Mr. Rockefeller, as rich as you are, our family can boast of something you don't have."

Rockefeller was impressed by the youth's remark and asked the obvious question—"What?"

"We don't have Jews living next to us," said Milton.

Getting back to Milton's long cock. When my book appeared, Milton beamed when he first saw me.

"After sixty-five years in the business, it took you to make me a star."

Milton is the fastest comic on his feet of anyone I know. One night at a party, Milton, Sammy Davis, and I all stood urinal by urinal in a men's room.

"If Truman Capote were here, he'd be singing 'Stranger in Paradise,'" said Milton.

Then Sammy, who is well hung himself, got his first good look at Milton's monstrosity. This was in the days when Sammy was having a torrid affair with Kim Novak. Sammy, effusive as always, went into absolute rhapsody at the size of Milton's cock.

Said Milton:

"If Kim Novak ever gets a look at this, you'll be back fucking Hattie McDaniel."

He Didn't Mention The Gipper

Bob Hope is a real friend. I travel with him all over the world—Vietnam, Thailand, Singapore—and Wilkes-Barre, Pennsylvania. You name it—I've been there with Hope.

To show you what a nice guy Hope is, here's what he once did for my ego. A few years back, he did a TV special from Notre Dame University, my alma mater. Naturally, he took me back with him. It was my first visit there in twenty years.

Some of my old pals still on campus and faculty members were quite impressed that I would return with a superstar.

That would have been enough, but Hope did even more. What Hope did on his opening monologue for that top-rated special thrilled me like nothing before in my life.

He began like this:

"What a thrill it is for me to be here on these hallowed grounds where once walked Knute Rockne, Frank Leahy (and then an emphatic pause)—and Jim Bacon."

When that show aired, you can't imagine the phone calls I got from all over the country—some from classmates I hadn't heard from in forty years.

Without exception, they all made the same comment:

"Bob Hope mentioned your name and he didn't even mention the Gipper."

Thanks for the memory, Bob.

He's Out Walking His Rat

I take part of the credit for launching Don Rickles. My God, what have I done?

I was invited to the Slate Brothers' nightclub one night for a Lenny Bruce opening.

Lenny, despite what his cultists and the Dustin Hoffman movie said, was dirty and sick. He had no redeeming social values. In fact, this opening he pulled a line that I won't even use in this book. And God knows I've used every four-letter, and some eight-letter, words so far.

The line was so bad and so sick that Henry Slate jumped on the stage and fired him right in the middle of his act. Now, if you know Henry Slate, you know what Lenny said was offensive because Henry Slate can make George Burns blush.

I had never seen this happen before or since.

With nothing left but a band, Henry came up to me and asked:

"Who in the hell am I going to get in here for the next two weeks?"

I had a brilliant idea.

"I saw a young comic up at the Zomba on Hollywood Boulevard the other night. He's closing tonight. He would be great. His name is Don Rickles."

Henry said:

"You're the second guy tonight who has told me about this guy. Sam Wall (the Slates' press agent) told me the same thing you just did."

That settled it. Rickles, a complete unknown, was booked into the Slates for the next night.

Rickles had come west hoping to make it in the movies. He had studied at the American Academy of Dramatic Arts with Grace Kelly as a fellow student. A natural comedian, he turned to nightclubs when the acting jobs got scarce. After all, Don is no Tyrone Power.

Don opened and was very funny. There were few celebrities in the audience but he worked over some of us whom he knew. He was a hit, but nothing like the hit he was to become a week later.

I was out on the town that night with Frank Sinatra and Lauren Bacall, whom Frank was squiring since the death of Humphrey Bogart. I talked Frank and Betty into going over to the Slates to catch this new comic.

Well, when you come into a nightclub like the Slates with Sinatra, you don't sit ringside. Henry Slate put a table for us on the stage.

Rickles, the Merchant of Venom, is working me over and some of the other people in the room. He never touched Frank or Betty.

Frank was enjoying him. Finally, as Rickles wound up his act, he turned to Frank and said: "Remember the good old days, Frank, when you had a voice?"

Every eye in the place turned on Frank to watch his reaction. When Sinatra is around, no one laughs unless he laughs.

A slight pause and then Frank laughed uproariously. The whole room, as if on cue, laughed too.

Rickles was made.

After that night, he became a special protégé of Frank's. He played the Slates for months, years.

Frank brought in big parties to catch Rickles. Before long, Don was in the lounge at the Sahara in Las Vegas.

One night Frank brought in Dean Martin and a group that looked like a Sons of Italy meeting. Rickles took one look and said:

"Dean, what do we need Italians for? I'll tell you. They keep the flies off our fish."

And to Frank:

"Make yourself at home, Frank. Hit somebody."

And when Frank came in with Tony Quinn and Ricardo Montalban, Rickles said:

"Tony, we need Mexicans. Jews like to eat lettuce."

Soon it got to be the big thing in Los Angeles or Las Vegas to be insulted by Don Rickles.

People often wonder why no one has ever taken a poke at Rickles. There's a good reason. Rickles offstage is the kindest and gentlest man alive. A devoted family man, there is no more religious Jew in show business. The congregation at his synagogue is always amazed to see this acerbic wit deep in prayer every Sabbath.

A musician at the Riviera in Vegas, where Rickles now has a $1-million contract in the big room, once told me that of all the performers to play there, Don is the ultimate gentleman.

"When the curtain goes down, he never fails to turn around

and say to the band, 'Thank you, gentlemen.'

"It may not seem like much, but when you don't hear it from anyone else, it means a lot."

Ernie Kovacs, Genius of Comedy

One of my favorite comedians was the late Ernie Kovacs, whose imaginative work has been an inspiration for many comics through the years.

Ernie really knew how to live. Like Mike Todd, he was often broke but never poor. Ernie never made the big money of a Bob Hope, but he came closer to living like a king than anyone in town.

For instance, Ernie's Havana cigars were made of vintage tobacco. Most cigar smokers would be satisfied just to have that "Made in Havana" label on the box. Not Ernie.

He once made a trip to Cuba, pre-Castro, and contracted for a certain leaf, grown on a certain side of the hill and in vintage years, to be made into his cigars.

Back in the fifties, Ernie was paying $3 a cigar. A lot of money then. George Burns once told him that before he would pay $3 for a cigar, he would want to fuck it first.

When Ernie and Edie Adams moved into their house off Coldwater Canyon in Beverly Hills, first thing Ernie built was a wine cellar. To make it look authentic, he had special effects people from ABC-TV come over and make artificial cobwebs. It was like going into Dracula's wine cellar.

Ernie and I shared a love of good wines and cigars. About once or twice a month, he used to order a case of a moselle we both loved called Bernkasteler Doktor. It was considered among wine connoisseurs as the best of the moselles.

How many wonderful afternoons Ernie and I spent drinking that wonderful wine and smoking those vintage Cuban cigars. In those days, it cost $18 a bottle.

When Ernie was killed in that traffic accident, his widow

sent me what remained of the Bernkasteler Doktor.

"I know Ernie would want it to go to you," said Edie.

Unfortunately, Ernie and I used to knock off a case or two a month so there were only twelve bottles left when he died. But I have always appreciated Edie's gesture, nevertheless.

Ernie and I were great friends but he never could understand why I lived in the San Fernando Valley.

"You're Beverly Hills and Bel-Air. It's written all over you," he would say.

Once he told Sammy Davis at a party at the Kovacs house one night:

"Sammy, you've got one eye, you're black, and you're Jewish. The only thing you've got going for you is that you don't live in the Valley."

There's quite a bit of snobbishness on the Beverly Hills side of the Santa Monica Mountains.

I was at the Bistro in Beverly Hills one night when all of us were discussing *Fortune* magazine's list of the fifty wealthiest men in the nation. Only one from show business made it— Bob Hope. A Bel-Air millionaire who couldn't even carry Hope's deposit slips observed patronizingly:

"Why, he lives in the Valley. How could he be that rich?"

But back to Ernie Kovacs.

"I'm Hungarian. That's why I love to live. My poor mother, when she took care of me by sewing dresses, she would never think of having anything for my dessert but chocolate mousse. We always lived beyond our means."

And when Ernie made it in the movies and television, he really lived beyond his means. It took Edie years to pay off the cigar companies and wine merchants after his death. But she never regretted it.

Too bad Ernie had to go so young in life. He had style.

He came to town from New York and Philadelphia with a reputation of being one of television's most inventive comics—a writer, producer, star, and director of the shows that became television classics.

Before long his $100,000 home had $600,000 in it. Besides

the artificial cobwebs in the wine cellar he installed a waterfall too. And in his narrow driveway, it cost him a fortune to put in a turntable like a railroad roundhouse. You would drive your car onto the revolving driveway and soon you were headed back down the hill—else you would have been backing and turning for fifteen minutes to get out of there.

Long before Mel Brooks' *Silent Movie*, Ernie did a silent TV show with not one word of dialogue. It was a classic.

His gourmet taste in food was revered by headwaiters at Romanoff's, Chasen's, and LaRue's. he knew wine like the winemaster at Chateau Lafite-Rothschild. His taste was so exquisite that he searched for the finest cook in town and hired her away from a fancy restaurant at a salary that only corporate executives were getting.

"She is so great that I never dine out anymore. I'm afraid I'll miss what she's having for supper."

Like all people with such taste in living, he was one of the town's better-known gamblers. I once went to a poker party at his house that began Sunday afternoon and was still going strong at 3 o'clock Monday afternoon. Wife Edie interrupted and said he had an urgent phone call from his agent.

"Why the hell is that bastard calling at this time of night?" stormed Ernie as he left to answer the phone.

Once a gambling friend called him from New York and Ernie asked if he had a deck of cards handy. The voice 3,000 miles away replied yes.

"Okay," said Ernie, "cut them. I say red for $500."

There was silence, then profanity on the other end of the line. He next gave his caller a bet that the next card turned up would be a spade, also for $500. A couple of days later, there was a check for $1,000 in Ernie's mail.

Ernie was just about ready to hit real big in the movies when his skidding station wagon hit a telephone pole in 1962 coming home from a party at Billy Wilder's house. It was raining and the car just skidded. Wilder said Ernie had had little to drink since he had come late from a TV show to the party.

His movie price was up to $200,000 a picture, very good for a comic and character actor.

And he got there the hard way—by telling Harry Cohn to go fuck himself.

All the actors in Hollywood who ever told the tyrannical boss of Columbia Pictures even to go to hell and survived could be counted on the thumb of one hand.

It happened during Ernie's first movie—*Operation Madball.* I was on the set the night they were shooting a party sequence. Director Richard Quine, in order to make it authentic, had the GIs drinking real champagne.

The scene called for lots of drunken soldiers chasing pretty French girls with that most ulterior of motives. The scene was shot all night at Columbia studios. No one ever expected Harry Cohn to show up but he did, around 4 A.M.

Ernie didn't know who in the hell Cohn was so when the boss walked up to him and said, "I hear you have been having a ball chasing all these pretty starlets around the set all night," Ernie looked down at Cohn and said: "Go fuck yourself," and walked away.

I told Ernie who in the hell he had said that to. It didn't bother him.

"I figured it was none of the guy's business."

Later, Ernie told me that remark endeared him to Harry and they became friends.

"Don't ask me why," said Ernie.

The Great Exit Lines

Some stars are so colorful in life that they can't die without exit lines that make them dying as well as living legends.

Take the great Ed Wynn, of whom Jack Benny once said that "Ed Wynn in the Ziegfeld Follies was the funniest man who ever lived—and that includes W. C. Fields."

Death is a horrible subject, but without it—and Bonds for

Israel—George Jessel wouldn't have a stage to perform on. I have known George to deliver four eulogies a day, sometimes over people he despised. So it is not surprising that Ed Wynn awakened from his final coma, spotted son Keenan by his bedside, and beckoned him to bend down so his father could whisper his dying message.

"Not Jessel," Ed muttered, and then died happily.

Author Gene Fowler, intimate and biographer of John Barrymore, was at the great actor's side when he died.

Now I have read that Barrymore's dying words to Gene were:

"Aren't you the illegitimate son of Buffalo Bill?"

Pretty good, but not what Gene told me Barrymore said.

"It's true he said that to me when I first entered the room, but his last words were to a fat and homely nurse who came in and felt his pulse.

"Jack looked up with that famous one-eye look of his and said: 'You're not much, but jump in anyway.' "

And while on the subject of Barrymore, I heard David Niven once on the Mike Douglas show say he didn't believe the Errol Flynn-John Barrymore death story.

David, who used to be Flynn's pal and roommate, apparently had a terrific and unpublicized falling out with Flynn before he died because David has been bad-mouthing Flynn for some time.

That's beside the point because both David and Errol were and are the charmers supreme. Both were good friends of mine. David still is and whatever happened is strictly his own business.

But Errol told me the story in great detail—and it's not the kind of ghoulish story one invents.

When Barrymore died, all his pals held an Irish wake for him in the funeral home. Fowler, Flynn, Raoul Walsh, Dave Chasen, Tony Quinn, and others.

As Errol tells it:

"We all loved Jack. To him, I was always 'Navarre.' I don't know why, but he always called me that. And I loved it.

"We all got very drunk at the funeral home. I left first because I was meeting some sweet cooz on the way home. I felt to get drunk and fucked after Jack's wake was the best way I could pay my respects to this greatest of actors.

"But that son of a bitch Walsh bribed a young funeral attendant with $500 to lend him Barrymore's body for a few hours. He and some of his nefarious pals transported Jack's corpse from its coffin to my house. There they propped him into a chair in front of the fireplace and put a drink in his hand.

"Can you imagine the shock I felt after being at Jack's wake to come home and find that son of a bitch sitting there in my favorite chair with a drink in his hand?

"I aged thirty years on the spot, drunk as I was. It scared the living bejesus out of me but you know what I did? I just sat down in the chair next to him and had a drink with him.

"The funeral attendant then showed up and took Jack back to his coffin. And then Raoul, that prick, came in and had a big laugh. So did I. It was the crazy sort of thing that Jack would have appreciated. I told Raoul that he must have loved Barrymore as much as I, else he wouldn't have gone to all that trouble.

"And then we had more drinks."

The Stuttering Wit

The guy I miss most on Vine Street is Joe Frisco.

Joe was an old-time vaudevillian and nightclub performer who was one of the great wits of all time. For years, he was the most quoted man in show business.

Even when dying of cancer, he never lost that sense of humor. I remember once when The Masquers, a show-business club in Hollywood, threw him a testimonial when everybody knew he only had a few months to live. Everybody came to cheer Joe but he ended up hilariously cheering everybody else.

My favorite Frisco line came one day when I walked by him in front of the Hollywood Plaza Hotel.

"H-h-hey, kid," he yelled, "can you let me have a twenty until Amelia Earhart gets back from her trip?"

And then there was that time across the street in the Brown Derby when Joe was dining with George Seaton and Bill Perlberg. In the course of lunch, Billy Barty, one of the most famous little people in show business, walked up to the table. Billy's chin just reached the table top.

Frisco took one look and yelled at a waiter:

"Hey, who ordered John the Baptist?"

Look What Happened to Hildy Johnson

Sometimes I go on the wagon. Invariably I get in trouble because of it. Trouble I never get into drinking.

For instance. One night in Palm Springs I'm at the Bob Hope Desert Classic ball drinking plain soda. Hope comes by the table and asks me to come over to his house after the ball. Jackie Gleason, also on the wagon, will be there. Bill Fugazy, president of Diners Club, Howard Cosell, Evel and Linda Knievel, Jack Lemmon, and a few others were invited too.

All of them were drinking at the ball but Fugazy the least—or so it appeared. We all piled into Fugazy's car for the trip to the Hope desert home. There must have been about nine or ten of us in the car. Linda Knievel sat on my lap because Evel told me that he had so many broken bones he couldn't hold her. Fine.

I was in the back seat seemingly safe. Everybody was talking and making no sense. They never do when you are sober and they are not.

All of a sudden, Fugazy is driving somewhat erratically. Within seconds the flashing red lights of the police car are upon us.

I felt safe because I was not driving—until Evel spoke first:

"We're riding, officer, because we're too drunk to walk."

Next came Humble Howard:

"How dare you stop a car in which I am an occupant? Don't you know who I am? I, sir, am Howard Cosell. What is your badge number so I may have this matter adjudicated?"

By this time, poor Fugazy was out walking a straight line— and doing very well.

He was yelling to Cosell and Evel to shut up. Just when he quieted them, Lemmon woke up and yelled: "Fuck you, offisher!"

Fugazy just about died. And so did I. I knew I was going to land in jail with a bunch of drunks after not having one drink myself all night.

Just then an amazing thing happened. The cop was so struck by the bizarre behavior of Knievel, Cosell, and Lemmon that he just burst out laughing and handed Fugazy back his license and told him to drive carefully. Fortunately, we were only a few blocks from Hope's house, so we got there safely.

I told Gleason what happened.

"Incredible, pal. Incredible. It don't pay to go on the wagon."

Then as we both sipped Diet-Pepsis, I told Jackie the Hildy Johnson story.

When I started to work for the AP in Chicago right after service as a naval officer in World War II, there were still some of the real-life characters from *The Front Page* working in the Criminal Courts building in the Loop. Even Walter Howey, the real-life counterpart for Walter Burns, the managing editor in the classic play, was still functioning as M.E. of the evening Hearst paper. His was the only name changed by Ben Hecht and Charlie MacArthur in the play. No doubt for fear of reprisal and mayhem.

But back to the beat reporters of the play. I think it was Murphy of the *Times* who handed me a bottle of bourbon one day when we were working the Suzanne Degnan kidnapping case.

I told him I was on the wagon.

"Don't ever go on the wagon, kid. Look what happened to Hildy Johnson."

Hildy, of course, was the hero of *The Front Page*.

Ironically, it was Lemmon who played him in Billy Wilder's latest movie version of the great hit.

Hildy also was one of Chicago's legendary drinkers. When Hecht and MacArthur held the premiere of the play in Chicago, they reserved a special box for their old news buddy. At the final curtain, the lights went up and the spotlight played on Hildy's box. The audience, on its feet, wanted to see what Hildy's reaction was.

Ben Hecht told me that Hildy had passed out in the box, an empty bottle by his side.

"I don't know if Hildy has ever seen his own play," said Ben.

But back to Murphy of the *Times*.

"One day, Hildy decided he should go on the wagon. The first day he did, he was walking down Randolph Street and a truck jumped the curb, pinned him against a building, and killed him right on the spot.

"Hildy would be alive today if he hadn't gone on the wagon."

Murphy took a long swig on the bottle, wiped it off with his hand, and then handed it to me once more.

I took a swig. Hildy would have wanted it that way.

The World's Most Famous Hobo

For years, the best-selling author Sidney Sheldon and Groucho Marx were close friends and neighbors.

Then as Groucho got well into his eighties, he started making a daily habit of visiting Sidney's house each afternoon for a snack of an apple and piece of cheese.

"It became such a ritual that Jorja and I looked forward to it every day. Groucho would eat his snack and then walk back to his own house," Sidney recalls.

After the success of *The Other Side of Midnight* and *Stranger in the Mirror,* Sidney and his wife leased the house and moved to Rome, where he worked on a new novel.

One day in Rome, he got a letter from the new tenant, who wrote:

"We love the house but there is one strange thing. Every afternoon, there's a little old man, about 85 or 90, who knocks on our kitchen door and asks for some cheese and an apple.

"He's too well-dressed for a hobo. Can you tell us who it is?"

Johnny Carson: Another Hollywood Legend

Johnny Carson will never have me on the *Tonight* show discussing this, but it will forever remain one of the more memorable nights in Hollywood history.

The Friars Club threw a stag roast for Buddy Hackett one night in a fancy hotel. Johnny was the roastmaster and he started off brilliantly.

The dais was amply supplied with bottles of scotch, gin, vodka, and bourbon. When Carson wasn't at the podium making with the funny one-liners, he was sitting on the dais doing guzzler's gin with real bottles. As the long evening wore on and on, Carson got drunker and drunker. He was funnier than Foster Brooks ever was.

Finally came the climax of the evening: someone was presenting the plaque to Hackett and Buddy was standing at the podium. Seated next to him was Carson, who had never left the dais all night. As the somewhat serious speech was being made, Hackett kept looking down on Carson.

Suddenly, Hackett screamed:

"Johnny's pissing on my leg."

Sure enough, the smashed Carson had to take a piss and what better place to do it than Hackett's leg in the middle of his big night.

At this, the comics had a field day. Jack Carter brought over a champagne bucket. Carson filled it.

Next day I wrote a whole column about the incident, never once mentioning what Johnny actually did but calling him a Hollywood legend nevertheless.

First call came from Johnny.

"Funny column," he said.

He meant it, too, because I had written it in tongue-in-cheek style for what it was—a damn funny incident before a group of astonished but amused men. No one was offended except Hackett and he didn't really give a damn.

All the other columnists there—and some who weren't—reacted typically. They were horrified and raked Carson over the coals.

Such horseshit.

Why W. C. Fields Hated Christmas

Everybody knows that W. C. Fields hated kids and Christmas, but no one knows why.

All actors hate kid actors. That explains why Fields put the gin in Baby LeRoy's orange juice. John Barrymore once tossed the young Virginia Weidler across a room. Barrymore was delivering the most important speech in *The Great Man Votes,* and he was delivering it as only one of the greatest of all actors could.

But on the first take, Virginia, age ten, was fingering and twisting Barrymore's tie. It was such a scene-stealing piece of business that even Garson Kanin, who was directing, was watching Virginia and not listening to Barrymore.

Barrymore, whom I knew in Chicago, once advised me:

"If you ever become an actor, never play a scene with a child or a dog."

So now you know why W. C. Fields hated child actors—all of them except one, that is.

That would be Will Fowler, son of the immortal Gene. Will learned to drink martinis with Fields at age thirteen.

Will and Papa Gene visited Fields' house one Christmas Day years ago and took him a gift. Fields was indignant that Gene would pull such knavery. But the martinis were poured anyway, and after a pitcher or two, Fields mellowed and came up with a rare confession.

"I used to believe in Christmas—until I was eight years old," he said. "While carrying ice in Philadelphia, I'd saved several quarters to buy my mother a new wash boiler for Christmas."

In the days before electric washers, housewives used to boil the laundry before scrubbing on a washboard by hand.

"I hid the money in-a milk bottle in the basement. And the night before Christmas, I went down to get the money for my mother's present and there was my old man stealing the money to buy booze. Since then I've remembered nobody on Christmas and I don't want anybody to remember me."

"But you should have outgrown that childhood bitterness," Gene told him. Fields then told the Fowlers the real reason he hated Christmas.

"Holidays like Christmas point up a thing called loneliness. A performer on the road—as I was for so many years—finds himself all alone in a dingy hotel room when everyone else has friends and companionship.

"It's no fun to be in Australia, or in Scotland, or in South Africa, as I have been, all alone on Christmas Day, and to see and hear a lot of happy strangers welcoming that daffy old crook, Santa Claus, who passes you by."

And as if fate were compounding Fields' loneliness, he died on Christmas Day, 1946.

Possum Plays Dead

The movies are filled with bizarre but little-known specialties—like Harry Possum, who played a corpse in more than three-hundred-fifty pictures, until a few years ago, when he took his job too seriously. Harry is no longer with us.

Harry Possum was only his stage name. Actually he was Harry Ray, one of the top makeup men in the business. At the time of his death, he was Jack Lemmon's powder-puff man.

But back in the twenties, when Harry first started in the business, he was no different from the rest of us. He wanted to be a star. His first role was in a Jack Hoxie western, where he did a live scene standing in front of a cigar-store Indian.

That debut inspired a long-forgotten director to comment:

"You make the wooden Indian look like he's overacting."

That's when Harry decided on his specialty. He played nothing but corpses after that.

"I made more money dead in movies than most actors alive."

Harry once told me his most challenging role was playing a tagged toe in a city-morgue scene. Somehow that struck me as funny but Harry was dead serious.

"I didn't come here to be made sport of," he stormed. "It's not easy to play corpses. I have to lie there and hold my breath for closeups.

"I can make a skin diver look like he has asthma."

Harry was so serious about his calling that he used to practice at home and scare hell out of his wife.

"I practice holding my breath in my swimming pool, which I bought and paid for out of my acting money. Sometimes I would go under for two minutes or more. My crazy neighbors were always calling the fire department when they would see my body lying at the bottom of the pool. They were not in show business and they didn't understand about rehearsals and stuff."

Harry also had perfected a deathly stare. He did that with strict control of his eye muscles. He also practiced keeping his eyes open for long periods of time.

Once a cop wanted to cite him for a 502 (drunk driving) when Harry went through a red light, but Harry convinced him that it was a perfectly natural state. Besides, he only had two beers.

Harry missed the biggest opportunity of his life in the thirties when Fredric March wanted him for two weeks' work in *Death Takes a Holiday*. Ordinarily, a corpse—unless he is established in a long scene—seldom works more than a day.

Harry, so thrilled at March's call, went down to Palm Springs to celebrate. He came back with a beautiful tan. He lost the job because, after all, what good is an acting corpse without a death pallor?

After that, Harry was the only male who ever went to Palm Springs with a parasol. Made a lot of new friends that way, too.

Harry was so good at his specialty that every time George Jessel saw him, he delivered a eulogy. Harry would listen deadpan and then assume an animated expression.

This startled Jessel but only momentarily.

"Whenever any of my corpses came alive," said George, "I immediately went into a couple choruses of 'Darktown Strutters Ball.'"

Harry said:

"I bet over the years George has sold me a couple hundred bonds for Israel. It would have been cheaper to play dead and listen to the eulogy."

It's amazing how much money Harry made playing corpses over the years.

"If you're dead in front of the scene, the scale was $75. In the background, you only got half that much. I told my agent to get me center camera or nothing. Highest scale of all was to lie in a coffin, center camera, wearing a tuxedo. The dress, extra scale, brought that up to $125 a day."

Harry became so famous at his calling that one year Forest Lawn wanted to name him Man of the Year. Harry turned it down.

"I never went in this business for the publicity."

Harry's pride was such that he often used to disguise himself for different pictures. Put a mustache on him and you'd swear it wasn't the same corpse.

Harry loved it when movies and TV stressed violence.

"You couldn't keep track of the calls from casting directors."

Like all extras, Harry always hoped the big break would come.

"Don't forget that Errol Flynn played a corpse in his first movie—and then came *Captain Blood*."

I once told Harry how I had written a story about Jack Norton, the screen's most famous drunk. Jack had never taken a drink.

"Well, what about me?" said Harry. "I haven't died vet."

But eventually he did. And there's never been anyone to take his place.

PART V: ALL ABOUT MY FAVORITE STAR

From the night I mislaid a Princess to a visit from
Ingrid Bergman at 4 A.M. in North Wales.

Was Knute Rockne Murdered?

Back in 1934, my sophomore year at Notre Dame University, I heard a remarkable story one night from Father John Reynolds, C.S.C., the rector of St. Edwards Hall, my residence hall on the campus.

Kitty Gorman, the center on the football team, and I were in Father Reynolds' office drinking beer—a strict violation of university rules for students.

But Kitty was an unusual student. He had come up through the Notre Dame Minims, once the elementary and high-school arm of the university.

I don't think Kitty had ever gone to any school in his life but Notre Dame—from the first grade through law school.

In 1934, the Minims were long gone but the memories weren't. Kitty, as a one-time Minims student, could do no wrong with the priests at Notre Dame.

The ordinary student would be expelled if he had beer on his breath on a Saturday night. Kitty, whose room was next to mine and also adjoined Father Reynolds', could come in drunk (as he often did), cuss, knock over the steel wardrobe locker in his room, and generally raise hell all night.

Father Reynolds, a strict rector, never stirred when it was Kitty causing a commotion. He was a Minim, one of the chosen few still left at Notre Dame.

So that explains how I was in the rector's office drinking beer: I came with Kitty.

Father Reynolds, who used to hoist a few himself in those days, told Kitty and me how he gave the last rites of the Catholic Church to Jake Lingle, the Chicago *Tribune* reporter who was killed by Al Capone's mob in the heyday of Chicago gangland executions.

Lingle, often called the world's richest reporter, was mixed up with the mob himself. He was the bagman who carried the payments from the Capone headquarters in suburban Cicero downtown to the crooked politicians and judges in City Hall and the Cook County offices.

Then Jake forgot to drop off a payment, or maybe he pulled off some other kind of a double-cross. At any rate, he was standing on the Illinois Central platform at the foot of Randolph Street when he was executed, gangland style.

The Chicago, South Bend, and South Shore interurban railroad also used that station for its terminus on the two-hour run from South Bend to Chicago.

Just as the South Shore unloaded its passengers, Jake Lingle got his. Father Reynolds, on a trip to Chicago, rushed to the stricken Lingle and gave him the last rites, hearing his confession.

Father Reynolds didn't even know whether Jake was Catholic or not. In fact, he had no idea who he was, just that he had been slain in front of the priest's eyes.

It was all reported in banner headlines in all the papers. The story got wide play because it was one of the few times, not counting innocent bystanders, that the hoods had not killed one of their own.

Of course, Lingle was one of their own, but the general public didn't know that. To the public, he was a newpaper reporter for one of the biggest newpapers in the country.

Father Reynolds then told Kitty and me a horrendous tale of his harassment by gangsters, all of whom wanted to know what Lingle had divulged to him during that last confession.

The priest gave all of them the same answer—that the seal of the confessional prevented his revealing what was said.

This only increased the phone calls and the mysterious visits.

But Father Reynolds never told.

Threats were made on his life and person.

Still he never winced.

Then one day he was walking across the campus and bumped into Knute Rockne. The two chatted and the famous coach told the priest that Universal Pictures in Hollywood had just called him to make a fast trip to Hollywood.

The studio was making a movie called *The Spirit of Notre Dame*, starring Lew Ayres and Andy Devine, and needed

Rock's expert advice on some phase of the production.

Rock was moaning that he couldn't get an airline reservation and would have to take the long train trip instead.

Father Reynolds said he had—in his pocket—reservations and tickets for a flight from Chicago to Los Angeles the next day.

The priest was in no hurry to get to Los Angeles and told Rock to take them. Father Reynolds would take the train trip.

Rock and Reynolds were old friends. Both had been track stars at Notre Dame.

Rock was to football what Babe Ruth was to baseball in those days, a superhero of the Golden Age of Sports.

So it was not surprising when the banner headline around the world on March 31, 1931, told of Rockne's death in a fiery plane crash over the Kansas farmland, near Bazaar.

A farmer, plowing his field, was an eyewitness to the crash, which also killed eight others. He said the plane exploded in midair, as if by a bomb.

Father Reynolds told us:

"My name was on Rock's tickets and reservation. He didn't have time to change them. And then all those threats on my life. Did those people plant a bomb on that plane for me? I don't know.

"I know if I hadn't given Rock my tickets, he would have been alive."

Last I heard of Father Reynolds, he was a Trappist monk someplace in Utah.

A Visit From Ingrid Bergman at 4 A.M.

Jim Denton, once director of publicity at 20th Century-Fox, had a funny way of packing a suitcase. No socks, underwear, or toothpaste. Just necessary things like scotch, gin, vermouth, and maybe a little club soda.

He made travel interesting. Like the time we got the

seventy-six-year-old widow drunk on a train ride to North Wales, embarrassing her sister the duchess and the vicar.

Or the time we toured Hamburg's notorious Reeperbahn with the same suitcase and almost wound up with cement shoes at the bottom of the Elbe River.

But let's travel to North Wales first.

Jim and I boarded the crack Royal Scotsman in London and soon found ourselves seated across from a widow who had a suitcase that ticked. The widow was one of those dotty English aristocrats straight out of a Margaret Rutherford movie.

I mentioned to Jim that perhaps we should do something about that ticking suitcase before we all got blown to Hell via the Midlands. So, casually and politely, I asked the eccentric widow what caused the ticking. She gave a most logical answer.

"This is my first trip outside London since my husband died fifteen years ago. My daughter was quite worried that I might miss my stop in Bangor, North Wales, so she put an alarm clock in my baggage. The alarm is set to go off at 6:10 P.M., exactly when we reach Bangor."

She smiled sweetly, satisfied that she had satisfied my curiosity. I didn't say anything for a moment. Then I said:

"It's highly possible that the train may be late or early. Why not let *us* make sure you get off at Bangor, because that's where we're going?"

She thought that was a great idea and opened her suitcase. Sure enough. There was no bomb. Just a ticking alarm clock. It relieved the tension so much that Denton opened his suitcase and said: "This calls for a drink."

He fixed scotches all around. The widow demurred at first.

"My husband and I used to drink sherry but I haven't had a drink in fifteen years. Do you think I should? My sister the duchess and the vicar are meeting me. And they are so strait-laced."

Denton, very gregarious and very persuasive, soon had her talked into taking a drink.

"It will make this seven-hour trip go like mad."

That was the understatement of the day.

When the train pulled into Bangor, we had a widow with bonnet askew who was smashed. Furthermore, she didn't want to go with the duchess or the vicar. She wanted to stay with us.

"I'll sleep between you," she said. "You won't be sorry. I haven't been with a man in fifteen years and I'm ready and willing."

Denton and I could see that the duchess and vicar saw no humor in this situation. We had beaten the bomb. Now it was time to beat the cops.

We fled to our waiting car, leaving behind a completely plastered widow who kept screaming in the station:

"I want to go with those crazy Americans. They have given me my first taste of life in fifteen years."

That made Denton and me feel very happy. We had done a dastardly but also a good deed.

We drove through the rugged Welsh mountainous countryside to a place I was not quite prepared for—Portmeiron.

Now North Wales is harsh and bleak, but Portmeiron was Portofino transplanted, even to the pastel buildings. It was charming. It was built by a Welsh architect who had seen Portofino in World War I and had vowed to build a replica in his homeland—but not until he had built a ruin first.

He was still alive when we got there and admitted that what he had done was pure folly.

"But man must have one folly in life—else there's no use living."

Bertrand Russell, the English philosopher who was his friend and neighbor, was with him when he told us about his folly. Russell agreed wholeheartedly.

The architect—and I can't remember his name—was as dotty as the widow but he told a delightful story of how this all came about.

"I was an officer in the Royal Welsh Guards during the First World War and was quite impressed with what I saw in Italy. I especially loved the Roman ruins.

"How sad for us Welshmen. You know the Romans never could conquer us so we had no ruins.

"In 1921, I decided to rectify all of this and applied for retirement from the Guards. My fellow officers wanted to throw me the usual regimental retirement dinner and give me the usual silverplate. I shocked them somewhat by saying I would prefer the money instead. 'What in heavens for,' they demanded to know.

"I told them that I wanted to build a ruin in North Wales. They, of course, thought I was mad but they gave me the money.

"And I got my ruin."

He later showed us the ruin, and as ruins go, it was quite a lovely ruin. Since the people of North Wales had never seen a ruin before, crowds flocked to the place.

That's what prompted him to build his supreme folly—the replica of Portofino, which has everything its Italian counterpart has except sunshine.

He then showed us a letter from a member of the House of Lords, which read:

"I would like to build a folly myself but due to somewhat straitened circumstances because of the Labor government, I can only afford a small folly. I would welcome any suggestions from you on how this could be done."

I have often thought about that architect's remark—"man must have one folly in life."

Those are words to live by.

Portmeiron is one of the most popular resorts in North Wales, which seems to have more rain than a Panamanian jungle. But Portmeiron, quaint and charming as it was, was not Paris after dark. After dinner and drinks, Denton and I asked our driver what to do for excitement. It was now 10 P.M. and the pubs were legally closed.

"Well," he said, "you can either go out and watch the tide go out in the Irish Sea or ——"

Before he could finish, we heard the damnedest roar—like an earthquake. We rushed out to the inlet on which Portmeiron was built and the whole damn thing was rushing out like God had siphoned it. It was a sight to see. In a matter of minutes, only a muddy bay remained of what had once been a beautiful inlet. It was still daylight in that northern summer clime.

After looking at the mud for a few minutes, we then asked what the hell else we could do. The driver said we could drive to the next village, which had a Welsh name about thirty-five syllables long. It seems there is an old wayfaring law, which goes back to the stagecoach days, which says an inn cannot refuse the weary traveler a drink, no matter what time of day or night.

So we got into the car and headed for the village some ten or twelve miles away. A whole string of traffic was coming in the opposite direction. Those were the pub crawlers from the other village coming to ours to take advantage of the wayfarers' law. God, no wonder Richard Burton is so fiercely Welsh.

After a rousing time in the neighboring pub, we returned to our cottages in Portmeiron. Our driver had gotten drunk so I drove back. It was my first experience in driving on the left side of the road but it was easy. I had had enough to drink so I just drove like I always did in the States.

Probably should tell you what we were doing up in this God-forsaken place. Fox was shooting a movie called *Inn of the Sixth Happiness,* a story that was set in China. If that sounds illogical, you don't know how Hollywood operates.

That explains the pounding on my door at 4 A.M. I yelled "Come in" since it wasn't locked. Who should walk in but a radiantly beautiful Ingrid Bergman?

What a great press agent that Denton is, I thought. First he has a suitcase packed with booze and instead of broads, he sends movie stars.

"Jim," asked the astonished Swede. "What are you doing here? I thought this was the makeup room."

Then she turned and left. I went back to sleep—alone.

Later we went to the location. It was China. Hundreds of Chinese extras were milling about. The company had brought them up from London and Cardiff. The locals had never seen Chinamen before. Lots of those villagers had never been ten miles away from home in a lifetime.

One sad aspect of the location visit. I had a nice chat with Robert Donat, the Oscar-winning Mr. Chips.

A week later, he finished the picture—and died.

Denton refilled his suitcase and we headed back to London. We got to the station at Bangor a half hour or more before the Royal Scotsman, taking us back to London, was due. Nothing to do but open up the suitcase on the train platform and have a picnic. It was quite unusual but, as the trainmaster said: "It's a jolly good idea."

It was such a good idea that the Royal Scotsman came and went without our noticing it.

That called for new travel instructions since the Royal Scotsman was the only direct train to London. The trainmaster gave us a complicated set of instructions about changing trains at various stops like Holyhead where my grandfather had landed 100 years before on his first stop from Ireland to America.

We made Holyhead all right but that wild suitcase caused us to miss three or four trains there. Finally after about four more changes of trains, we finally were on a train that was going to London.

Both Jim and I noticed that everytime we got on and off a train all the way from Bangor a young African got off and on with us. He didn't look like a detective shadowing us but that's what he was doing. Finally, I asked the guy how come he kept getting on and off trains with us. He told us he was the son of a tribal chieftain in Africa and a first-year student at Bangor university. When he had arrived to study at Bangor, his plane had landed in Cardiff, South Wales, and he had never been to London before.

"This is my first trip to London so I asked the trainmaster for directions. He pointed to you two gentlemen and said that I should follow you and that you would get me to London. I am so happy he did because this trip is so complicated I never would have made it without you."

Turned out he had a ticket for the Royal Scotsman too.

That called for another opening of the suitcase and the three of us became great friends. Jim and I have often wondered about him—whether he is now a president of one of the new African nations. We got quite chummy on the trip after a few rounds. This was in 1958, long before the black revolution in the United States. He asked us where we were born and when Denton said Mississippi, he was astonished.

"We black people in Africa have heard such terrible things about Mississippi but after meeting you, Mr. Denton, I feel as if I will have to change my opinion about Mississippi."

So the round trip accomplished two good deeds. We cheered up a lonely widow going North and changed the image of Mississippi going South.

Jim and I had a horrendous experience a few years later in Hamburg, the wickedest city in the world. Naturally, the two of us were on the Reeperbahn, the wickedest part of the wickedest city.

I later told Peter Lorre that just the two of us had made a night of it on the Reeperbahn. He was shocked. Can you imagine anything shocking Peter Lorre?

"I vas only there vunce," he told me, "but I vould not go alone. I had six plainclothes policemen mit me."

Peter Lorre scared? It's incredible.

The night started interestingly enough. We went into one place where naked women wrestled in mud and a camel came over to our table and got drunk drinking beer out of a pail. It's something the SPCA should investigate because that camel got absolutely smashed. It really was not an edifying experience.

The next place we stopped was one of those strip joints that are absolute ripoff joints. You find them the world over, not only on the Reeperbahn. Actually they are worse in Germany because the strip artists can't even walk in tempo, let alone dance and strip.

Between strips, they showed a travel movie of a young guy and a particularly gorgeous young girl driving along the Italian Riviera. The travel film fascinated us because we kept hoping it would turn into something dirty. It never did. It was strictly a G-rated travelogue.

All the time we kept drinking Rhine champagne because that's all they would serve us. Between the two of us, we must have consumed three bottles at the most. Our suitcase was confiscated.

It's not very good champagne and we expected a tab of no more than $50, even at clip-joint prices.

The tab was 350 American dollars.

Naturally, we squawked. Finally the manager showed up. He spoke English and looked like a Nazi Storm Trooper.

"I am going to call the police," said Denton.

"The police are afraid to come in here," said the manager. At that about half a dozen burly waiters and strongarm men moved around us menacingly.

Something about the tone of that guy's voice gave us both the idea that mayhem was about to commence. Something was mentioned about a swim in the Elbe River, cold at that time of year.

"Pay the money, Jim," I said. He was on studio expense account.

We did and got out of the Reeperbahn fast. I'll probably go back there some day. Adventure intrigues me.

A *Time* Cover? Great! But What Have You Got Tomorrow?

Hollywood press-agentry is a much maligned and much misunderstood profession. It's a frantic profession but it performs one of the most important functions in the movie industry. It sells the product.

The press agents are, in effect, the super salesmen of Hollywood. And Hollywood, being the weird town it is, will always lay off the press agent first. Can you imagine General Motors laying off its salesmen at the first sign of a slump?

And here's an even more flagrant example. Arthur Wilde, one of the veterans in the business and a real pro, made a contibution to Paramount Pictures that earned them upwards of 8 million dollars on a picture called *The Bad News Bears.*

You remember the picture—a story about Little League baseball starring Walter Matthau and Tatum O'Neal. The studio had a real problem. The picture was a box-office smash in the United States, but except for Japan and Latin America, where they play baseball, the rest of tne world would never understand what it was all about.

Wilde came up with the suggestion that they precede the picture with an animated short in the various languages showing what baseball was all about. The studio bosses were ecstatic but not ecstatic enough to pay Wilde for the idea. He considered it part of his job and took that philosophically.

But a few days later, he got in a beef with his boss's secretary. It was either Wilde or the secretary who had to go. Naturally, it was Wilde. His bosses even ordered a moving van so he could move out faster.

Wilde, being the pro that he is, was snapped up by Universal the next day.

No other denizen of the Hollywood jungle gets sniped at as much as the press agent. On one side, he has the Hollywood press, which has some of the most obnoxious prima donnas you can imagine. And no-talent ones at that.

Most Hollywood columnists hate each other's guts, and when one is fed a good exclusive, all hell descends on the press agent who planted it.

And on the other side, the press agent must deal with the monumental egos of stars, producers, and directors.

As a class, the producer is much more of a publicity hound than the actors he hires.

"A *Time* cover? Great! But what have you got tomorrow?"

How many times has the press agent heard that?

Frustration is a way of life. A publicity man may have a big break all set and then a major news story will knock it out of print.

There is comic frustration, too.

Bill Pine and Bill Thomas, later to become producers, were assigned to a Mae West picture called *It Ain't No Sin*. Pine and Thomas concocted a brilliant publicity stunt for the movie. They bought 300 parrots and every day for two months the two press agents kept repeating *It Ain't No Sin* to the parrots. God knows how many man hours they put in on the task. The object was to mail the parrots to the movie editors of the country, who would open the cages and hear a parrot plug the picture. The very day that Pine and Thomas had the parrots crated to ship, a memo came from the front office changing the title of the movie to *The Belle of the Nineties*.

One of my favorite press agents was a fellow named Bob Yeager, who never took himself or the town seriously. Unfortunately, his career was cut short when he was senselessly murdered by teen-age prowlers. He specialized in great publicity stunts throughout his career, and I was involved in most of them because Yeager and I seemed to be the only ones in town who had fun with their jobs.

When Yeager called me to tell me what he had in mind, I always went along with him in the same tongue-in-cheek vein.

In *Pal Joey*, Yeager noticed in the script that Frank Sinatra had a pet mongrel, which he fed bagels. That's all Yeager needed. First he approached Sinatra with the idea of having a dog bagel-eating contest to cast the part, with Frank as the sole judge. The only place to have it was Nate 'N' Al's delicatessen in Beverly Hills. Frank bought the idea because it came from Yeager. Frank loved Bob. I was chosen as the guy to write the story because working for the Associated Press's 8,000 newspapers, I had the biggest circulation in the world. Also Frank's press list was the smallest in town and I was the surviving member.

Well, can you imagine a couple dozen dog owners parading their mutts before Sinatra in a delicatessen? Naturally, most of the dogs just sniffed at the bagels and nothing more. Then the cutest, littlest mongrel you ever saw came up to Sinatra and devoured the bagel. It got the part and was one of the stars of the movie.

Yeager had taked the precaution somehow to give this particular bagel an Alpo flavor.

Yeager knew all about the winning dog's history. It had just that afternoon been rescued from the gas chamber in the dog pound. That gave the story human interest.

It hadn't, of course. The dog was actually the pet of one of Harry Cohn's kids. Cohn was the tyrannical boss of Columbia Pictures, where the picture was made, and also Yeager's boss. Bob knew a lot about job security.

The story made page one around the world. Roy Roberts, the famous editor of the Kansas City *Star*, wrote me that it was the funniest story ever to come out of Hollywood. I just wrote it. Yeager invented it.

Most of the contemporary stars look down on publicity and the Hollywood press, unlike the great superstars of the Golden Era.

Yeager didn't let that bother him. His job was to get the title of the picture in the papers. So he made up his own stars. There would be Al K. Hall playing the town drunk in *The Devil at 4 O'Clock* and Ed Shrinker playing a psychiatrist in *The Last Hurrah*.

My favorite was Robert Rooster, who was cast in a Ross Hunter movie starring Bobby Darin and Sandra Dee. Rooster would play the owner of a chicken farm. What else?

I called up Hunter and disguised my voice

"Mr. Hunter," I said, "I'm actor Robert Rooster, a member of the Screen Actors Guild for twenty-one years. The other day I saw in *Daily Variety* where I was cast in your movie. I was wondering why I haven't received my call yet."

Hunter started sputtering and mumbling. Then he went off the phone for a moment and came back with this:

"Well, let me explain. I have this crazy press agent. . . ."

Until Yeager and I explained to Ross it was all a put-on, Hunter was looking for a part for the nonexistent Robert Rooster·

Another time, Yeager called me and said that Barbra Streisand, in *On a Clear Day You Can See Forever,* refused to give interviews. He suggested that we do a story on one Wong Keye, a mythical tone-deaf Chinese piano tuner who was tuning all the pianos on the Streisand movie.

Great. The story was written with appropriate tongue-in-cheek. It told how Wong Keye had started out in life as a fortune-cookie stuffer in a Chinatown bakery, then sold exotic fish for a while until he found his niche in tuning pianos. Since then he had been in great demand around the studios because he was such a superb piano tuner.

Not long after my column appeared, I started getting calls from piano owners wanting to get in touch with Wong Keye. Then the London *Daily Mirror,* one of the biggest papers in the world, joined the fun. They immediately cabled Paramount and said they would love a picture of Wong Keye.

That didn't faze Yeager. He grabbed Alan J. Lerner's son-in-law and put him through makeup and wardrobe. Before long, the *Daily Mirror* printed a picture of a heavily made-up nineteenth-century Chinese coolie with his ear cupped, bending over a piano. It took up most of the page of the tabloid *Mirror* with this caption:

"The man behind the Hollywood musicals—a tone-deaf Chinese piano tuner named Wong Keye."

In the story with the photo, the *Mirror* commented that Wong Keye's skill was just one more of those inscrutable Oriental mysteries.

But the funniest repercussion of all came when Streisand—who had refused to give interviews in the first place—complained to Producer Howard W. Koch because the piano tuner on the movie was getting more publicity than the star.

Yeager had another beauty on *Plaza Suite,* which Koch also produced. (Somehow either Sinatra or Koch was always our partner in crime.) He was Francis Xavier Schwartz, who had one of the most breathless jobs in movies all bottled up. F. X. Schwartz was a sound specialist in imitating popping champagne corks for the screen.

It may surprise a lot of you to know that on film, the real popping of a champagne cork sounds like a burp after a Hungarian dinner. Schwartz obtained his special effect by inhaling deeply. Then with his cheeks expanded like a glass blower, he would release his breath in an exploding, popping sound. It was beautiful to hear and I told him so. No finger was ever used.

"You, sir," he said, "are a connoisseur of champagne because the pop you just heard was my Dom Perignon '59 pop. I only use it in big-budget movies like *Plaza Suite*. Also Cary Grant movies."

As I said in my eulogy at Yeager's funeral, how can you ever thank someone who has given you a million laughs? I miss you, Bob.

Sometimes a publicity interview can take an unexpected and spectacular turn, like the time Maury Foladare invited me to have lunch with Edy Williams. Now Maury for years has guided the public relations of Bing Crosby and Danny Thomas. Among his other clients was Dimension Pictures, who had made a movie called *Dr. Vixen*, starring the curvaceous Miss Williams.

Before the lunch was over, Edy became the first girl ever to go topless in the Polo Lounge of the Beverly Hills hotel, a sort of Irish pub for the very rich and very famous.

It happened twice. And each time, waiters dropped trays, diners gawked in mid-fork, and Marty Allen yelled: "Just one more time, Edy."

Maitre d' Nino actually blushed, which is very hard to do when you are Italian. Maury swallowed three pills for high blood pressure. Earl Wilson the columnist missed it the first time and it was he who cleverly arranged the encore. Even Muriel Slatkin, one of the owners of the hotel, saw it. She left the Polo Lounge shaking her head and saying to herself:

"It didn't happen here, did it?"

Edy measures 37-23-37 and has one of the most spectacular bodies since Marilyn Monroe. She creates excitement even with her clothes on—which is seldom.

This day she came looking very innocent. In keeping with the title of the picture and her title role of Dr. Vixen, she wore a medical smock and a stethoscope. She took my pulse over a glass of champagne, asked a few medical questions, and then handed me a box of Ex-Lax. Edy should have been a press agent. Then she started talking seriously:

"This is the first time in my career that I have actually played a lady. For once, the producer and director did not look upon me as a sex object like they have in the past. I won the part strictly on my ability as a serious actress, which really is what I am.

"Look at this costume and this severe hairdo. It's the way I dress for the daytime scenes in the movie."

The next question I never should have asked.

"What do you wear for the nighttime scenes?"

That did it. She unbuttoned her smock and there in full glorious sun tan was what she wore for the nighttime scenes. Nothing but her magnificent breasts and navel. She held the pose for what seemed minutes. The she buttoned up again.

Had I asked: "Is that all?" I am sure she would have gone bottomless.

A couple of booths away, Wilson asked Marty Allen what he was applauding. Earl then stammered, "But I missed it. I missed it."

He soon joined our table. Earl, for all his years on Broadway, is still a country boy from Rockford, Ohio. He was disbelieving.

"Come on, Edy. You're kidding. That was a see-through blouse, wasn't it? What's-her-name said it was." "What's-her-name" was Rosemary, Earl's B.W., who was sitting with him.

At that, Edy did it again.

Once again Walter the waiter dropped his tray and Nino, the maitre d', came over to the table and said: "Mr. Bacon, you are our favorite customer because such strange things happen whenever you come in here."

Earl got up shaking his head and beckoned to what's-her-name to come along.

Press agents sometimes have to do more than publicity. Like escort some of the lady columnists who can't get dates to parties. But often there are better assignments.

Jay Bernstein, in his early days in the business, got a dream assignment. The young, beautiful Joan Collins was afraid of the dark and Jay was assigned by his boss to sleep in her apartment as part of his job.

"But," recalls Jay, "my boss told me that if I ever tried to fuck her, I would be fired the next day. I never tried. I'm sure Joan thought I was a fag [which he isn't] but I kept my job and got paid overtime on the assignment."

Lots of movies would wind up on the bottom end of a double bill if it weren't for super press-agentry. Some years back, Hecht-Lancaster bought a TV play starring Rod Steiger playing a homely butcher who couldn't find a girl. One night at the Mocambo, Burt Lancaster was telling me about plans for the movie version.

"We're doing it strictly as a tax write-off.

"We made so damn much money off *Navajo* and *Vera Cruz*, we'll do this one strictly for art."

Fine. Except he forgot to tell Walter Seltzer, the Hecht-Lancaster publicity man. As you all know, *Marty* was the story of a homely butcher and a homely wallflower. From a publicity standpoint, it was hardly Elizabeth Taylor and Richard Burton.

But Seltzer came up with a publicity campaign that is still a model for the industry. He had Ernest Borgnine slicing meat all over town and columnists saw previews of the movie in their own home with their friends and neighbors. Booze and buffet all furnished by Seltzer along with the film and projectionist. It made the columnist the big man on the block. And all were appreciative in print.

Punch line, of course, is that *Marty* won a bunch of Oscars, including best actor for Borgnine and best picture. It was not a tax write-off but the biggest grosser in Hecht-Lancaster history. Borgnine, unknown before *Marty*, came off the stage and handed Seltzer a miniature Oscar made of gold.

"You deserved it, win or lose," said Ernie.

Harold Hecht, clutching the best picture Oscar, gave Walter hell because there were photographers around Borgnine, and not him.

Russell Birdwell was the most flamboyant of the old-time movie press agents. He once was profiled in the *New Yorker* magazine. Next day all his clients, who never had a *New Yorker* profile, fired him.

Russ also was one of the highest paid. He collected $275,000 plus expenses as a fee from John Wayne to publicize *The Alamo*. Birdwell delivered. The picture got an Academy Award nomination.

Once when Porfirio Rubirosa gave Zsa Zsa Gabor (a Birdwell client) a black eye in an argument, Russ bought a fifteen-cent eye-patch and called in the photographers. Zsa Zsa and her black eye-patch made front pages around the world.

He once had a love affair with Anne Baxter. He must have had the cigar institute as a client because he came out with a story that Anne smoked nothing but cigars. The granddaughter of Frank Lloyd Wright and an Oscar winner went along with it—all for love. When they broke up, Birdwell said he couldn't stand Anne leaving cigar butts around the house.

Russ was a former newpaperman and as a press agent he made news with his publicity stunts. It was he who engineered the worldwide search for Scarlett O'Hara in *Gone with the Wind* and it was he who made Jane Russell an international celebrity five years before Howard Hughes' *The Outlaw* ever hit the screen.

One of Russ's stunts in which I was involved backfired in one way and in another it didn't because he got publicity for his movie. Joseph Stalin was one of the characters in the movie. And they had an actor who was the dead image for the dreaded Soviet ruler. Russ suggested that I take the actor to lunch in the Stalin wardrobe and see what happened. We went to one of Los Angeles' busiest restaurants and then walked the streets with a photographer.

Now remember this was at the height of Stalin's reign in

the Kremlin. We ate and walked and, outside of a few gawks, there was no real reaction from the Los Angeles crowd. All of which gives you an idea of what a weird town Los Angeles is.

Even Garbo, when she first came out here, ran through the Hollywood publicity mill. When she first arrived from Sweden, Pete Smith of the MGM publicity department posed her in starting position with the University of Southern California track team. That picture is still around. I see it every now and then.

There was even a shot of her frying eggs for a home layout.

Garbo didn't quite know what the hell was going on but she did what she was told. Then one day a columnist interviewed her. She talked openly and honestly about her live-in arrangement with Director Mauritz Stiller.

It would be nothing in today's permissive society, but in the late twenties, it was shocking. That did it. Louis B. Mayer issued an edict. All Garbo interviews were forever banned. That didn't disturb Garbo, who was basically shy anyhow.

Some long-forgotten genius in the MGM publicity department came up with that famous quote:

"I vant to be alone."

And this greatest of movie actresses has been ever since. Even Howard Hughes could have taken lessons in reclusivity from her.

Who was the first movie press agent?

Naturally, he came out of the circus, where the art of press-agentry was founded. His name was Harry Reichmann. In the circus, he publicized the tattooed man. But Harry got fired when the tattooed man got too fat. It made all the Apostles at the Last Supper look like they were laughing.

About this time the first Tarzan movie, starring Elmo Lincoln, came out. Harry convinced the producers that he could get the name of the movie in every paper in the country and even the world. He was hired.

Harry registered himself in the Astor Hotel in New York City as Mr. T.A.R. Zan. Then each day Harry ordered fifty pounds of raw meat sent up by room service. After a few days, the hotel got suspicious and called the cops, who were followed by police reporters. In the room, they found Mr. T. A. R. Zan and a lion, who was eating the raw meat.

When that story broke all over the world, mentioning the name of the movie, Hollywood press-agentry as a profession was born.

Most classic of all Hollywood press-agent stories is that of J. Ned Farrington, an eminent but mythical movie producer from New York. For years, Farrington made periodic trips to Hollywood and always announced a new picture. In subsequent stories, he would name a director, a music scorer, a writer, a cameraman, a star or two, and so on. All these people had one thing in common—the same press agent.

The late Dave Epstein, one of the pioneer movie press agents, had invented Farrington to get his clients' names in the trade papers. For years, Dave got away with this. Then one day writer Jimmy Henaghan, then an editor of one of the Hollywood trades, deduced that not one J. Ned Farrington movie had ever been made. Henaghan thought Epstein's creation was too imaginative to be kissed off with a mere dressing down over the telephone. Only one way to do it.

Henaghan wrote a beautiful obit for J. Ned Farrington, who on his latest visit to Hollywood had suffered a fatal heart attack in his suite at the Beverly Hills Hotel. It was a touching story; it even had Farrington graduating *magna cum laude* from Harvard, rare for a producer. All pallbearers were the same Epstein clients.

Henaghan said nothing to Epstein and Epstein said nothing back. Within a year, Henaghan left the paper for another job.

Next day, the same paper ran a story about J. Ned Farrington, Jr., just in from New York. He had inherited all his father's screen properties and was casting all of the same people and some new ones Dave had acquired. There will always be a press agent.

I once had lunch with actress Piper Laurie and almost gagged as I watched her eat a whole bowl of carnations. She almost threw up, too, but she kept smiling. Piper in those days was only eighteen and very shy. She was very hard to publicize, but she was the special protégé of Leonard Gold-stein, one of the most important producers on the Universal lot.

The publicity department went nuts trying to come up with something. One day Freddie Banks of publicity saw Piper pick up a weed and put it in her teeth. Next day a story went out that this actress actually ate flowers.

Great, except that AP, UP, and INS all wanted pictures. It was carnations for AP, daffodils for UP, and daisies for INS.

Piper developed into an extremely talented, serious actress. Remember how brilliant she was in *The Hustler*, with Paul Newman and Jackie Gleason? She was an Oscar nominee that year and she told me that she didn't have a chance to win because Hollywood always remembered her as the starlet who ate flowers. Maybe *Carrie* will help.

I was in on the birth of the most publicity-minded of all Hollywood personalities—the late Jayne Mansfield. I was even responsible for getting her started.

I was sitting all alone at my desk in the AP office on a day before Christmas in the early fifties. All of a sudden, I felt a warm kiss on the back of my neck. It felt strange in the all-male newsroom.

Looking up, I gazed on a beautiful young blonde, twenty-one at most, with the most beautiful pair of breasts I had ever seen. They were falling out of her low-cut dress. Then she bent over and gave me a warm kiss on the lips. I kept my eyes open because I couldn't take them off those gorgeous breasts.

"Here's a present from Jim Byron," she said, and wiggled out the door.

Byron was an old friend, the press agent for Ciro's night-club on the Sunset Strip. I called him immediately and asked who in the hell that girl was.

"Would you believe," said Jim, "this girl walked in my office off the Strip and said she was a coed at UCLA and wanted to be a movie star. I had your present on my desk so I told her to deliver it to you and I'd get your reaction. What can I do with her?"

I had on my desk at the time an airplane ticket to Silver

Springs, Florida, where RKO was about to premiere a new Jane Russell movie called *Underwater*. I couldn't make the trip and told Byron I would call Nat James at RKO and also Howard Hughes, who owned the studio and who was a great tit man.

If they agreed, Jayne could take my seat on the flight. I called Howard first. He was much easier to get on the phone in those days. After I described Jayne, he agreed on the spot.

As a matter of formality, I called Nat, the publicity man in charge of the junket, and told him what Hughes had said.

Jayne was on the flight. The other girls who went along were Debbie Reynolds, Mala Powers, and Lori Nelson, all beautiful but none with the assets that Jayne had.

Jane Russell, the star of the picture, was delayed a few days in New York. She couldn't have cared less for cheesecake shots at this stage of her career.

So, for the photographers, Jayne had a wide-open field and she handled it like O. J. Simpson. She wore a bikini that was twenty years ahead of its time and when all the photographers were focused, a strap conveniently broke. And before long, the magazines and newspapers were filled with pictures of Jayne Mansfield, a new international star who had yet to be even interviewed for a movie. Unfortunately for Jayne, that heady debut caused her to eventually ridicule herself out of the business.

I first noticed this happening at the famous reception for Sophia Loren when the glamorous Italian star made her first visit to this country. Sophia, full-bosomed, presented a threat to Jayne. Naturally, the photographers all wanted to get shots of the sexy Italian import. This infuriated Jayne, who acted as one possessed.

Every time the photographers shot the seated Sophia at her table at Romanoff's, Jayne would rush over and lean over her with her big breasts almost drooping on Sophia's shoulder. It resulted in one of the most remarkable pictures ever taken, with Sophia peering down into Jayne's huge mammaries.

Toward the end of her tragic life, Jayne could get little work but opening supermarkets and shopping centers. But she was no dummy; her fee was never less than $5,000 a shot.

I was very fond of Jayne because, basically, she was a lovable girl. Often I would try to advise her but she would never listen.

She had the talent to make it big even without publicity, but you could never make her believe it. Only thing I ever talked her out of was when she decorated her big honeymoon mansion on Sunset Boulevard. She wanted everything heart-shaped—the bed, the bathtubs, lighting fixtures, even the toilet seats.

I told her the toilet seats wouldn't work.

"Why?" she pouted.

"Because you haven't got a heart-shaped ass," I said.

All the toilet seats remained oval.

Speaking of Romanoff's a few paragraphs back reminds me of the time I put a press agent and a famous German star into panic. Curt Jurgens came to Hollywood for the first time and immediately hired Rogers and Cowan to make it an auspicious debut. It was the biggest publicity firm in the business and when they tossed a party, like the one they did for Curt at Romanoff's, the whole movie colony turned out. Everybody but Eric Linden was there. If you don't remember Eric Linden, he was The Fonz of 1932.

Next day, my weird sense of humor got the best of me so I called Warren Cowan.

"Warren," I said, "I'm writing my story of the Jurgens party and I want to check one fact with you."

"Wonderful," said Warren, envisioning a story around the world on the AP wire. "What is it?"

"Did Curt shoot down twenty-two or was it twenty-three U. S. planes during the war?"

There was silence. Then Warren said:

"I'll get back to you." His voice was four octaves higher than usual.

Five minutes later the phone rang. It was Jurgens, who went into a long explanation about how he wasn't a Nazi but he did entertain troops during the war—like your U. S. O."

I explained to him that I was just playing a little joke on Warren. Curt laughed, a little hysterically as I recall.

I was once involved in a publicity stunt even before I got to Hollywood—and even before Jean Peters had heard of Howard Hughes. It was around 1946 and I was working in Chicago for AP. A "95" message came over the wire from Los Angeles. That was the code number for "urgent."

A young Ohio State coed by name of Jean Peters had won a beauty contest and the prize was a screen test at 20th Century-Fox. The beautiful young girl had waited around her hotel room, heard nothing from the studio, so decided to take the Super-Chief home. By coincidence, just as the Super-Chief was to pull into Chicago, the studio had seen the test and wanted her back· immediately for a picture with Tyrone Power. I believe it was *Captain from Castile*.

It seemed odd that the studio would use the AP to get the good news to her instead of just wiring her direct on the train, but I went out to the depot anyway. I found Miss Peters in the compartment where I was told she would be. She was overjoyed at the news but not too surprised, as I recall. She took a return train back to Hollywood.

A year or two later, I was assigned to Hollywood and met the famous Harry Brand. Harry is the press agent who got Fatty Arbuckle worldwide publicity by urging him to give a party in San Francisco. Harry went on to become director of publicity for 20th Century-Fox.

I kidded him about the Jean Peters incident. Harry said:

"Well now, if I had sent out a story that Jean Peters made a successful screen test and was signed to a 20th Century-Fox contract, who the hell would have used it but the Columbus, Ohio, *Dispatch?*

"I let you handle it and it was in every paper in the world."

I agreed because that is what press-agentry is all about.

You could write a book about Harry Brand, but let's just give one more story. In the early thirties, Lawrence Tibbett, the great Metropolitan Opera star, made his movie debut. At the first showing, Harry sent one of his publicity guys over to Grauman's Chinese with an automatic counter. His job—count how many women went to the ladies room during the Tibbett picture. The underling promptly returned and said he counted 34 for the entire picture.

"He'll never make it," said Harry. "Valentino used to make 200 girls pee an hour."

And he was right. Tibbett, after a few pictures, returned to the opera.

And then there are actors who are their own best press agents. One of my favorites in that category is Hugh O'Brian, founder of the Hugh O'Brian acting awards, which, incidentally, Hugh has never won.

When Hugh was a $75-a-week contract player at Universal, he cultivated all the columnists and never waited for the publicity department to plant news about him. Hugh planted it himself. He was not phony about it.

More important, he cultivated the columnists' wives. How many times have I heard a wife say: "Why don't you write about Hugh O'Brian? He's the only actor who knows my name."

It paid off for Hugh. He became big and made a fortune off the TV series *Wyatt Earp*.

One day after he had hit it, I ran into Hugh at the Sands Hotel in Las Vegas. Coming up on the plane I had read a complimentary piece in Louella Parsons' column about Hugh. So when I saw him, I commented on the item. Hugh was genuinely surprised. It was obvious that he had not read it.

"Christ," he said. "Now I know I've made it. Somebody else is planting me."

For several years, Hugh carried on a torrid affair with Soraya, once the Empress of Iran. One day I had an interview scheduled with Hugh. He emphasized several times that I show up at his home on Benedict Canyon at 3 P.M. sharp, not a minute later or a minute before. This was in the early days of his romance with Soraya, right after her divorce from the

Shah of Iran. No one was supposed to know that she and Hugh were fooling around. Obviously, it must have killed Hugh to have this international hunk of publicity go unnoticed.

When I arrived at his house at exactly 3 P.M. to the second, Soraya almost knocked me down running out of the house. That night the whole world knew that Soraya's new romance was Hugh.

Hugh is rich and famous today but the old instincts are still there. Just recently, at the Sands Hotel again, I was in a house phone cubicle when I saw Hugh enter the one next to me. He didn't see me but I heard him ask the operator to page Hugh O'Brian. Soon all over the casino, you could hear the loudspeaker blaring: "Paging Mr. Hugh O'Brian."

Almost simultaneously, Hugh appeared at the top of the casino landing where the hundreds of gamblers and tourists could see him.

There's only one Hugh. And I love him for being so honest about promoting his favorite product—Hugh O'Brian.

Another one of my favorite press agents over the years was Jerry Juroe, who became a good friend in the days when he was an apprentice at Paramount. Jerry, like every other press agent in the business, knew how to raise his salary to that of senior status via the expense account.

He often called me up in the morning and said, "I took you to dinner at Romanoff's last night, didn't I?"

Finally, one day the comptroller of Paramount stopped me on the lot and introduced himself.

"I have always wanted to meet someone who could eat seventy-seven lunches and dinners in one week," said the money man. Lots of press agents had put me on phony expense accounts that week.

But Jerry was an imaginative press agent. Back in 1951, Paramount made possibly the worst movie ever made, called *Aaron Slick From Punkin Crick*.

The picture was made because Y. Frank Freeman, the guy who ran the studio, had starred in the play during his senior year at Greenville, Georgia, high school way before World War I. He wanted it made into a movie and studio bosses were big enough to indulge their nostalgic wishes in those days.

No producer on the lot would touch it, because it was so corny it made *Hee Haw* sound like Noel Coward.

But Bill Perlberg did and his partner George Seaton directed it. As Perlberg once told me:

"I knew it would be a dog but George and I had our eyes on a couple of good properties the studio owned (like *The Country Girl*) and we knew if we did this for the old man, we would have carte blanche on the lot."

And they did. The prime stuff always went to Perlberg and Seaton first. But even such a talented director as Seaton, one of the greatest in the business, couldn't salvage this corny story.

Dinah Shore was one of the stars. I don't think she ever made another movie. *Aaron Slick* was so terrible that it drove Dinah into the infant, television, where she still remains one of the medium's great superstars.

But Juroe, under the gun, asked me if I would do an interview with Dinah to plug the boss's picture. Even though I had seen the picture, I agreed out of friendship. Juroe and I drove out to Encino, where Dinah, then married to George Montgomery, was living. Unfortunately, Dinah had also seen the movie the night before. When we got to the Montgomery home, Dinah was nowhere to be found.

She was just too damn embarrassed to talk with me. George made all sorts of excuses but I understood perfectly and, in fact, sympathized with her.

In those days, George was big at making furniture. I asked him to show me some of his work around the rustic house. They were magnificent masterpieces of cabinetry. Seeing that I was interested, he then took Juroe and me over to his furniture shop in another part of the San Fernando valley and we saw more. Juroe saw a story developing on the craftsmanship of Montgomery's furniture—with no mention of *Aaron Slick*.

Which was exactly what was happening.

Finally, George showed us a beautiful piece he had just

made for Clark Gable for $15,000, a lot of money in those days. Juroe, ever the press agent, blurted out:

"What a beautiful *Aaron Slick* finish!"

It was so funny that the line stayed in the story and 8,000 newspapers around the world heard about *Aaron Slick* in a furniture story.

Another Juroe gem happened in 1958 when he was sent to Paris with Cecil B. DeMille to open *The Ten Commandments* in that city. I happened to be in Paris at the same time and was astonished to see huge posters advertising the picture on the massive doors of Notre Dame cathedral. In fact, there were few churches in Paris that didn't carry the blatant advertising usually reserved for billboards and construction fences.

I knew it was Juroe's work, so I called him immediately to find out how he had pulled off such a feat.

"Very easy," he said. "Instead of taking DeMille around to the Paris press when he arrived, I took him immediately to visit the cardinal-archbishop of Paris.

"C. B. so charmed the cardinal that the rest was easy."

Now that's press agentry.

Bacon the Ham

Robert Redford shows a complete lack of concern about this, but—I've acted in six times more movies than he has.

Counting both feature and TV films, the last count was 331. By the time this book is published, you can add twenty or thirty more. That's been the yearly average in recent years.

Duke Wayne is pushing me in quantity. I don't push him in quality. Let's say that I'm in running for the title of King of the Bit Players. Usually I work one day at a time. Longest I ever worked was with Elizabeth Taylor and Richard Burton in *Lucy Meets the Burtons.* That took five days—including rehearsals.

This was one of the funniest of all the Lucy shows, but it

almost wasn't. Lucille Ball, so overwhelmed at getting such a distinguished movie couple to appear on her show, gave them all the best lines, especially Richard.

After the dress rehearsal, which, as with all Lucy shows, was done before a live audience, the great comedienne came to me and asked if I would speak to Richard about the way he was delivering his laugh lines. With typical British underplay, Richard was throwing his punch lines away. When you work before that live TV audience, you have to hit them over the head like a Milton Berle.

I explained to Lucy that it would be presumptuous for me to tell one of the world's great actors how to deliver lines. I argued that he had great respect for Lucy's comedic talents. I did mention casually to Richard that a TV show before a live audience was a whole different ball game from doing Shakespeare in the Old Vic.

He agreed and wondered himself why the laughs didn't come as he expected at the dress. I then told Lucy that Richard was a pro and why not sit down with him during the break between the dress and the actual show.

"How in the hell can I tell Richard Burton how to deliver lines?" she asked.

"Very easy," I answered.

Lucy, the great comedienne, had counted twenty-three belly-laughs in the script for Richard. At the dress, Richard got twenty-three chuckles.

So Lucy and Richard talked during the break.

Came showtime and Richard came off like a stand-up comic in Las Vegas.

After the show, he turned to Lucy and said: "You're right, Luv. There were twenty-three belly-laughs. I counted them."

I was in all five of the very successful *Planet of the Apes* movies. In four of them, I played an ape, which is very frustrating. You can never find yourself in the movie.

In *Escape from the Planet of the Apes,* I played a four-star U.S. Air Force Chief of Staff summoned by the President of the United States for an emergency White House meeting when two apes landed in the U.S. from the apes' planet. Aftei the picture played the theaters, Producer Arthur Jacobs showed me a flock of letters from Air Force personnel. All of them asked where they found a size 46 uniform for an Air Force general.

In the first ape movie, which starred Charlton Heston, I showed up on the set wearing the ape jumpsuit and carrying my ape mask under my arm. Heston greeted me, quite seriously, and asked: "Are you working in the movie, Jim?"

I said, "No, Chuck, I just escaped from the San Diego zoo and I'm looking for a banana stand." He never laughed.

My first movie role—the one that got me a Screen Actors Guild card in 1951—was *Black Tuesday*, a gangster picture starring Edward G. Robinson and Jean Parker.

Although I had done considerable Little Theater acting, I had come to Hollywood as a writer, not an actor. But this particular movie called for Robinson to walk up to the electric chair and be executed. Since I covered a few executions in my legitimate days as an AP man, Producer Leonard Goldstein asked me to be a technical advisor.

I'll never forget the first time Little Caesar, the screen's all-time tough guy, saw that death-room set. He actually trembled. That's because Eddie was the most gentle and sensitive of men.

Anyhow, came time to shoot the execution scene and Eddie, the consummate actor, forgot his trembling and walked up to the chair like the cocky Little Caesar so familiar to movie audiences. I shook my head. Goldstein called a halt and asked what was wrong.

"Leonard," I said, "at every execution I ever witnessed—and I know reporters who have seen dozens more than I—no one walks cockily to the electric chair. It always takes about eight to ten cops to drag them there. Would you walk under your own power to the electric chair?"

Leonard conferred with the director. Then he returned to me and said:

"How would you like to be an actor? We'll pay you $200 and buy your SAG card."

I became one of the reporters covering the execution. I was out as technical advisor and I didn't really give a damn. Eddie once more was the cocky Little Caesar that movie audiences loved. As I recall, the picture didn't have the black guy on Death Row singing "Swing Low, Sweet Chariot." That was a minor victory.

Gangster movies are fun. One of my all-time favorites was *Al Capone,* starring Rod Steiger. This film, made on a low budget, has become a cult film. Steiger once told me that college audiences and film buffs ask him more questions about this movie than any other he has ever appeared in. Steiger cast the movie himself and asked me personally to play a reporter in it.

Erskine Johnson, one of the most widely syndicated columnists of those days, wrote: "James Bacon's delineation of a reporter in *Al Capone* is simply superb. I loved every minute of it."

I loved that so much that I even took out an ad in *Daily Variety* quoting him. And then in small type below the tag line was this line: "Currently appearing in Irwin Allen's *The Big Circus.*"

How hammy can you get? Naturally, I reciprocated the favor later for Skinny. Columnists liked each other in those days. Shows that give you the most recognition are those in which you play yourself.

In *77 Sunset Strip,* starring Efrem Zimbalist, Jr., I had a good scene in Dino's Lodge with Efrem and James Garner, who also played himself. He was then the star of *Maverick.* I think everybody in the world watched *77 Sunset Strip,* one of the most popular private-eye shows of the fifties and early sixties.

Once I was walking down the Champs Elysées in Paris when I was stopped by a group of young French girls, all chic and gorgeous. They wanted my autograph. I asked them if they hadn't gotten me confused with Sydney Greenstreet.

One of them spoke in halting English. They had seen *77 Sunset Strip* the night before and they recognized me from it. I was flattered, of course. We all stopped at a sidewalk cafe, had a drink or two, and then did the town together. It's fun being a celebrity, if only a minor one.

The next day the prettiest one in the group—she couldn't speak a word of English—showed up at my hotel alone. She was my companion for the next three days. Love is a universal language.

It was my first taste of celebrity fucking, one of the great fringe benefits of movie work. Travel sometimes with a big superstar and you'll find out, as I have, that some of the most beaútiful society women in America will take the train in from Connecticut for a little friendly matinee in the hay with a star. Then back on the train and home in time to have a martini waiting when her Wall Street tycoon husband gets home from a hard day's work making millions.

The horny stars—are there any other kind?—love it because there will be no paternity suits and their own wives will never hear about it. It's much better than fucking extras on the set who have everything to gain and nothing to lose if they talk.

Some of these gorgeous socialites do this sort of thing for a lark. All good clean sport. Once I was sitting with Frank Sinatra in a New York restaurant when a gorgeous socialite, whose picture is always in *Vogue* or *Town and Country*, left her husband and came over to Frank ostensibly as a fan and pressed a note into his hand.

Frank read the note, which gave her phone number, and what hours to call. It said "I'll come up to your hotel room and suck your cock like it has never been sucked before."

Must ask Frank sometime if he ever called her.

But back to the movies.

My greatest acting performance was in a movie called *The Outfit,* starring Robert Duvall and Joe Don Baker. It was a story about how two small-time hoodlums, in a vendetta, knock off the Outfit, which is another name for the Mafia or the Syndicate. I played a bookie for the Mob. Duvall and Baker come in and knock over the joint. Director John Flynn staged a few rehearsals, in which Duvall just pointed the gun at me. I showed fright but I was no Larry Olivier.

Came the take and Duvall, an intense and superb actor,

came up to me and jammed that gun right in my ribs. Boy, did that smart. Naturally, I wasn't expecting it and gave out with a painful reaction that made Flynn say later:

"I never realized that you were such a good actor."

I took the compliment modestly and said: "It's easy to act when you're working with someone like Duvall."

Duvall had made me a Method actor in thirty seconds.

That picture, incidentally, opened to sensational reviews but no one ever saw it. It was quickly pulled out of release when someone high in the Mafia called the MGM brass and said the boys didn't like being made fools of. They preferred pictures like *The Godfather,* which made them look semihuman. Also, it didn't help any when MGM opened *The Outfit* in Chicago and Detroit first.

Most historic movie I ever made was *MacArthur,* starring Greg Peck. I was cast as a rear admiral in the surrender of Japan aboard the actual site—the U.S.S. *Missouri.* Only this time, Big Mo was tied up to a dock in Bremerton, Washington, Naval Yard as part of the mothball fleet.

When Director Joe Sargent lined up the scene—so authentic it was eerie—Peck spotted me. He turned to an assistant director and yelled:

"Give Jim another star."

I can always tell my grandchildren that I got a battleship promotion to Vice-Admiral from MacArthur himself.

At one rehearsal, Greg went through the signing process— the Japanese, the Russians, the English, etc. Then he said: "Will Vice-Admiral Bacon please sign?"

I marched up, took the pen, and signed the most famous signature of World War II—"Kilroy was here!"

It wasn't in the picture. But what a thrill to be a Vice-Admiral after once being the oldest living ensign in World War II.

I have played in a number of black movies, which is hard to do when you are an Irishman. In *Black Samson,* I was a drunk at a bar whose opening shot was through the crotch of a beautiful nude go-go dancer.

And in another, the title of which I forget, I played the

obnoxious redneck who kept calling all the black actors "Boy." At the sneak preview in Harlem, I was booed by the audience for five minutes. Thank God I wasn't there. I would have been lynched. But I consider it one of my better critical notices.

Like all actors, some of my finest work was left on the cutting-room floor. In the movie *Pepe,* the great Mexican star Cantinflas and I improvised a scene that even had Harry Cohn belly-laughing. No one before or since had ever seen the tyrannical boss of Columbia Pictures laugh out loud in the rushes—or anyplace else. I was in the projection room at the time and I was ready to give up writing and head for Las Vegas.

George Sidney was the director of the movie, but Cantinflas took over my scenes because my 8,000 newspapers included thousands in the Spanish-speaking world. It was a hilarious scene—right out of Laurel and Hardy—but it had absolutely nothing to do with the plot.

Came the night of the premiere of *Pepe,* I was still barely in the movie but my big scene was not.

The picture was not that hot, and the next day when the diastrous reviews came out, Cohn paid me the supreme compliment:

"We should have released your scene with Cantinflas and thrown away the goddamn picture. Then we would have had a hit."

Other actors, who secretly resent my moonlighting as an actor, often ask me who my agent is.

"My column," I answer.

But I once had an agent. And only I would have ever come up with an agent like this one. He called me up one day and said he would like to talk to me about representation. We set a lunch date. Well, this guy shows up with a full growth of beard, bloodshot eyes, and a harried look. He apologized.

"I just got out of jail."

Then he described a horrendous tale of how he had been picked up on his third 502 (LAPD code for drunk driving) in a year. I was amazed that he even made the luncheon. Only I could come up with an agent like that.

Naturally, I signed with him.

When sober, he was a very good agent. He got me parts and even had me set for an audition for the Sterling Hayden role in *The Godfather*. The casting director was convinced that I looked like a crooked Irish cop.

There was one drawback. The role called for a minimum of eight weeks on location in New York. It's a hard place to write a Hollywood column so I had a crisis. I turned down the audition. Not long after that the agent, whose name was Bob Brandeis, got me an audition for the role of a henpecked rancher in a western called *To Hell You Preach*.

As I gave a cold reading to Rick Robinson, a twenty-five-year-old director, he stopped me.

"Are you putting me on? How come you're doing John Wayne on me?"

I told him I wasn't sounding like Wayne consciously but maybe it was because it was a western.

"To hell with you playing a dirt farmer. You're going to be one of the Dalton gang."

And I was. Even had a scene with the local whore—closest I ever came to playing a love scene in all my movies. But that was frustrating too. I had just taken off my pants when the shooting began in the saloon so I had to join in.

Funny thing happened on that movie. I hadn't been on a horse since I was a kid in the rural community of Jersey Shore, Pennsylvania. The script called for me to gallop into town, stop on a dime, shoot guns in the air, and everything the bad guys do when they hit the saloon. I had some apprehension.

Then Richard Gully, a friend of mine who is an astrology buff and always sends me my horoscope, gave me one for Taurus that said, for the very day I was to do all the fancy riding: "Beware of a serious fall today."

That didn't help any.

But the show must go on. I rode that goddamn horse like

Duke Wayne on his best day. I dismounted and walked over to the director, who was sitting in his chair on the porch of the saloon on the western street at Carefree, Arizona.

I sat down on the railing, never for a minute realizing it was a prop railing. I dropped on my ass to the ground four feet below in a fall a stunt man wouldn't do for less than $500.

Fortunately, I didn't get hurt because I fell so relaxed it almost looked like slow motion. I put a little more stock in astrology than I ever had before.

A lot of people think that *At Long Last Love* was the worst movie Burt Reynolds ever made. It wasn't. I was in the worst. It was called *Skulduggery* and was shot entirely in Jamaica. Universal called me up one day and said they had three days' work for me in Jamaica. They preferred I leave the day before I was to shoot so that I could get a script on my arrival and rest a day before shooting.

I was booked on a Delta flight that arrived in Ocho Rios around midnight. A driver took me to the luxurious resort hotel that housed the company, including Reynolds and Susan Clark. When I arrived, there was a solitary figure at the bar. It was Chips Rafferty, the noted Australian actor and an old friend.

Never accept the offer of a nightcap from an Australian, because before you know it, it's breakfast.

About 6 A.M., I got to bed, happy in the thought that I could sleep all day and get a script and study my part later. I also had a little booze in me to make me sleep better.

Around 7 A.M., there's this horrible pounding on my door. I figured it was Rafferty, whom I left at the bar. It wasn't.

It was Newt Arnold, the first assistant director.

"Get the hell up," he yelled as he shook me. "You're in the first scene."

It was obvious that the studio doesn't always get the word from the location. In less than a hour I was in the middle of a fucking riot with the worst hangover in history. I was supposed to play Walter Cronkite or Dan Rather describing a riot scene outside a courthouse in this little Jamaican village. I hadn't read the script because I had never seen one.

John Ford would have sent me home on the next plane but, fortunately, Gordon Douglas was the director. Gordie is Frank Sinatra's favorite director and now I know why. He immediately ordered a couple of beers from the prop department, and also cue cards.

Then to make my hangover worse, what started out as a movie riot scene turned into a real riot.

The company had hired about 1,000 natives at $20 a day. Now some of these poor devils don't see $20 in six months. So another thousand or two showed up looking for this Yankee gold mine. When they were turned down, they started screaming, yelling, and threatening mayhem.

And here I was on top of a mobile camera truck nursing the worst hangover in creation, with 2,000 Carribbean blacks rioting and rocking my truck. I thought sure it was going over.

I don't think the movie ever made the theaters. I saw it on television and I was the best thing in it. I looked like I was describing a riot—and I was. That gives you an idea.

One thing you learn in 300 movies is that many are made but not all are released.

I was in one in Rome called *The Appointment.* It had everything to make it good. Sidney Lumet, certainly one of the screen's great directors, and Omar Sharif and Anouk Aimée, certainly two fine artists. And it had me. I was the most important actor in my scene—the lead tray in a cafeteria scene. Nothing could move until I slid my tray.

I also learned something, girls. Omar gets that soulful look in his eyes with the help of drops before each take.

The Appointment, as far as I know, was shown only at the Cannes Film Festival. When the lights went up after the show, Sharif was the only one left in the theater.

My biggest budget movie was *The Towering Inferno,* in which I was upstaged by the fire. So were Paul Newman, Steve McQueen, Faye Dunaway, Bill Holden, Fred Astaire, and a few thousand more Irwin Allen hired.

Outside of the Burtons, the biggest international star I ever worked with was Sophia Loren in *The Cassandra Crossing* in Rome. I did one scene with the beauteous Sophia and Richard Harris.

But my big scene was done with Lee Strasberg, O. J. Simpson, Martin Sheen, Lionel Stander, and a few others. I got the part quite by accident. I had come on the set strictly as movie reporter. Then George P. Cosmatos, the young Greek director, looked me over.

"You look like a corporation executive. How would you like to be in this movie.?"

That was like asking Dean Martin if he wanted a refill.

The suspense movie concerns a train racing across Europe à la *Murder on the Orient Express,* except that this time, it's not murder, it's an outbreak of the plague.

For this particular scene, the train's destination has been changed drastically and suddenly. I'm an American tycoon with an important business meeting in Paris and the train is headed in another direction. Naturally, I raise hell with the conductor, Lionel Stander, and threaten to pull the emergency cord.

O. J. plays a priest. He's the calming influence in the frantic situation. It took several takes because every time O. J. called me "My son," it broke me up.

But it was one hell of a scene. The picture is not released at this writing but I hope it's still in the picture.

O. J. saw the rushes and said it played great.

Have to give you the advice Strasberg gave me before the scene started. He is, of course, America's greatest acting teacher and one hell of an actor himself. I asked him for a free lesson on the spot.

"I can give it to you in two words," said Lee. "Don't act." Now was that sound advice—or had he seen me act before?

One of my favorite parts was playing a bartender in a movie about motocross racing called *Sidewinder One.*

It took all day to shoot the scene. Now you fake the whiskey drinks in these scenes—water for vodka, iced tea for scotch or bourbon. But you can't fake a can of beer.

By the day's end, I had every extra at the bar plus the bartender flying high on beer.

Elmo Williams, the producer, saw the rushes the next day and said it was the most authentic barroom scene he had ever seen.

I told him it was because he had a Method bartender.

When Marlon Brando did *The Young Lions*, playing a Nazi officer, he had a drunk scene. For some strange reason, he asked my advice on how to play it. I told him to take a few belts first. So we brought out a bottle of vodka, and Marlon, who can't drink, got loaded.

Take a look at that scene sometime on the late, late show. It's one of the best drunk scenes in the movies.

And watch Clark Gable in *Teacher's Pet*, with Doris Day. Gable and I prepared for his drunk scene by having lunch at the old Lucy's with six martinis apiece. It's a classic drunk scene too.

The Brave Bulls

I'm one American who loves bullfights. That's because I saw my first one in Madrid in the mano-a-mano combat between Dominguin and Ordonez, so beautifully immortalized by Ernest Hemingway in *The Dangerous Summer*.

Jack Paar, the former TV star who went with me to the same bullfight, was affected differently. He fainted.

No one with a weak stomach should ever go to a bullfight. Better to read Hemingway.

Bullfighting is colorful, dramatic, gory, barbaric, and—for a matador—one hell of a way to make a living. The bulls seldom win and the matadors who do win often become millionaires.

Even when a matador loses, he gets the kind of funeral Al Capone used to give his dear, departed rivals.

In a preliminary to the Dominguin-Ordonez main event, a matador got gored. If there had been goal posts, the bull would have scored three points for a perfect field goal. Surprisingly, he landed on both feet with the whole ass out of his pants. There was more derrière exposed than in the Lido show in Paris. He managed to kill the bull before leaving·the arena in a stretcher to cheers. Somehow that bare ass took away from the glamor of Hemingway's prose.

The Latin feels sorry for the matador, who has to face death every Sunday afternoon. He doesn't even wear a jockstrap under those silk pants. That's one of the reasons matadors get more girls than Warren Beatty.

The Anglo-Saxon feels sorry for the bull. That's why bullfighting is strictly a Latin sport.

I'm neutral. I'll cheer a brave bull anytime. Of course, the bull seldom hears the cheers as the mules draw his carcass out of the ring. A bull, after all, is destined to die. Isn't it better to go with cheers than a slaughterhouse execution?

In case you have never seen a bullfight, here is how it works. The bull, strong enough to derail a freight train, comes charging fiercely, to be met by the *cuadrilla*—the matador and his retinue—whose main duty is to distract the bull by cape work. At this point the bull is so mean and full of bull that the *cuadrilla* makes a few swipes and then runs like hell for the nearest barricade.

I have seen bulls jump the fence and chase hell out of the sideline people, who all wished they had gotten less choice seats.

Eventually the *cuadrilla* will work the bull into position for the picadors. These are stout men on horses with long poled knives.

As the bull charges the horse, the picadors push the knives into the bull's back and neck. One sadistic picador performed this act right in front of us. He kept pushing his knife into the same wound. This is not kosher and he got booed by the aficionados.

It also made Paar faint. And I refused to order rare steaks for a while.

After the picadors have broken or weakened the bull's neck

muscles, the matadors in *cuadrilla* place six gaily ribboned darts called banderillas into the bull's shoulders.

By this time, the bull has lost his friskiness.

And Jack Paar was revived. His first words were:

"I'll fight Floyd Patterson (then heavyweight champ) for the title anytime if I can have a couple of those guys jabbing him with knives before I come in the ring."

But the picador provides a useful service. If he didn't do what he does, the bull would win every time. It's just a matter of equalizing the contestants.

Personally, I wouldn't go in there alone even if the bull was having a cerebral hemorrhage. I once was down in Mexico with Duke Wayne and one day after a bottle of scotch or two, he got in the ring with a baby bull at a ranch outside Durango. The Duke got knocked on his ass so fast that he jumped the fence and hasn't been in a bull ring since, except as a spectator.

But what makes bullfighting such a glamour sport is what Hemingway called the moment of truth. That's when the matador faces the bull alone. It's a ritual, if done right, that equals classical ballet for grace. You know the matador must kill or be killed. It's as simple as that.

This particular day both Ordonez and Dominquin were working close to the horns with their capework. The two great matadors risked death every Sunday afternoon during that Hemingway summer. It was something to see. I have never seen bullfighting like it since and probably never will.

I don't buy the American notion that bullfighting is barbaric. Look at the Indianapolis 500, where 150,000 spectators sit there secretly hoping to see a crash, not the mechanical performance of an experimental machine.

And prize fighting becomes fun only when someone gets his brains bashed in.

Still, one wonders if bullfighting would have survived if Hemingway had taken up three-cushion billiards as a spectator sport—and written about that instead of *Death in the Afternoon*.

In Spain, a football game draws 150,000 people. Most you ever see at a bullfight is twenty to thirty thousand.

Get Me Giesler

Lots of lawyers buy my books, so I will include a chapter on the greatest criminal lawyer of them all—the late Jerry Giesler of Los Angeles.

When Jerry was alive, the movie crowd—whenever they got into trouble—had one cry: "Get me Giesler."

When Cheryl Crane stabbed Johnny Stompanato, Lana Turner's lover, Lana called Giesler, whom she had never met before she called the police.

It was typical. Standard procedure in Hollywood.

Jerry, who knew the law like a Supreme Court Justice, wrote more California law than anyone in the legal history of the state.

Yet if a casting director were to cast a lawyer type for a movie, Jerry couldn't have gotten past the front door. He was a country boy from Wilton Junction, Iowa, until the day he died.

Amazingly, Giesler got his start with two of the greatest criminal lawyers this country ever produced. He was an office boy for Earl Rogers, then the greatest criminal lawyer on the West Coast and father of writer Adela Rogers St. Johns.

Clarence Darrow, the greatest of them all, was charged with bribing a jury in the famous Los Angeles *Times* bombing case of 1910. He hired Rogers and his office boy to defend him.

At one point in the trial the two famous lawyers asked Jerry to research a point of law. Jerry came back with a well-documented forty-page tome. It impressed the lawyers. Darrow was acquitted and Jerry was promoted to associate counsel.

Next Giesler and Rogers defended heavyweight champion Jess Willard on a charge of manslaughter after he had fatally knocked out Bull Young in a fight in suburban Vernon. As the case neared its end, Jerry heard Rogers tell the court:

"Your honor, my associate, Mr. Giesler, will address the jury."

Jerry was eloquent and Willard was acquitted.

But Jerry didn't make it on his own until 1931 in the famous Alexander Pantages case. Pantages owned theaters that still bear his name around the country. He also owned the famous Pantages vaudeville circuit. He was already behind bars, convicted of raping a girl in his plush Hollywood office, when he hired Giesler.

Pantages was on his way to twenty years or more in prison when Giesler, studying the trascript of the trial, noted a prosecution flaw. The state, in asking the maximum penalty, had spoken of the girl's "prior chastity." But the question of prior chastity had never come up in the trial. Giesler, in his appeal, argued that the defense never had a chance to cross-examine the girl on prior chastity.

Giesler won the millionaire showman another trial and got him acquitted the second time around.

From then on, it was "Get me Giesler."

In 1936 the famed Busby Berkeley's car crossed the center line on a busy highway and the dance director was charged with murder after three people were killed in the head-on collision. The state said that Busby was drunk.

Jerry paraded a flock of witnesses from tire companies who convinced the jury that a blowout caused the collision. Berkeley was acquitted.

I covered many Giesler cases in court. He was all things to all people. He could play it country or he could play it big city. And always he was courteous. He was never sarcastic with a witness.

In Charlie Chaplin's Mann Act case, the federal government accused the famous comedian of transporting Joan Berry to New York for immoral purposes. Jerry, businesslike, then showed Chaplin's cancelled checks, showing payments for drama coaches, voice teachers, and script writers. Miss Berry, Giesler argued, was a career protégé of Chaplin's. He was acquitted too.

In a later paternity suit, Chaplin hired another lawyer. He was decreed the father of Miss Berry's child.

Bob Mitchum, arrested in 1948 for a marijuana party he never quite made, paid Giesler $25,000 and got sixty days in jail.

Said Mitchum: "I could have gotten sixty days in jail with a $50 lawyer."

It was Howard Hughes, Mitchum's boss, who hired Giesler, who based his defense solely on the transcript of the grand jury that had indicted Mitchum.

"I advised Mitchum," Giesler once told me, "that he was a hero to many moviegoers. A long, messy trial might alter that status. I also told him that I would try to prove that his arrest was a frameup, a point the District Attorney's office investigated on its own some months after the trial.

"I let Bob make the final decision. It turned out to be a smart one. He took his medicine like a man, gained public sympathy, and today is a bigger star than he ever was."

Even Mitch concedes today that Giesler was right.

Jerry's greatest headlines came with Errol Flynn. Two teen-aged girls alleged that Flynn had criminally attacked them on his yacht a year apart although the charges were filed within a week of each other. Errol denied all.

It was the girls' word against Flynn, but Errol had Giesler. He got Errol acquitted after devastating the girls' pasts, which were less than virtuous.

Meanwhile, during courtroom breaks Errol romanced another teen-ager, Nora Eddington, who was selling cigarettes and candy in the courthouse lobby. She was the daughter of the number-two man in the Los Angeles county sheriff's department.

Errol married Nora after the trial.

One night I was visiting with Elizabeth Taylor in her bungalow at the Beverly Hills Hotel. I had parked my car on Crescent Drive near the bungalow.

Around 2 A.M., I wandered out of the bungalow and momentarily forgot where I had parked the car. In seconds a Beverly Hills police car stopped and hauled me in. No one walks in Beverly Hills after dark.

At the police station they charged me with vagrancy, although I had $300 in my pocket and all sorts of credentials and press passes.

I demanded my one phone call. It was to Giesler, of course. He got me released by phone.

One hell of a lawyer.

No Bacon Allowed in Israel

Once Joe Levine invited me to travel to England with him aboard the *Queen Mary* along with Carroll Baker, who was starring in Levine's *Harlow*.

It was my first trip aboard a luxury liner. Closest I had ever come to it before was during World War II as a naval officer. A U.S. Navy pilot landed me on the carrier *Enterprise* as it lay bobbing in the Pacific Ocean during World War II. That was considered a luxury ship by navy standards.

Before the *Queen Mary* departed its New York docks, Joe tossed a tremendous party aboard. All the important press and celebrities were invited and it was a wingding. As departure time drew near, I invited a group of people down to my stateroom for some champagne. It was the only way to go.

Next thing I knew I was asleep in my bed and the ship was at sea. I woke up before long and saw an amazing sight in the bed next to mine. There was a particularly gorgeous girl, who worked for the *Saturday Evening Post*, who had been a guest at the cocktail party up above, and who had been invited along with a dozen others to my private champagne party. I knew she was not supposed to make the trip to England, so I shook her awake. She was in tears when she realized the ship was at sea. I told her not to worry, that the *Queen Mary* had stores aboard and she could be outfitted in clothes in the morning. She kept sobbing:

"I'll be fired if I don't show up for work in the morning."

I couldn't stop her hysterics, so rang for the steward and explained that this young girl had had too much to drink and had passed out in my bed. What could we do?

He said: "Follow me."

Soon we were on the bridge where once again I explained the girl's plight to the skipper.

"It's a good thing you didn't wake up five minutes later, else you would have had a companion for this crossing."

One look at the girl and I cursed myself for not sleeping later, but there was still time to make the pilot's boat back to New York. And my new friend, still a little woozy, was lowered down the side someplace around Sandy Hook and transported back through New York harbor. No doubt she showed up at work the next morning with a horrible hangover and told her friends how she almost made it to England on the *Queen Mary*. And no one believed her.

I'll always remember that crossing. It was like being transported back in the Gay Nineties. Never—and I have been to some lavish parties and places—have I seen such elegance as we experienced in first class aboard that great ship. It's a style of life we'll never see again.

Dinner companions at my table included the chairman of the board and president of Vat 69—the scotch, not the pope's unlisted phone number. These two executives had been in the United States introducing the firm's new Vat 69 Classic Gold.

"It's not a true scotch." said the executives, "because you Americans won't buy a true scotch. You want it light, like J & B or Cutty Sark, which are the big sellers. In order for us to meet that competition, we have introduced Classic Gold, which is blended with neutral spirits to make it light for the American taste."

So you see the crossing was not all revelry. It was educational, too.

One night Joe Levine staged a huge *Harlow* party in the thirties style aboard the ship. It was fabulous, mostly because

Joe bought a bottle of good French champagne for every passenger from first class to tourist. It must have cost him $20,000 for the champagne alone, but Joe always was fast with a buck.

A funny thing happened to me on that crossing. I never once got seasick, but as soon as I landed in London and got settled in my room at Claridge's, the room started going around. It was the most amazing feeling, and one of the worst nights I have ever spent.

The next morning I got up to one of those dreary London rains. That didn't help matters. In Hollywood, I would have gone to Palm Springs, but I was in London. So I did the next best thing. Went to Israel, which is similar to Palm Springs except you see more Arabs.

That afternoon I was on El Al airlines flying nonstop to Tel Aviv. I was the only person in first class that whole flight.

The plane landed at Tel Aviv airport and as I started down the first-class gangplank, noted that there were TV cameramen, reporters, still photographers by the dozens, all waiting for the cabin door to open.

I knew I had a certain amount of celebrity status but this was overwhelming. I came down the gangplank with a Jimmy Carter smile and walked right past the small army of newsmen, who never even glanced at me.

Golda Meir had made the same flight in economy.

Worse, I got in the airport and went through immigration. A very attractive Israeli girl took my passport, glanced at it, and then without a smile asked:

"Is Bacon your right name?"

I told her it was. Then she said:

"I can't stamp your passport. I'll have to stamp your finance card instead."

Still not a smile. Dead-faced serious. I asked her why not.

"Because we don't allow bacon in Israel."

And still straight-faced.

A driver met me and drove me up to a beautiful little hotel in Galilee on the shores of the Mediterranean. After I deposited my bags in the room, dropped into the little bar. There was Peter Finch, the noted Australian actor. He was shooting a movie with Sophia Loren nearby.

"How about a drink, my good man?" beckoned Peter.

He ordered wine.

"I don't drink spirits anymore," he explained.

When the smoke cleared, there were about twenty empty bottles of wine around Peter. He was out completely. He was too big to carry to bed so I left him there and walked to my own room a little haltingly.

That night the room went around just like it did in Claridge's. By this time I figured out it was kind of a reverse seasickness on land. At least in Israel when you wake up, there's brilliant sunlight.

The phone rang and it was my driver, Paul, a veteran of five years in Dachau. He said he survived because he was young and strong and the Nazis had to have someone to do the manual labor. He said he was taking the British actor Jack Hawkins on a tour of the Holy Land sites where Jesus lived and preached. Would I want to go along?

I was dressed in a minute, grabbed a fast breakfast, and took a look in the bar. Finch was still asleep in his chair, but he had remained true to his vow—no spirits.

One of the first places we stopped was at Tiberias on the Sea of Galilee. Hawkins, Paul, and I stopped at a waterfront cafe on the shores of the holy lake for some wine. Paul was explaining that Syria had gun emplacements across the sea aimed at Tiberias. He no sooner had spoken than a shell burst in the water about fifty yards away. Paul grabbed my arm and said: "Don't worry. They can't shoot any farther than that."

We couldn't give the same message to Hawkins. He had disappeared under a table someplace.

So for about a half hour, Paul and I sat there calmly sipping our wine while the Syrians fired from the Golan Heights—fifty yards from us on every burst, just as Paul had said.

The shooting stopped and we found an ashen-faced Hawkins and left for Nazareth.

Just as we were about to enter the home of the Holy Family where Christ played as a child, an Arab riding a burro came down the narrow street and knocked me right on my ass.

I have always felt that all my sins were forgiven and eternal salvation granted me at that moment.

Why Don't You Have a Name Like Westbrook Pegler?

For twenty years, Jim Bishop and I have been confused with each other. Neither of us knows exactly why. Naybe it's the similarity of syllables—Jim Bacon, Jim Bishop. Maybe it's because we are both white-haired, both syndicated columnists, and both authors—although we live on different coasts.

But it happens so much that both Jim and I laugh it off. Recently I was awarded the Al Freeman award for journalism at the MGM Grand Hotel in Las Vegas. Jim read that I was to receive it. He made a special trip to Las Vegas to present it to me.

First time this confusion manifested itself came after a retreat held by the Catholic Press Council of Southern California at a Franciscan monastery in Malibu. Next day a reporter for the Los Angeles *Herald-Examiner* stopped me in the elevator and said:

"Boy, you really have had an inspiring life."

I asked why.

"One of the priests read your life story during meals at the retreat I attended over the weekend. It was beautiful." Then he went into details about the life story, which, while inspiring, wasn't mine. I called the monastery and talked to the priest.

"It wasn't your life story. It was Jim Bishop's."

A few days later, Bing Crosby, an old friend, stopped me on the Paramount lot to congratulate me on a story I had written for *Look* magazine on Jackie Gleason. I told Bing I hadn't written anything on Gleason recently.

"Hell you haven't," said Bing. "The byline said Jim Bacon."

I looked up *Look*. It was by Jim Bishop, of course.

Next time it came up was over on the Goldwyn lot where Pearl Bailey, working there in *Porgy and Bess,* stopped me:

"Man, I'm always seeing you swing around Las Vegas. And then you turn around and write a book like that. Man, you're something."

"Like what book?" I asked.

"The Day Christ Died," answered Pearlie May.

This went on for a year or two. Finally, I was invited to Al Horwits' house in Beverly Hills for a party in honor of Jim Bishop. I had never met him. I got there before Jim. When he came in, Clare Horwits, Al's wife, introduced him around. When she came to me, she introduced me to Jim Bishop as Jim Bishop.

We both laughed and Bishop said: "You've got to be Jim Bacon."

Then he told me amazing tales of how he had been confused with me. Once he was attending a banquet in New York when Ed Sullivan, the emcee, announced: "In the audience, we have that great syndicated columnist, Jim Bacon."

Ed looked straight at Bishop as he said it.

"I looked around to see if the real Jim Bacon was in the audience. When you didn't get up, I stood up sheepishly and took a bow."

Lots of humorous things have taken place over the years. Once Bill Kennedy, who is one of Detroit's top TV personalities and an old friend, called me while he was on the air live.

"Jim," he said. "That's an amazing column you had on Errol Flynn. Will you tell our viewers the background of how you came to write about it?"

Now the minute he mentioned the column I knew it was Jim Bishop's, but here was Bill Kennedy on the air live in Detroit. Was I about to ruin an old friend's show by saying that I didn't write the column? Fortunately, I had read Bishop's column and was knowledgeable about the subject matter. So for the next fifteen minutes I was talking to a million people in the Detroit area as Jim Bishop. He would have done the same for me.

Sometimes I think that the reason my first book, *Hollywood Is a Four Letter Town*, made the best-seller lists is that half the people who bought it thought it was by Jim Bishop.

One of the funniest incidents occurred at the El Rancho Vegas in Las Vegas one night when my old friend, Joe E. Lewis, put me in his act like he always did.

I was sitting ringside and Joe E. started singing. He looked down at me and said: "My old drinking buddy, Jim Bishop, says I have a voice like the all-clear signal in a floating crap game."

I didn't laugh. I just hung my head. Joe was disturbed. He soon found out why.

As I left the El Rancho Vegas that night, there was Joe E. down on his hands and knees by the door, saying:

"I don't even know Jim Bishop. Why in the hell can't you have a name like Westbrook Pegler?"

All was forgiven.

But the most amazing confusion of all came when my own mother, then living in Lock Haven, Pennsylvania, called me and said:

"Jimmy, that was the most wonderful column you wrote about your Irish father, but that wasn't your father, that was your grandfather."

I could only say:

"Mom, that wasn't my column. It was Jim Bishop's."

"Oh," she said. "I won't have it framed then."

The Night I Mislaid a Princess

One night singer Joni James and her arranger husband Tony Acquaviva threw a party for Princess Lalla Nezha, sister of the King of Morocco.

Everybody was there but I never saw the Princess.

Burt Bacharach and Liz Whitney Tippett and I got into a big discussion about horses. Both own big stables. I made the only profound remark of the discussion—that the only guy who makes money at the track is a pickpocket.

Mama Jolie Gabor, mother of the famous Gabor sisters, was telling how she drove into the exit instead of the entrance of the Racquet Club in Palm Springs. The spikes blew out all her tires. An hour later, Frank Sinatra did the same thing. Not one of his tires was damaged, which made me believe more and more in the divinity of Sinatra. He's the only guy who calls Dial-a-Prayer and asks if there are any messages.

It was a terrific party but I never saw the Princess. So wrote about it the next day—how everybody but the Princess showed up. As soon as the paper hit the streets, everybody called up—from Tony Acquaviva to the Moroccan Embassy in Washington. No kidding. It seems the Princess did show up after I had left. And that's a story in itself.

Charlie Fawcett, one of those mysterious soldiers of fortune, was a friend of the Moroccan royal family, so he volunteered to drive the Princess to the party. He did it in a Volkswagen camper, which shows a certain amount of nonchalance. As Charlie drove the Volkswagen up the Beverly Hills street, not sure where he was going, he spotted a house with a lot of cars parked outside. Naturally, he assumed this was the Acquaviva party, so he and the Princess and a lady-in-waiting or two went in.

"We were received warmly and given some drinks and sat down and chatted for an hour or two. Suddenly I realized we were at the wrong party. It was a birthday celebration for a charming lady who was celebrating her 100th birthday. Both the Princess and I thought it would be terribly rude to leave abruptly, so we stayed awhile. Then we left and went to the right party."

The people who gave the party for the 100-year-old lady will now find out that they entertained royalty—and didn't know it.

I later apologized to the Princess for mislaying her and she was most gracious.

"I was most happy, even if it was inadvertent, to help honor someone who had lived such a long and eventful life."

Writing the Book Isn't the Half of It

Going out on the road and selling your book, like I did last year for *Hollywood Is a Four Letter Town,* is an experience you won't believe. Authors will know what I'm talking about, but the general public will find it a revelation.

In one month, I did 200 talk shows, from San Francisco to New York and back again a couple or three times. One day in San Francisco, I did eleven shows in one day, had three newspaper interviews, and wrote my daily column—all from 7 A.M. to 7 P.M.

And then to read the reviews of your book, especially since I had been in the business of giving them instead of taking them for thirty years.

The reviews in the New York *Times* and *Daily Variety,* the Hollywood show business bible, were so great that I honestly could not have written them better myself.

In the black press, I got blasted because I only wrote about Sammy Davis, Jr., and his involvement with a white girl, Kim Novak. One syndicated black columnist blasted me for not writing about Sidney Poitier and Harry Belafonte, both of whom have white wives.

Some of the reviews that generally liked the book hit me for the chapter on the affair with the young Marilyn Monroe. How many times was I to see "kiss and tell" in headlines. It was the one inevitable question that was asked me on talk shows: Why did I kiss and tell?

If a girl interviewer asked the question, I always said:

"What if you had had an affair with Paul Newman, could you keep it quiet?"

This was always followed with a smile and no answer. And if a man asked, I just substituted Elizabeth Taylor.

I guess the reason I put the chapter in the book was because so much has been written about Marilyn's affairs with JFK as president, Frank Sinatra, and others, that I just had to let the world know I was there first.

The next question inevitably would be: "Wasn't Marilyn Monroe, as an actress, using you to further her career?"

I admitted that the fact that I wrote for 8,000 newspapers was part of my charm but also I was younger, slimmer, had coal-black hair and few other attributes.

"Yes," I answered, "she was using me but what nice usage."

And then they invariably asked: "Do you have regrets about writing that chapter?"

"Yes, after I did it. I felt sorry I wrote—not that Marilyn would have minded in the least—about our affair."

But the publisher felt it was the most commercial chapter in the book. And he was right. It caused the most comment and helped make the book a best seller.

Surprisingly, a chapter I never dreamed I would ever be questioned about on the air was the chapter on the biggest cocks in Hollywood.

I started my tour in Minneapolis. The first night I arrived, a talk-show host by name of Henry Wolf, who had a Kissinger-like accent, had the dubious honor of asking my first question of the tour. It was:

"Do you think anyone is interested in the size of Milton Berle's sexual organ?"

I was stunned but only for a second.

"Yes," I answered. "Mrs. Berle."

You would be amazed at how many times that chapter came up throughout the Bible Belt.

The author's big headache is to do all these shows in a city and then have no books in the stores. As a syndicated columnist, I found the towns well stocked where my column appeared. Where it didn't, it was another matter.

Dr. Wayne Dyer, who wrote the best-seller *Your Erroneous Zones,* took a page out of Jackie Susann's book and solved that problem nicely. Dr. Dyer took four months off from his teaching duties and loaded his station wagon with at least 400 copies of his book. When he hit a city like Philadelphia, he visited all the main bookstores and told them of his TV and radio appearances in their city. Then he loaded them with books on consignment. If they sold, it was money in the bank for them. If they didn't, send them back to the publisher and no sweat lost.

The result was that *Your Erroneous Zones* sold 400,000 hard covers and the paperback rights went for $1.1 million.

Pretty good for a guy who had only written textbooks before.

Unfortunately, I write six Hollywood columns a week and it's hard to do from places like Philadelphia, Baltimore, Washington, etc., for four months.

Maybe I should give up the column at the prices Dr. Dyer got.

Biggest thrill of the whole tour was walking down Times Square and seeing my name in lights on a fourteen-story sign on Number One Times Square, the most photographed building in the world. The sign read: "Broadway's Earl Wilson welcomes Hollywood's James Bacon to Number One Times Square, June 6."

My friend Alex Parker, who owns the building, did it to advertise a party he and publicist Joel Preston arranged with Earl as host to launch my book in New York. The sign was so huge you could see it down Seventh Avenue from Central Park South.

Even people from my hometown of Lock Haven, Pennsylvania, saw it.

On the day of the party, Alex put my name and the title of the book on the news ticker that gave Times Square its name when the New York *Times* was published in the building.

What a thrill.

Everybody from Henny Youngman to Robert Merrill of the Met showed up at the party, which Alex sprung for me on the twenty-first floor of his building. It was a huge sendoff.

The next day Youngman and I toured all the important book stores on Fifth Avenue and Henny moved my books up high on the best-seller table. If a store had stocked only a handful of copies, Henny would say: "I wanted to buy twenty-four to give to my friends as gifts. I'll have to go to your competition."

Then he would walk angrily out of the store, followed by

me. It pays to have friends like Youngman, Marty Allen, and Sidney Korshak. The famous Beverly Hills and Chicago lawyer bought 100 copies as gifts for his friends. Marty and his wife Frenchie bought at least 100 and tossed me a big book-launching party at Hunter's Book Store in Beverly Hills, where we sold 400. It was a class-A party, because Henry (The Fonz) Winkler showed up. When the Fonz shows up, it gives the party stature.

After the party at Number One Times Square, I went on the *Tomorrow* show with Tom Snyder. It was rather a hilarious session because of the champagne at the earlier party and the fact that I got bleeped several times, rare for a 1 A.M. audience.

Snyder, true to form, asked me about the chapter on the largest cocks.

"When I was in Hollywood," said Tom, "I used to play golf all the time with Forrest Tucker and I didn't know he was co-champion with Milton Berle."

"Did Tuck use a club?" I asked.

Surprisingly, that was not bleeped. But on another question he asked, I said: "Together, they form the Alaskan pipeline." That was bleeped.

My luck was such that the *Today* show was shooting in Los Angeles instead of the customary New York. So after *Tomorrow*, I had to take the red-eye to Los Angeles and show up at Burbank at 4 A.M. to do the *Today* show. I did Merv Griffin the same night and then took another red-eye to Philadelphia to do Mike Douglas the next afternoon.

From Philadelphia to Pittsburgh to Detroit. In the latter city, Earl Wilson, who was promoting *Sinatra,* appeared with me on the syndicated Lou Gordon show.

Lou is tough on his guests. That's his act and he has an interesting show. Jackie Susann once walked off right in the middle of his show, he was so rough on her.

I must have said the magic word, for just as we reached the five-second countdown to showtime, I said to Lou:

"Destroy me."

He was exceptionally kind to me and destroyed poor Earl, who is the nicest man in the world. ·

Next stop Cincinnati where I had a great warm-up comic on the Bill Braun 50-50 show—Bob Hope.

Then back to Los Angeles again for the Dinah Shore show, which is one of the most relaxing on the air. That's great coffee they serve in those cups.

Next to Chicago where columnist Irv Kupcinet introduced Earl and me as "The Sunshine Boys" of talk shows.

By this time airline stewardesses were calling me by my first name. They couldn't believe my schedule. Usually, you would finish a city like Cincinnati around 9 P.M., grab the 10 P.M. flight to Cleveland and be on an early morning news or talk show at 7 A.M. and then all day long.

On the whole tour, I had one free night—in New York. Henny Youngman and I did the town and I got my pocket picked. It was the fourth time I had been robbed in New York City, once with the gun in my ribs at Sixth Avenue and Fifty-second Street.

On that latter mugging, I walked across Sixth Avenue, $350 poorer. A hooker stops me and says, "I'll spend the night with you for $50."

I said: "See that guy running down the street? Get him. He's loaded."

I had twenty cents in my pocket.

But tough as the book tours are, it's still fun. For me it was an eye-opener to find out how good regional television and radio is in this country. They've got shows in Houston and Dallas and San Francisco and Detroit and other cities throughout the country that are on a professional par with the best Hollywood has to offer.

If *Hollywood Is a Four Letter Town* never did anything else, it got my name up in lights in Times Square. Told Alex, after it was up a month, he should put up a Spanish version.

You don't hear too much *ingles* spoken in Times Square these days.

Index